Understanding
ADHD
Attention
Deficit
Hyperactivity
Disorder

Also by Dr. Christopher Green
Published by The Ballantine Publishing Group

Toddler Taming
Dr. Green's Baby Book

Understanding

ADHD
Attention
Deficit
Hyperactivity
Disorder

Dr. Christopher Green
and Dr. Kit Chee

Illustrated by Roger Roberts

FAWCETT COLUMBINE
THE BALLANTINE PUBLISHING GROUP
NEW YORK

Publisher's Note

The authors believe the information contained in this publication to be accurate at the time of writing. We emphasize that it is not intended that the work be substituted for the individual opinion obtained from consultation with a professional practitioner. Where drugs or prescriptions are referred to, care should be taken to note same in conjunction with current and ongoing specifications issued by the relevant drug houses.

A Fawcett Columbine Book
Published by The Ballantine Publishing Group

http://www.randomhouse.com

Library of Congress Catalog Card Number: 98-96349

ISBN: 0-449-00152-0

Cover design by Cathy Colbert
Cover photo © Bokelberg/The Image Bank
Text design by Jie Yang

Manufactured in the United States of America

First American Edition: October 1998

10 9 8 7 6 5 4 3

Contents

About the authors

Dr. Christopher Green, MB, BCh, BAO, FRACP, MRCP(UK), FRCP(I), DCH

Christopher Green is a pediatrician, Head of the Child Development Unit at the New Children's Hospital, and clinical lecturer at the University of Sydney, Australia. Over the last 15 years Dr. Green has been prominent in introducing modern attitudes toward treatment of ADHD to Australia. More recently he has been influential in bringing this same message to parents and professionals in the United Kingdom.

He is the well-known author of two internationally bestselling books on childcare, *Toddler Taming* (1984, 1990) and *Dr. Green's Baby Book* (1988, 1996). Outside his clinical practice, Chris lectures widely in Australia, New Zealand and the United Kingdom. He has also been a speaker at CHADD conferences in the U.S. He is a former columnist with the *Australian Women's Weekly* and a presenter with Australia's top-rating, daytime television program, the *Midday Show*.

Chris is married to Hilary, a part-time general practitioner and full-time mum. They have two sons. When not working, he enjoys sailing, swimming, and outdoors Australia with his family.

Dr. Kit Y Chee, MB, BS, FRACP

Kit Chee is a pediatrician specializing in the behavioral and learning problems of children. She is honorary physician at the Child Development Unit at the New Children's Hospital, Westmead, and consultant at the Sydney Learning Clinic.

Kit has a research interest in children's learning, language, ADHD, and the effect of stimulant medication. Kit is married to Arthur, also a pediatrician. Outside work, every minute is taken up looking after her two young children, but she still finds time to enjoy classical music, the arts, and exploring Sydney.

Author's Note

In this book there may seem to be an overuse of the word *he*. The truth is that ADHD mostly affects "hes," and when it comes to extremes of behavior, the "hes" usually get the gold medal.

There is also a certain amount of repetition, with the same information appearing in different lists and chapters. We have aimed to create a book that is useful to those who don't wish to read from cover to cover. For this reason each section is as complete as possible, but this has necessitated some duplication.

Thanks to Dr. Mary Lynn O'Brien, pediatrician in Portland, Oregon, for her advice and support in preparing this American edition.

Introduction

Thank goodness most professionals have now accepted Attention Deficit Hyperactivity Disorder (ADHD) as an important condition of childhood. All around us ADHD causes clever children to under-function at school and, despite good parenting, to behave poorly at home. With the current awareness of ADHD, professionals and parents are wanting practical, up-to-the-minute information on how to help these children, and this book aims to fulfill that need.

Understanding ADHD presents a clear overview of a far-from-simple condition. This new edition tries to emphasize that ADHD is not just about inattention or overactivity—it is a four-part condition. The first part is the problem of attention, memory, and academic underachievement. The second is the active, impulsive, poorly controlled behaviors. Then there is a third part, the associated comorbid conditions (e.g. dyslexia, Oppositional Defiant Disorder, Conduct Disorder) which are not true parts of ADHD but for many add to the problem. The fourth part is the influence of the child's living environment, where the child who is accepted and nurtured will do much better than those children who are met with force, hostility, and criticism.

There is still debate over the best way to diagnose ADHD, the relative importance of various types of therapies, and the presumed but as yet unproven long-term benefits of stimulant medication. These, and other unresolved issues, are unimportant as long as we all pursue the same goal: to help these children enter adulthood with the best possible education, good self-confidence, useful life skills, and intact family relationships. If we all work together toward this end, the next decade will be a lot easier for these children and their stressed parents.

This book provides an easy-to-read text, full of well-tried, practical suggestions that work both in the home and classroom. For those who wish to take it further, the Appendices at the end are full of additional information, such as summaries of the most recent research findings, current diagnostic criteria, parent/teacher questionnaires, information on computer programs, and where to get help.

What you are about to read is a very personal, yet up-to-date perspective of ADHD. There will be people who dispute some of our ideas. All we ask is that if you can relate to the text and it helps with a child in your care, please read on.

Christopher Green
Kit Chee

ONE

ADHD—The Facts

Attention Deficit Hyperactivity Disorder (ADHD) is not new: it was first described almost 100 years ago, and the beneficial effects of stimulant medication have been well known for over half a century.

Today when we talk about ADHD we refer to a slight but demonstrable difference in normal brain function that causes a clever child to underachieve academically and to behave poorly, despite receiving the highest standard of parenting. This cluster of behaviors was once called Hyperactivity, then Attention Deficit Disorder, and now Attention Deficit Hyperactivity Disorder.

With so much current interest in ADHD one might think that we are in the midst of an epidemic. But ADHD is occurring no more frequently than in the past—we have just become more skillful at recognizing a very real condition that previously was missed and misdiagnosed.

Despite our better knowledge of ADHD, many children still remain undiagnosed. Bewildered parents watch as their children underachieve at school and create immense tension in the home. Professionals are often equally unaware, some continuing to believe ADHD to be a trendy noncondition or a poor excuse for incompetent parenting.

A few of the old school of child psychiatrists still see ADHD as a sign of the dysfunction and troubled mind of the child's parents. Fortunately, parent punishing is well on the wane, with entrenched ideas being overtaken by science.

As ADHD is caused by a subtle difference in the normal brain, the seeds of ADHD are present at birth. The extent of the difficulty depends on the severity of the child's problem and how well their behavior and education are managed. We can't change this inborn predisposition, but we can most certainly modify the home and school environment to help our children behave and achieve to their maximum potential.

The facts about ADHD

With so much misinformation still confusing today's parents, let's start this book by outlining the essentials of ADHD.

- ADHD is a real condition which to some extent affects approximately 2 percent to 5 percent of all children.

- The concept of ADHD is said to be controversial, but in the late 1990s there is controversy only in the media, not in reputable professional circles.

- When the media describes some disastrous behavior or criminal activity as typical of ADHD, they are misrepresenting the truth. ADHD, by itself, does not cause a child to be malicious or deliberately antisocial. The problems presented are severe Oppositional Defiant Disorder or Conduct Disorder. These can be associated with ADHD, but they are not a true part of the condition we describe.

■ ADHD is a biological, brain-based condition which is caused by a minor difference of fine tuning in the normal brain (a slight brain dysfunction).

■ The dysfunction of ADHD is thought to be due to an imbalance in the brain's neurotransmitter chemicals, noradrenaline and dopamine. This imbalance is mostly found in those parts of the brain responsible for self-monitoring and putting the brakes on unwise behavior (the frontal lobes and their deep connections, which are the basal ganglia circuits).

■ These areas of dysfunction are now being demonstrated by researchers who use the latest brain scanning techniques, Positron Emission Tomography (PET), and volumetric and functional Magnetic Resonance Imaging (MRI).

■ ADHD presents in two ways, impulsive, poorly self-monitored behavior (referred to as hyperactive-impulsive behavior) and in problems of attention, short-term memory, and learning (attention deficit-learning problems). A child may present with one of these in isolation, but most ADHD children have a mixture of both.

■ These behaviors and learning problems are not exclusive to ADHD. They occur in all of us, but to a much lesser extent. To qualify for a diagnosis of ADHD, a child must be significantly out of step with others of the same developmental level and standard of parenting.

■ The cutoff point between a normal but difficult temperament and ADHD is not clearly definable in black and white. For a diagnosis of ADHD, six out of nine difficult behaviors should be present. (See Appendix I, "The Criteria for Diagnosing ADHD (DSM-IV)".) The child with four or five of these difficult behaviors may not fit the full criteria, but they will still be a handful to manage.

■ Factors in the child's environment do not cause ADHD, but do affect its severity and outcome. A child with six difficult behaviors, who has an exceptional teacher and a saint for a mother, may not need to be treated for ADHD. The child with five out of nine characteristics officially does not qualify for diagnosis, but may require treatment if they are being less well managed in a noncoping home and school situation.

■ Diet is no longer seen as an important part of ADHD. A few children react adversely to some artificial and natural food chemicals. This can also occur in those who do not have ADHD. Food intolerance does not cause ADHD, though occasionally it makes it worse.

■ ADHD is a strongly hereditary condition. Most ADHD children have a close relative (usually male) affected to some degree by the same problem. Developmental Reading Disorder (dyslexia), which is often associated with ADHD, is also a strongly hereditary condition.

■ ADHD is mostly a "boy" problem. Boys are six times more likely to be referred for help than girls. It is suggested that the true ratio in the community is actually 3:1. Many girls remain undiagnosed, as by nature they tend to be less disruptive and suffer more silently than the male of the species. They may not be referred to a clinic for bad behavior, but they may still be failing at school.

■ ADHD is a long-term condition which affects learning and behavior right through the school years. About 50 percent of these children will carry some of their ADHD with them into adulthood. With age ADHD tends to move away from the restless impulsive behaviors, toward those of inattention, inability to sustain work output, deficient short-term memory, and frustration with learning. Some do remain extremely impulsive, and this can do immense damage to their adult relationships. The treatment of adult ADHD is an exciting success story at this time.

■ It is believed that the incidence of ADHD is approximately the same in most countries and races. The rate of ADHD differs between areas depending on the level of professional vision or blindness. (See Appendix XV, "ADHD in other cultures.")

■ A few parents know their child is different from the moment the child is born or even when still in the womb. About half the parents say their child has been "unusually active and into everything" from the moment they first walked.

■ Some preschoolers are incorrectly labeled as "hyperactive." In fact they have no problem other than the normal "busyness" and lack of common sense one finds at this young age.

■ Most parents first suspect their active-impulsive ADHD child is out of step between the age of two and a half and three years. However, due to the more laid-back, less demanding life of preschool, most of these children manage well until the first or second year of school.

■ A small minority of two-year, three-year, and four-year-olds will present for treatment. At this age the behaviors that force us to intervene are low frustration tolerance, unpredictable outbursts, assaults on other children, and suspension from preschool. (See Chapter 18, "ADHD in the Underfives.")

■ Where ADHD is causing strife at a young age, this must be taken seriously. When parents find a three-year-old impossible to manage, they lose confidence or become excessively punitive. The use of force and hostile-critical parenting lead to resentment, which sows the seeds for irretrievable relationship problems. If a difficult child finds early acceptance, nurture, and support, this greatly reduces the risk of oppositional behavior and other negative outcomes.

■ Teachers of ADHD children tell us that at school, "This child is distractable, disruptive, and needs one-to-one supervision to achieve." Teachers are confused when a clever child behaves poorly and underfunctions for intellect.

■ Playground problems are common as the child misreads social cues, "comes on too strong," and overreacts to teasing. Sometimes teachers describe an ADHD child as "known by all but liked by none." This has immense implications for self-esteem.

■ Approximately half of the children who present with ADHD are also troubled by specific learning disabilities, for example dyslexia, Language Disorder, or a weakness with mathematics. These are not caused by the ADHD but are associated or "co-morbid" conditions. The treatment of ADHD does not treat the specific learning disability, but it makes the child more receptive to remedial teaching.

■ At school the two parts of ADHD (hyperactive-impulsive behavior and attention deficit-learning problems) present in different ways. The hyperactive-impulsive, poor self-monitoring behaviors result in the child rushing through work, settling slowly after a break, tapping and fidgeting, calling out in class, and failing to check work before it is handed in. The attention deficit problems affect organization, getting started with work, listening skills, sustained work output, distractability, and short-term memory.

■ Problems of short-term memory make memorizing homework difficult. The information is locked in the night before but forgotten by the time of the test. Learning times tables is a particular hassle. The memory problems can cause a weakness in reading comprehension, where ADHD children forget what was at the beginning of the paragraph by the time they reach the end.

■ Most ADHD children present with a mix of the hyperactive-impulsive behaviors and attention deficit-learning problems. A surprisingly large number are now being diagnosed as ADHD—predominantly inattentive (i.e. having mostly problems of learning). The extreme of this group, ADHD—purely inattentive, are quiet, dreamy, slow moving, disorganized, inattentive, and underachieving. They remain undiagnosed until about the age of 10 years, when self-motivation becomes vital for school success. They cause no behavior concerns; they just "space out" and sink silently.

■ Hyperactivity by itself is not a troublesome behavior. In these hyperactive-impulsive children the difficulty comes from lack of impulse control and from incessant demand. It is not activity that makes them so unpredictable and hard to handle.

■ ADHD children are sought out by school bullies as they overreact to taunting. Though they did not start the incident, they are blamed for the fight that follows.

■ Poor impulse control leaves the ADHD child both physically and verbally accident-prone. They frequently trip, fall, act stupid, and put their "feet in their mouth." ADHD children nag and demand from dawn to dusk—this incessant pressure generates great tension.

■ Most ADHD children have the social and emotional maturity of a child two-thirds their age. Lack of emotional understanding, independence, and common sense are frequent complaints.

■ Professionals are taught that poor parenting causes a child to develop bad behavior. In ADHD it is the difficult child that makes good, competent parents appear inadequate.

■ Fathers are generally more effective in managing the ADHD child than are mothers. They are not a superior parent, they just have a louder voice and are less exploitable because they are less often at home.

■ ADHD is a strongly hereditary condition. When it affects a parent, management of their own ADHD child may not be calm and considered. As mothers provide the consistent structure of most homes, behavior management may be easier if the ADHD-affected parent is the father, not the mother.

■ Treatment of ADHD involves behavioral advice, support at school, and the use of stimulant medication.

■ ADHD children act before they think and are less satisfied with rewards. This makes the behavioral techniques that work so well on our other children much less effective when used on those with ADHD. As nothing seems to work, parents often pull back on discipline, and this is then incorrectly blamed for causing the difficult behavior that made the parents pull back in the first place.

■ Any behavioral expert who recommends a standard behavior program or suggests a parent effectiveness course probably has little experience with the management of ADHD.

■ Stimulant medication is pivotal in the treatment of ADHD. A major multicenter study under way in North America is currently looking at the relative benefits of various combinations of medical, educational, and psychological treatments for ADHD. Rumors at this stage suggest that without first priming with medication, most of the other techniques are relatively ineffective. Stimulants help a child to focus, listen, and be reached. You have to reach before you can teach.

■ The benefits of stimulant medication are often misrepresented in the media and by misinformed professionals. When stimulant medication is used correctly it is both safe and remarkably free from side effects. It is without doubt the single most effective form of therapy available for ADHD. (See Appendix XVI, "Recent Review Papers.")

■ The stimulants Ritalin and dextroamphetamine sulfate have been used for 40 years. At the last count there have been over

155 reports of controlled trials which show their benefits and safety (see Spencer et al. 1996 in Appendix XVI). Between 80 percent and 90 percent of children with significant ADHD will be helped in the short term by one of the stimulants. Long-term benefits are presumed but as yet unproven.

■ Stimulant medication may be a relative of amphetamine, but it does not cause the ADHD child to substance-abuse or become addicted. Medication brings the unfocused child into full-focus reality. You don't get addicted to reality.

■ Natural remedies are often promoted as safer than stimulants and equally effective in the ADHD child. These have not been subjected to the same scientific trials and safety checks that would be required for a medication. Just because a product comes from a plant does not mean it is safe: opium, digitalis, magic mushrooms, and tobacco are all natural substances.

■ Medication is given only after a full explanation and the informed consent of the parents. If there is ever any doubt about benefits or any worrying side effect, the parents must stop the preparation at once and talk to those who prescribed it. Parents are in charge, not doctors.

■ With any medical treatment the benefits must be carefully balanced against all potential risks. Critics of medication quote the obscure, small-print side effects but do not mention the major risk of failing to treat. Every year impulsive, unthinking ADHD children are injured or killed needlessly in accidents. Countless families of untreated children fall out of love with the difficult child and these wrecked relationships may never heal.

■ Oppositional Defiant Disorder (ODD) is a comorbid condition found in 40 percent to 60 percent of children with ADHD. The ADHD child acts impulsively, without thought, and is remorseful after the event. The ODD child is openly hostile and may show no regret. When ADHD and ODD exist together treatment will be much more difficult. The behaviors of ODD do not respond to stimulants or any other medication.

■ The ADHD child is not deliberately difficult, they just act before they think. Successful parents make allowances but still ensure that children with ADHD know they are responsible for their own actions. ADHD is an explanation, it is not an excuse.

Diagnosis and treatment are important

ADHD must be recognized and treated properly. If this does not happen, it will continue to severely disadvantage tens of thousands of our children. The best time to diagnose and give support is early. In ADHD there is a limited window of opportunity to help—once this is closed gains will be much smaller. Poorly managed ADHD can lead to serious long-term problems:

- Most children with undiagnosed ADHD feel inferior and believe that they are dumb.

- With academic and social failure comes shattered self-esteem.

- Children who are poorly managed in their early school years lose their drive to succeed and the will to learn.

- Family relationships can be irretrievably damaged by the stress of living with an ADHD child. Many parents feel guilty when they start to wonder if they have any loving feelings for their child.

- The poorly managed ADHD child has a great chance of entering their adult life badly educated, socially inept, and lacking in confidence.

- Those children who make a successful transition into adulthood often channel their immense drive, determination, and single-mindedness to be outstanding in business or public life. We need to follow their lead and, for all ADHD children, to turn their difference into an advantage.

ADHD needs to be taken seriously. It is no longer good enough to pretend it is a trivial noncondition. Whatever means we use, our aim should be to help these children enter adulthood with the best education, esteem, and life skills that are possible. It is also vital to keep family relationships intact. If we miss out here, all the rest of our efforts are pretty pointless.

TWO

ADHD—An Old
Condition Rediscovered

ADHD has been heavily promoted recently in the popular press. Although it has now become the behavioral "flavor of the month," it is not a new condition. Churchill, Einstein, and some of the most influential people of all time had one thing in common: they channeled their ADHD activity, drive, and single-mindedness to achieve greatness.

The history of ADHD

ADHD was first described almost 100 years ago. Some of the earliest work was done by a famous English pediatrician, George Still. He remains a respected father figure who is now remembered, not for his work on ADHD, but for his classic description of arthritis in children, which continues to be called Still's disease.

Others had seen these behaviors some years before, but it was Still who, in 1902, was the first to recognize and describe the condition. He noticed a group of his patients, mostly boys, had difficult behaviors which had started before the age of eight. Most were inattentive, overactive, and were different from other children in their resistance to discipline.

Still described these children as having a poor control of inhibition, being full of aggression, and, in his Victorian language, suffering from "a lack of moral control." Still saw this as a chronic condition, biological (inborn) in nature, and not caused by poor parenting or adverse environment. What George Still described at the turn of the century is probably what would nowadays be called ADHD with Oppositional Defiant Disorder (ODD) or Conduct Disorder (CD).

It is interesting to note that at this time the United Kingdom led the world in its understanding of ADHD. As the twentieth century moved along, British researchers became preoccupied with a more psychoanalytical style of psychiatry, which left the job of sorting out ADHD to the North Americans.

ADHD and brain damage

Interest in ADHD came next in the wake of the great influenza epidemic of 1918–19. This epidemic killed over 20 million people worldwide, and its associated encephalitis (an inflammation of the brain) left many people neurologically impaired. Some of these people went on to develop Parkinson's disease (as described in the film *Awakenings*, with Robin Williams), while others showed immediate signs of disinhibition and dysfunction that had some similarities to the problems first described by Still. From this experience, ADHD was now seen as being the result of brain damage.

It was a long time before this injured brain idea lost favor and research returned to the in-built, biological nature initially suggested by Still.

Stimulants and ADHD—a chance finding

In 1937 a group of behaviorally disturbed in-patients were subjected to an unorthodox treatment. They were given the drug amphetamine and to everybody's surprise their difficult behaviors
improved. It took almost another 20 years before stimulant medication became widely used, but this chance finding was to greatly influence the direction of future treatment.

Minimal Brain Damage—Minimal Brain Dysfunction

Researchers in the 1950s and 1960s began to realize that most of
these ADHD children had never suffered any brain damage. They
softened the name from Minimal Brain Damage to Minimal Brain
Dysfunction. This implied that the brain was effectively normal,
but there was some subtle malfunction which accounted for the
behaviors.

Pediatricians then became obsessed with hunting for minor neurological differences. Until relatively recent times much of the assessment of ADHD consisted of looking at the flow of movement in
the fingers, the dominance of eye, foot, and hand, and a multitude
of other trivial tests. This form of assessment is still popular in some
centers, but most have moved on from this unhelpful preoccupation with "soft neurological signs."

Minimal Brain Dysfunction was never a satisfactory term, but at
least it implied that ADHD was made up of a cluster of behaviors
and it placed the blame on the brain, rather than the parents.

Hyperkinesis and Hyperactivity

During the time when the term Minimal Brain Dysfunction (MBD)
was being used, other medical professionals were starting to look at
specific behaviors. In the early 1960s the Hyperactive Child Syndrome was first described. The symptoms were somewhat unclear,
but the condition was seen as being part of the child's individual
makeup and not caused by brain damage. Through the 1960s and
1970s the terms MBD and Hyperactivity were both used, Hyperactivity being the name that caught the attention of the public and the
press.

Hyperactivity and the Feingold Diet

Dr. Ben Feingold, a former professor of allergy in San Francisco, first suggested a relationship between diet and Hyperactivity in 1973. He claimed that the reported rates of Hyperactivity were increasing in proportion to the number of additives which legally polluted our food. Feingold was quickly championed by the press and such was the overreaction, the American government was obliged to set up committees, and detailed research projects, to investigate the claims.

Feingold believed that 50 percent of Hyperactive children might be helped by his diet. When the results of carefully controlled trials were analyzed, it appeared that no more than 5 percent of these children were adversely affected by food. (See Chapter 13 for an up-to-date overview of diet and ADHD.)

These years of obsessive interest in diet distracted professional attention from the complex package of problems that made up ADHD, and from the already proven benefits of stimulant medication.

Stimulants—in and out of fashion

The beneficial effects of stimulant medication have been well known for over half a century. The benefits of amphetamines were clearly documented in the late 1930s, but stimulants were not widely used until the late 1950s and 1960s. The main breakthrough came with the introduction in 1957 of a new stimulant, methylphenidate (Ritalin), and in the next decade many carefully controlled studies showed that stimulants were both safe and effective.

The use of stimulants increased rapidly, impeded only by the occasional feeding frenzy in the media. In one early 1970s article, which is still often quoted, the rate of prescribing was misrepresented by 10 times its correct level. This media misinformation helped the sale of newspapers but it also frightened parents from a form of therapy that for some would have revolutionized their relationship with their children.

The greatest assault on stimulants was made in the late 1980s from an unexpected source, the Church of Scientology. This organization sent press releases to the media through its lobby group "the Citizens' Commission on Human Rights." Although most of their activities took place in the United States, this group's actions also affected many families in Australia.

Newspapers and radio stations were quick to transmit the commission's dramatic claims. Ritalin, it was asserted, was a dangerous and addictive drug, often used as a chemical straitjacket to subdue normally exuberant children because of intolerant educators, parents, and money-hungry psychiatrists. Ritalin could result in violence, murder, suicide, Tourette's syndrome, permanent brain damage, emotional disturbance, seizures, high blood pressure, confusion, agitation, and depression. Great controversy was said to exist among the scientific and professional communities concerning the use of medication (see R. A. Barkley, *Attention Deficit Hyperactivity Disorder—A Handbook for Diagnosis and Treatment*. New York: Guilford Press, 1990).

This unexpected assault by a religious subgroup set back the appropriate treatment of ADHD by years. Parents believed what they read in the press and refused to put their children on the medication. Even worse was the attitude of many top educationalists, psychologists, psychiatrists, pediatricians, and policy makers. They were swayed by what they saw in the media rather than reviewing the numerous studies in the scientific literature.

It was only at the start of the 1990s that we fully recovered from the aftershocks of this antistimulant campaign. In the meantime, many children had been prevented from receiving the treatment they needed.

Parents must still be on their guard, as even today press releases and "letters to the editor" continue to come from Scientologists with antimedication attitudes.

From Hyperactivity to Attention Deficit Hyperactivity Disorder

In the early 1970s a Canadian, Virginia Douglas, promoted the view that attention deficit was a more important symptom than hyperactivity. By the end of the 1970s her publications were so impressive that the American Psychiatric Association in 1980 used the term "Attention Deficit Disorder" in their diagnostic and statistical manual (DSM-III). In 1987 the American Psychiatric Association put out DSM-III-Revised, which now talked of Attention Deficit Hyperactivity Disorder. In 1994 the association released its latest classification DSM-IV, which describes Attention Deficit Hyperactivity Disorder (ADHD) without active, impulsive behaviors; ADHD with active, impulsive behaviors; and ADHD with a combination of both. Many parents, teachers, and legislators still use the popular term ADD, but to be strictly correct this condition should be referred to as ADHD.

Conclusion

In this century, our definition of ADHD started with Still's cluster of behaviors which were of biological (inborn) origin and had a poor prognosis. This was followed by a time of presumed brain damage. Next all the focus was on hyperactivity. Then diet seemed all-important in a condition that was believed to resolve itself before high-school age. The current definition describes a cluster of in-built behaviors of which inattention is paramount and impulsivity and overactivity are usual. The problems are long-term and symptoms often continue into adulthood. Medication is now accepted as an important part of therapy.

We have come a long way, but ADHD remains a highly variable, complex, and imprecisely defined condition. The danger for today's parents and professionals is to become lost in the uncertainties, rather than focusing on what we know to be true and using this information to help our children.

Summary: one hundred years of ADHD

1902:	Clear description of ADHD behaviors. Not caused by brain damage or poor parenting.
1930s:	Brain damage causes ADHD behaviors.
1937:	Stimulant medication first used.
1950s–60s:	Now believed to be a brain dysfunction— "Minimal Brain Dysfunction". Psychoanalytical child psychiatrists see ADHD in terms of parent and environment problems (for some this attitude continued until the 1990s).
1957:	Methylphenidate (Ritalin) introduced.
1960–70:	The "Hyperactive Child Syndrome" becomes popular. Ritalin widely used and many research papers on stimulants.

1970–75:	Inaccurate media claims raise concerns with medication.
	Feingold Diet becomes popular.
1975–80:	Medication regains considerable popularity.
1980:	American Psychiatric Association uses term "Attention Deficit Disorder" (DSM-III).
1987:	American Psychiatric Association uses term "Attention Deficit Hyperactivity Disorder" (DSM-IIIR). Anitmedication campaign misleads many parents and professionals.
1990:	Positron Emission Tomography (PET scan) shows significant difference in function between the ADHD brain and the non-ADHD brain.
1994:	American Psychiatric Association redefines "Attention Deficit Hyperactivity Disorder" DSM-IV.
1997:	ADHD seen as an interplay of four factors: attention and learning; impulsive, poorly controlled behaviors; the presence or absence of comorbid conditions; nurture or hostility in the child's environment.

THREE

ADHD—The Cause

Researchers still disagree on the exact cause of ADHD, but two things are certain. First, it is a hereditary condition. Second, the problems of ADHD result from a subtle difference in the fine tuning of the brain.

Most of the current debate centers around the exact nature of this brain difference. Some doctors see ADHD as a part of the normal spectrum of temperament, but the majority believe that it is a syndrome which is separate from temperament. Most researchers now believe that it is due to the underfunctioning of those areas of the brain that put the brakes on unwise behavior, the *frontal lobes* and their close connections, the *basal ganglia circuits*. In addition to this, there seems to exist an unusual imbalance in the message-transmitting chemicals of the brain, the *neurotransmitters*.

Whatever the rights and wrongs of these theories, two old ideas have certainly outlived their day: this condition is definitely not caused by diet or by poor parenting.

Heredity/genes and ADHD

When we look carefully at families in our practice, we notice most children with ADHD seem to have a close relative with a similar problem. Often we see a father who found his early school years difficult or who underfunctioned academically for his abilities. Some of these adults have done well in life but are still restless, inattentive, and fitted with a dangerously short fuse.

There is good research evidence to prove this genetic influence. Identical twins are created sharing the same genetic material. If one twin suffers ADHD, research shows an almost 90 percent chance the other will also have this problem.

Unidentical twins have the same risk of ADHD as the brother or sister of any ADHD child. The risk between siblings is somewhere between 30 and 40 percent depending on who you believe. These are high figures when compared with a rate of ADHD in the general population, which is somewhere between 2 and 7 percent. An

ADHD child of a parent with both ADHD and dyslexia often inherits both the attentional and reading problems.

There is no doubt that genes play an important part in the inheritance of both ADHD and specific learning disabilities, but why one child in a family inherits and another does not remains a mystery.

The brain difference

In this noisy world, most of the unimportant messages that enter into the brain are screened out at a low level without ever coming to the attention of "middle management." Important information is taken in and looked at by the specialist parts of the brain, which interact together to give a properly coordinated response. Finally, the chief executive (frontal lobe) takes an overview of the middle-management decisions, approving or disapproving on the grounds of appropriateness, priorities, future implications, and their effect on others.

In the ADHD child's brain it seems that the information rushes in without much filtering, which leaves the television screen of the mind in a bit of a buzz. The information is integrated, but action is often taken before the chief executive has approved the decision.

This is an oversimplification of a complicated process, but there is no doubt that these children do become distracted with too much competing stimulation and they tend to respond without giving proper consideration. Though the research emphasis is all on frontal lobes and the basal ganglia circuits, it is probable that many other areas of the brain are also involved.

Brain research in ADHD

At present the main research interest is in four areas: assessing *frontal lobe function* (the seat of executive control); investigating *areas of under- and overfunction* (SPECT, PET, and functional MRI scans); measuring levels of activity; and studying the message-transmitting *brain chemicals* (neurotransmitters).

Assessing frontal lobe function—neuropsychology

A more specialized breed of psychologists, the neuropsychologists, are constantly developing ways to study the subtle workings of the brain. One area of special interest is the executive control which resides in the frontal lobes.

Most knowledge of this part of the brain comes from studies of adult accident victims. When their frontal lobes have been injured, they may respond to situations without proper consideration. Most of the tests of frontal lobe function focus on "response inhibition," "planning," and "mental flexibility," as these seem to be the hallmark of problems in the frontal lobe.

In testing, the child is bombarded with a flood of distracting information, and in the midst of this they are repeatedly challenged to see if they will make a considered, not reflex, response. The ADHD child shows a weakness in knowing when to react, when to hold back, and when to modify their response.

This poor performance in response inhibition, planning, and mental flexibility confirms a weakness in frontal lobe function. Children who have ADHD without the hyperactive–impulsive behaviors, the "inattentive only" group, have the same weakness and, on top of this, their speed of processing information is very slow. These dreamy ADHD children have frontal lobe dysfunction and also show "slow-moving cogs" in their brain.

Brain imaging

SPECT and PET

Until recently medical methods of imaging the brain did little to help us understand ADHD. Skull X-rays showed problems in the skull bones but not the brain. Routine CAT (Computer Axial Tomography) scans showed the anatomy in detail, but in ADHD the brains were essentially normal.

In the late 1980s two exciting new developments arrived, firstly Single Photon Emission Computed Tomography (SPECT) and then Positron Emission Tomography (PET scans). These techniques assess the level of activity in the various parts of the brain where they show function rather than anatomy. (See also Appendix IX.)

The SPECT measures blood flow to different parts of the brain and emits much less radiation than a PET scan. In the PET scan a sugar is tagged with a radioactive marker and injected into the body. The sugar accumulates in the areas of the brain that are doing most of the work, which "light up" with high levels of the tagged radioisotopes.

Due to the amount of radiation used and the expense, these scans are not routinely used in children with ADHD, but research scans have come up with some fascinating findings:

■ The frontal lobes and their close connections are found to underfunction in ADHD.

■ The areas of the brain that collect auditory and visual input seem overloaded in ADHD, suggesting that they are being bombarded by a lot of unnecessary, inappropriate information.

■ When stimulant medication is administered, the ADHD difference seen in the brain scan can be largely reversed. This exciting finding shows that the effects of stimulant medication are certainly no figment of the imagination; they normalize the brain difference that is presumed responsible for ADHD. (See Appendix XV, "SPECT scans in ADHD" and "PET scans.")

MRI scans

The Positron Emission Tomography (PET) and Single Photon Emission Computed Tomography (SPECT) studies have their limitations, due to the levels of radiation. Researchers have recently moved to the techniques of volumetric and functional Magnetic Resonance Imaging (MRI). These give out little radiation and the hard copy of the MRI picture can be assessed impartially by experts around the world. Volumetric MRI is not cheap, with about 30 hours of labor needed to measure each scan.

In ADHD each volumetric MRI scan is measured in minute detail. These studies will reliably pick up about 70 percent of ADHD children due to a slight asymmetry in their frontal area and a constant difference in the caudate nucleus (part of the basal ganglia circuits).

When first published, these results created great interest, but critics questioned whether the stimulant medication administered to these ADHD children had caused the brain difference. The researchers went back to testing for a further year and have now found that whether medication has been used or not, 70 percent still show the difference. A further study is now looking at ADHD girls.

Measures of activity

Over the years there has been a preoccupation with the hyperactive part of ADHD. One group of researchers devised an instrument that could record the levels of activity throughout a day. The results showed that the problem in ADHD was not the level of activity, but the inability to adapt this to expectations of the classroom or playing field. All children were "hyped up" when they came in from the playground, but those without ADHD settled down on the teacher's command, while the ADHD child took time to calm and concentrate. This ability to self-regulate and to settle improved with the use of medication.

Measurements were then taken during team sports. Unmedicated children with ADHD surprised the researchers by being less active on the sports field. Evidently they stood around and found it hard to follow the game. When given their stimulants, they focused and were just as involved and as active as their non-ADHD classmates.

ADHD is not about general hyperactivity; it is about the self-monitoring of activity which allows quick calming in class and full throttle in sports.

Message-transmitting chemicals—the neurotransmitters

At the cutting edge of brain research there is great interest in the individual cell, the gap between each cell, and the chemicals that pass messages from cell to cell. How do these billions of individual cells communicate with their neighbors? What chemicals are released to spark off the next cell? Why do brain chemicals work in one part of the brain and not another? Why are some messages passed on and others blocked?

Synapses and neurotransmitters

Two brain cells (neurons) lie next to each other, separated by a small gap (synapse). For a message to pass from one cell to the next, the first cell (presynaptic cell) releases a chemical (neurotransmitter) which stimulates the second cell (postsynaptic cell). Once the transmitter chemical has done its job, all traces are immediately broken down by a fast-working enzyme system. This process sparks a chain reaction from cell to cell.

Researchers are interested in the neurotransmitter chemicals, the cleaning-up enzymes, and the switching substances (the phospho-proteins) which seem to turn certain pathways on and off. To date over 50 neurotransmitters and 100 different switch chemicals have been described, each apparently specific to certain brain regions and functions. This area of research is only in its infancy but it is all-important to our understanding of the treatment of ADHD.

Brain chemicals in ADHD

The basic difference between those who have ADHD and those who do not lies in the balance of the neurotransmitter chemicals dopamine and noradrenaline. In ADHD both these chemicals appear to be either produced in lower volumes by the presynaptic cell, or picked up less efficiently by the postsynaptic cell. This results in a relative reduction in dopamine and noradrenaline, an effect which we presume is only found in certain areas of the brain, particularly the frontal lobes and the basal ganglia circuits.

The neurotransmitters dopamine and noradrenaline both have quite different actions. Dopamine is probably the most important chemical in ADHD. It acts by sustaining readiness and not letting our own thoughts or outside activity distract us. Appropriate levels of dopamine allow us to inhibit what is unimportant and retain attention on a task. If dopamine levels are raised artificially high, a child may become stuck, and appear obsessive.

The role of noradrenaline in ADHD is much less clear-cut. This is the brain chemical that deals with the "fight or flight" reactions. It provides the protective animal instinct that allows us to quickly focus on what's important and then act appropriately. Noradrenaline keeps us on a high level of alert, sensitizing us to anything that is unusual, unexpected, or of immediate significance. Too little noradrenaline causes us to be indifferent, disinterested, and a bit withdrawn. Too much may produce a constant wish for a thrill and over-the-top excitement.

The neurotransmitter serotonin seems important for feelings of satisfaction, adequate sleep, and positive thought. Low serotonin levels are associated with depression. Though we understand some of the actions of these chemicals, we still need to know how they work together and how they are switched from one part of the brain to another.

Drugs and brain chemicals

The drugs methylphenidate (Ritalin) and dextroamphetamine increase the available levels of dopamine and noradrenaline. The action of these chemicals is isolated to specific areas, presumably by the switching effect of the phosphoproteins. The drug Ritalin is thought to have a slightly greater effect on aggression and impulse control, while the drug dextroamphetamine is thought to have marginally more effect on attention. The two drugs act on slightly different pathways, though they produce a reasonably similar effect.

The tricyclic antidepressants imipramine (Tofranil) and desipramine (Norpramin) act by inhibiting the breakdown of noradrenaline at the postsynaptic cell. This increases the level of noradrenaline and at the same time appears to have a slight dopamine-increasing action. The tricyclics are not as effective as the stimulants, but they do bring some benefit to those with ADHD.

The selective serotonin reuptake inhibitors, for example Prozac and Zoloft, work by increasing the effective level of the neurotransmitter serotonin. They have no significant dopamine effect and so are not of value in the treatment of ADHD. This serontonin-raising effect brings benefits to those with depression, Obsessive Compulsive Disorder, and, to some extent, to people suffering anxiety.

The development of drugs to modify these brain chemicals has recently revolutionized the practice of psychiatry. Though we have come a long way, there is still a lot to learn about the production, interaction, and switching of these substances.

Parenting as a cause of ADHD

Children with ADHD often behave badly and cause stress for their parents. The normal methods of discipline work less well and after some years of failure most parents back off and aim for the more peaceful path.

Some uninsightful experts, when seeing this lack of textbook discipline, misread the situation and attribute the child's behavior to poor parental management.

It is important for every professional to realize that a child's behavior affects the style of disciplining, just as the parent's discipline affects the style of behavior.

Genuine parenting problems

Where major family chaos exists, this will affect any child, whether they have ADHD or not. Statistics show that ADHD children have a greater chance of coming from a dysfunctional home setting. On face value it would be easy to see this family turmoil as the sole cause of the difficult behavior. But things are not always what they seem.

We know that major troubles in the home are much more likely if a parent has an intolerant, impulsive, socially inept style of temperament. These problems of personality make an adult hard to live with, but they may also be symptoms of residual ADHD.

This is where the confusion really starts. If a parent has ADHD, the child is at risk of inheriting the same condition. If this genetically more difficult child is then brought up in a home which is inconsistent, volatile, and full of stress, the behavior will be blown through the roof.

Where major environmental chaos exists alongside ADHD, it is often hard to work out which came first—the chicken or the egg. Genes and environment may both be responsible.

ADHD—normal, not pathological

Research from the late 1950s shows that each child is born with an individual temperamental style. Could it be that ADHD is just part of the wide spectrum of normal temperament? These behaviors may even have been of benefit in the past.

Until recent times, reading, writing, and sitting in a classroom would have been irrelevant for the average child and ADHD would probably not have been noticed. Going even further back, ADHD may have been an advantage in caveman times, when survival was all-important. While cooking a rabbit over a fire our ADHD ancestors would be quickly distracted by every breaking twig and rustle in the bushes. If danger appeared they would respond by reflex. On the other hand, our deep-thinking, attentive ancestors might focus so much on the rabbit that they would be wiped out before they knew of the danger. Possibly these active, impulsive people were the superhumans of their day, while those who are now well-behaved school achievers would have been quite disabled.

We know that Winston Churchill underfunctioned at school, but the immense energy and bloody-mindedness of his ADHD changed the course of history. ADHD is not due to a damaged brain, but it is probably an edge of the wide spectrum of normal. In the past it may have been an attribute, but today the demands of school and society have turned it into a problem.

Summary: the cause of ADHD

A hereditary condition

- Usually a parent or close relative has ADHD.

- If a parent has ADHD and SLD (specific learning disabilities), the child will often inherit both.

- In studies of identical twins, if one has ADHD, there is a 90 percent chance the other will have ADHD.

- Siblings carry a 30–40 percent risk of inheriting ADHD.

A problem of fine tuning of the brain

Neuropsychology

- Impulsive ADHD children show frontal lobe dysfunction: they can't "put the brakes on" behavior.

- Children who are purely inattentive (without impulsive, active behavior) show the same frontal lobe problems but also have a slow processing speed: "slow-moving cogs."

The PET and SPECT scans

■ Show underfunction of frontal lobe and close connections.

■ More unnecessary information arrives through ears and eyes.

The MRI scan

■ 70 percent of ADHD children show a "marker."

Measures of activity

■ ADHD children are overactive when they should be quiet and underactive when they should be busy.

■ It is not overactivity, it is poor self-monitoring of activity.

Brain chemical imbalance

■ An imbalance or reduction of noradrenaline and dopamine.

■ Stimulant medication appears to help normalize this imbalance.

■ This normalizing effect has been demonstrated using a SPECT scan.

Parenting and ADHD

■ Poor parenting does not cause ADHD.

■ Poor parenting can make the behavior worse.

■ Difficult children make their parents' discipline appear inadequate.

■ Major family dysfunction can occur with ADHD: part of the problem may be in the genes and part in the environment.

FOUR

The Behaviors That Bother Parents

In the official diagnostic manual (DSM-IV) produced by the American Psychiatric Association, two groups of behavior are described: the hyperactive-impulsive behaviors and those of attention deficit–learning problems. The aim of this chapter is to forget about the formal criteria and paint a Technicolor picture of how these children present to their parents and teachers. Once you recognize the shades that make up this disorder, move to Chapter 5 to see how these fit in with the modern view of ADHD.

Inattentiveness

Inattentive children quickly lose the focus of their attention. They become bored, get distracted, and may flit from task to task without achieving anything. Schoolwork takes a long time to complete or never gets finished. Teachers are mystified; the child does so much when stood over and so little when left alone.

This deficit varies from day to day: some days these children are in tune, and the next they are "off the planet." This behavior also changes from one situation to another; some of the most inattentive children we manage can leave their peers for dead as they focus on a video game.

This variability means inattention may often be missed by inexperienced assessors. Some ADHD children appear to concentrate well in the novel, interesting environment of our offices. Some equally inattentive children work well with the psychologist in one-to-one testing but fall apart when they return to a busy class of 30.

Inattention to verbal instructions and a poor short-term memory are particular problems. Parents send the child off to get two things, he reappears a minute later and says, "What was the second one?"

There is an interesting subgroup of inattentive children (ADHD—inattentive-only type) who are heavily distracted by their own thoughts. These children appear to drift off the air as their teacher starts to talk. Their minds are a million miles away, and as they sit placidly in class they cause no one any bother, but they don't seem to learn. They become "the quiet unachievers." Einstein was probably one of these, an intelligent school failure interested more in cracking the theory of relativity than in listening to his teacher.

Adults with residual ADHD often tell of their difficulty concentrating during a lecture. Their minds spin, full of thoughts about other subjects. As they read, the print passes their eyes, but their mind is elsewhere. Others cope with their poor short-term memory by doing things immediately or writing reminder notes. Most of these inattentive adults and children have difficulty with mental arithmetic or remembering a sequence of numbers.

It's hard to communicate with an inattentive child, and stimulant medication may help this problem. One of our patients recently said, "At school, when I don't take my medication, many people are talking. When I am on Ritalin I hear only one voice—that of the teacher."

See detailed description of the attention and learning problems of ADHD in Chapter 5—"Attention deficit (problems of executive control.")

What the parents say

"What I tell him goes in one ear and out the other. Can we get his hearing tested?"

"When we work at times tables and spelling lists, they are remembered tonight but tomorrow she knows nothing."

"It's not that he can't attend—he concentrates for hours, at Nintendo and watching television."

"She's off the air."

"With homework he slips off focus unless I stand over him."

"He's impossible in the morning. He goes to his room to get ready for school, half an hour later he has one sock on and is looking out the window."

"My husband can't even remember to pick up a quart of milk on his way home unless he writes himself a note."

"He can remember details of what happened last year but forgets what I said two minutes ago."

Inattention is not always ADHD

When any of us finds our work too difficult, we quickly lose concentration. This is called secondary inattention and is found in children who have problems of language, reading, writing, or mathematics. The child switches off when his mind is overloaded, but full attention returns once the stress stops.

Children who are intellectually disabled often appear inattentive, but their attention span is appropriate for their younger developmental age. Other children drift off when their minds are preoccupied by some stress, but this comes and goes with emotional events and is not associated with the other cluster of ADHD behaviors. There are, of course, occasions when emotional stress, specific learning problems, and intellectual disability can coexist with ADHD.

Impulsiveness

ADHD is a problem of unreliable self-monitoring and inadequate inhibition of unwise behavior. These children do not set out to get into trouble; they just shoot straight from the hip with no thought of the repercussions. These children are quite aware of what is right and wrong, but it doesn't register until a millisecond after they have reacted and by then it is too late.

Poor impulse control is the behavior that gets these children into the most trouble. Parents can't understand how someone so intelligent can behave so stupidly. No amount of reasoning helps the situation; the children are genuinely upset at what they've done but they will be just as unthinking the next time.

When the average child is shoved at assembly, they carefully check if the teacher is looking before they kick someone in retaliation. The ADHD child responds by reflex, gets caught, and is called aggressive.

Many of these children are accident-prone; they climb on roofs, jump out of windows, run across roads, and ride their bicycles without looking ahead.

It is not unusual for lawyers to ask us to appear when they are suing an insurance company claiming that a child has become inattentive as the result of a road accident. Sometimes when we talk to the school we find that the child was just as difficult before the accident; in fact, it was the impulsiveness of their inborn ADHD that caused them to run across the road and get injured. One teacher even took it a step further—she told us that the bump on the head had "maybe made him concentrate a bit better!"

Impulsive children interrupt and talk over the top of others. They are also easily frustrated and extremely impatient. Most have a short fuse and explode easily.

In school, incorrect answers are blurted out before the question has been completed. Instructions are only half heard before a response is made. Work is rushed through with lots of careless mistakes.

In the playground, these children are easily led and often over the top. Some have such poor playground behavior that they spend most lunchtimes sitting outside the principal's office. These children are not aggressive, but their behavior quickly escalates out of control and they don't think too deeply of the consequences of their actions. A number of older children find themselves suspended from school after a poorly managed blowup.

These sparky, "short fuse" children are difficult to discipline as their reactions are so reflex-bound. They learn slowly from experience and along the way cause great pain to their parents, teachers, and themselves. Unreliable impulse control causes stress to many adults with ADHD. Relationships are damaged by unthinking outbursts. Finances fail due to impulse spending. Volatility causes difficulty at work and increases the risk of accidents. It is this fallout from impulsivity that triggers many ADHD adults to seek professional help.

What the parents say

"As a preschooler you could never trust him out of your sight."

"He doesn't seem to learn from experience."

"She's eight but she still interrupts us like a toddler."

"When we visit friends, something always gets broken and somebody always gets hurt."

"He enjoys his bike, but he has no road sense."

"He's easily led and always gets the blame."

"At school other children seek him out to taunt. They know they always get him to react."

"When he's around, you never quite know what is going to happen next."

"He's got such a short fuse—it's like juggling dynamite."

"He's quite like his father."

"We worry that one of these days he's going to get a driver's license!"

Overactivity

Historically, it is hyperactive behavior which has been the main feature of ADHD. It is our opinion that overactivity in isolation is only a minor problem, but when overactivity and impulsivity come together, this busy, short-fused combination becomes absolute dynamite.

A few of these restless young people were unusually active even before they were born. A significant number were colicky and demanding in infancy. A surprising proportion were quite average or even exceptionally good as babies—presumably they were saving themselves! For most parents the change came when they started to walk; then they took the house apart and got into everything.

Many are busy at preschool, finding it hard to settle down at story time. Once school starts, hyperactivity is generally more subtle in its presentation. There is an overall increase in body movement, which gets worse as the day wears on. These children are restless, fidgety, and have difficulty remaining seated. Those who appear to be sitting still are jiggling their legs, tapping their fingers, or fiddling with anything they can touch. This restless squirming activity is described as "rump hyperactivity." These school children may not move from their seat, but their rump and fingers are certainly pretty active.

When busy children hit the playground they are like animals released from captivity. When they return to the structure of the classroom, many find it hard to settle down. At home they pace around, touch things, open and close the refrigerator door. Hyperactivity tends to ease in the early school years and is much less by the time these young people reach teen age. A few remain just as fast and furious in their adult years.

What the parents say

"He was hyperactive even before he was born."

"She was such a demanding baby she took up every minute of my life."

"This toddler is constantly on the move. He is like a pinball, bouncing from one thing to another."

"He's so noisy, he just erupts."

"When visiting he has to touch everything."

"I could never take him to the china department."

"She hates to be restricted, she loves to be outside."

"He is a teenager, but on a wet day he still paces around like a caged animal."

"His grandmother says I was just the same as a child."

Insatiability

These children intrude, demand, interrogate, and don't know when to back off. This insatiability, which comes with ADHD, is probably the most nerve-numbing behavior for parents. Once an idea gets into their minds, these children go on and on, long past the point when any other child would have let it drop.

It is a minute before dinner. *"Can I have a slice of bread?"* "No, your dinner is just about ready." *"Can I have a cookie?"* "No!" *"Can I have a banana?"* Soon their parent is ready for a straitjacket.

They quibble, nag, and demand on until the calmest parent is close to having a stroke. Insatiability is the behavior that causes the greatest stress—at the end of a family weekend the parents feel as if they have had a 48-hour workout with the KGB.

When stimulant medication is effective most spontaneously say "home life has become calmer." Easing the escalation and interrogation is what they mean.

What the parents say

"Why can't she put a lid on it?"

"Nothing I do pleases him; whatever he gets, he wants more."

"We don't tell him when we are going on a trip. If we did he would ask, 'Are we going on Wednesday? How will we get there? Are we really going on Wednesday? Are we going by car? Is it Wednesday we are going?' "

"I try to stay calm, but as he goes on and on, my chest feels tight, my neck tenses, and I wonder if I am about to have a coronary."

"He's like a mosquito, in my ear from dawn to dusk. I need some space!"

Social clumsiness

Though ADHD children are sensitive and caring, many are socially out of tune. They want to be popular with their friends but don't seem to know how to make this happen. They misread the accepted social cues, saying or doing something quite inappropriate. When in a group, their instability makes them come on too strong, which causes their friends to pull away and wonder, "What sort of a weirdo is this?"

In the playground they want to be part of the main game, but rather than let things take their natural course, they barge in, poke, taunt, and annoy. The more they try to be friendly, the more they become isolated.

These children function best in the small-group setting or with one good friend. Even here they can have problems, being bossy and always wanting to be top dog. Friends who come around to play soon leave in a huff.

Social problems hit a peak in primary school and start to ease in high school. In adolescence, however, any remaining insecurities make the normal social uncertainties of this age even greater. When adults bring the remains of their ADHD to their grown-up years, it is often this social clumsiness that causes particular pain.

What the parents say

"It burns me up, watching him play with his friends. He behaves like an impaired idiot."

"At school he is known by all, but liked by none."

"It embarrasses me that she doesn't have a clue how to behave when she is with other people."

"Other children don't seem to understand him."

"He's so hurt by being shunned by his schoolmates, though he brings it on himself."

"He says he has no friends."

"Before medication he was the only member of the class who was never asked to a birthday party. This year he's been to seven!"

"At times he's quite paranoid. The most innocent things others do are interpreted as deliberate attempts to get at him."

"My ADHD husband is a nice guy, but he seems blind to my emotional needs."

Poor coordination

Coordination problems come as *fine motor* (coloring, manipulating, handwriting, tying shoelaces) or *gross motor* (running, climbing, catching a ball, riding a bike).

Most ADHD children have difficulty with fine-motor tasks, particularly written work. The further they get down the page, the greater the untidiness and the more they cross out. Parents and teachers often despair over the quality of this handwork, becoming so obsessed with the writing they fail to spot the talent in the content.

A few ADHD children are genuinely clumsy but a larger number appear clumsy due to their poor impulse control. These children charge around like a bull in a china shop, bumping, tripping, and spilling as they go. Their knees and elbows are scarred, their lower legs covered with bruises.

Many ADHD children have a less obvious coordination problem—their difficulty is in planning what they do as well as the quality of their flow of movement. They walk, run, and climb efficiently, but it just doesn't look right. They have difficulty coordinating a sequence of movements or doing two things at one time. At the swimming pool they move their arms and kick their legs, but they don't seem able to breathe in rhythm. At the dance class they love the music but when it comes to formal steps they are lost. Aerobics are impossible as they try to kick, wave, shake, and smile all at one time. Shoelaces are abandoned in favor of Velcro.

When children have difficulty throwing and catching a ball, they feel unwelcome in the normal school-break play activities. A good occupational therapist will never turn this child into an Olympic athlete, but can improve his performance on the playground. On the positive side, many ADHD children are superb at sports, and this attribute gives an immense uplift to their self-esteem.

Some adults with ADHD are exceptional athletes. One of Australia's rugby greats was recently in trouble for impulsive outbursts on the field. A friend who gave a character reference said, "He is a wonderful guy, but like a large international airport with a very small control tower."

What the parents say

"He's so clumsy, he's last to be picked for any game."

"I know you tell me her coordination is normal but the way she moves is different from other children."

"Soccer does not suit him; he forgets what he is doing, spaces out, and is a poor loser."

"If there was one small brick in a big playground, she would trip over it."

"He took forever learning to tie his shoelaces."

Disorganization

Many ADHD children are highly disorganized. You can see this in their dress: clothes are back to front, inside out, and messy, while shoelaces are only half-tied. Dirty hands wipe through the hair and over the clothes, and some have "fiddly fingers," which seem to act without instruction from the brain.

Messages sent from school never get home. The school bag is left on the bus. Swimsuits are found later at the pool. Books are not brought home for homework. Many children are blind to the trail of mess that surrounds them.

By the early high-school years, ADHD children are generally tidier, but disorganization is still an impediment. When doing projects, they fiddle, procrastinate, and find it hard to get things started. During exams, they spend half their time on one question and don't finish the other questions. Many ADHD adults acknowledge this vulnerability and protect themselves by living life to a strict, almost obsessive routine.

When an ADHD child is disorganized from birth, their messiness will improve with age, and it is important that parents do not get too worked up along the way. When an obsessively tidy mother produces a completely disorganized child, there is the potential for major conflict. Fighting is pointless, as no amount of nagging will change this child in the short term.

What the parents say

"If I ask him to tuck in his shirt, the shirt goes in. As he removes his hand twice as much comes out."

"School projects are finished late."

"He can't see a problem before it hits."

"When doing homework she lines up her books, takes out a pencil, sharpens it, puts it away, takes out another, but can't get started."

"He leaves a trail of lost property at school, sports fields, and the pool."

"He's so disorganized, he's the sort of child who could eat a Mars Bar and brush his teeth at the same time."

"High school projects are finished late or at the last minute."

Variability

All children and adults have good and bad days, but people with ADHD experience extreme variation in performance and mood. These dramatic differences confuse parents, who have often asked if their child might have a double personality or even be schizophrenic!

Parents try to account for the bad days by blaming stress, lack of sleep, or some dietary difference. Even when these factors are carefully controlled, the behavioral fluctuations will remain. Their cause is not known, but they are certainly not intentional.

Teachers are particularly aware of this variation. On the occasional good day they are amazed at how so much work can be achieved. On bad days they say that the child might as well have stayed at home. Teachers have to accept that these fluctuations will occur and reward the occasional good day. The bad days have to be accepted as part of ADHD and not as a sign of laziness.

What the parents say

"Some days she is so easy to be with. Others she just doesn't know what to be up to."

"Homework is usually a hassle, then some days he finishes it in 10 minutes."

"On bad days his teacher sends him to help in the library. She realizes he is learning nothing in the classroom."

"His emotions are all over the place. One minute he's intensely irritating, the next he's devastated at a minor reprimand."

Poor self-esteem

It is a paradox, but most ADHD children are exceptionally sensitive. For this reason it is important to look below all their hustle and hype to see the soft, sensitive center.

Self-esteem is almost always low in ADHD children—it's no surprise, as they see so much failure. They put so much effort into their schoolwork, yet achieve so little. They want to be popular, but they are treated like an annoying outcast. Some achieve well at games, while others are banished to the sidelines as being too uncoordinated to play with their friends.

This combination of sensitivity, vulnerability, and inadequate esteem in those with ADHD must be taken seriously. By the age of 20 all their classroom problems will be behind them, but any ongoing weakness in socialization and self-esteem will have implications for the rest of their lives.

What the parents say

"He says he's dumb."

"She tells me she has no friends."

"He says he's ugly."

"No one seems to want to play with him."

"She now gives up without even trying."

"He finds it less competitive to hang out with younger children or others with problems."

Specific learning disabilities

Over half of all children with ADHD will have a significant weakness in some academic area. This may be in reading, writing, spelling, language, mathematics, or a combination of all of these skills. These problems of learning and language are so frequently associated with ADHD that it is important to consider them in every child. It is tough at school when you can't concentrate, organize your work, and stick to a task. It is even tougher when there are also unrecognized problems of learning and language (see Chapter 22).

When is it normal? When is it ADHD?

As you have read the list of behaviors covered in this chapter, we can hear you say, "But these are present in lots of normal children and adults." That's true—there is no clear cutoff point between the normal child with an active temperament and the one with a mild ADHD.

The diagnosis will be made by looking at which behaviors predominate, their magnitude, and how well they are being handled. No one is going to set up a behavioral program or give medication unnecessarily. <u>We treat only those whose behavior and learning are causing problems to themselves and those who care for them.</u>

The difference between the bothersome behavior of ADHD and that of a normal, busy temperament is the trouble it creates. Remember, "A problem is only a problem when it causes a problem."

Summary: behaviors associated with ADHD

Core behaviors

- *Inattention:* The child is easily distracted, forgets instructions, flits from task to task, is best with one-to-one supervision. A few have attention deficit of the purely inattentive type. These dreamy "space men" have slow-moving brains.

- *Impulsivity:* The child speaks and acts without thinking and has a short fuse.

- *Overactivity:* The child is restless, fidgety, and has "rump hyperactivity."

Frequent findings

- *Insatiability:* The child is never satisfied, nags, never lets a matter drop.

- *Social clumsiness:* The child is "out of tune" socially, acts silly in a crowd, misreads social cues.

- *Poor coordination:* The child is clumsy, has poor flow of movement, has difficulty doing two actions at one time.

- *Disorganization:* The child is blind to mess, is compelled to touch everything, has problems starting, sustaining, and completing work.

- *Variability:* The child suffers from mood swings, and has good and bad days to the extreme.

■ *Specific learning disabilities:* Examples are dyslexia, language problems, difficulties with mathematics.

Note: Now see Chapter 5, "The Modern View of ADHD." This shows how the problems of attention, behavior, learning disability, defiance, and factors in the child's environment all fit together.

FIVE

The Modern View of ADHD—A Four-Part Problem

When a group of parents discuss their ADHD children, any eavesdropper would realize that no two are identical. Some of these children are amazingly active, interrogating, and impulsive. Some are inattentive and dreamy, while the behavior of others is hostile and oppositional. Many are dyslexic, some have language problems, and most are underfunctioning at school. Occasionally one is involved in criminal activities. The modern view sees ADHD as a bit of a mixed bag.

The four-part problem

The condition most parents describe as ADHD is not true ADHD. They are seeing a blend of four parts, only two of which correctly fit the ADHD diagnosis. The two parts of true ADHD are *hyperactive-impulsive behaviors* and *attention deficit–learning problems*.

The two ADHD parts are then affected by the presence or absence of a third part, the comorbid conditions. These associated problems, for example dyslexia, Oppositional Defiant Disorder, and Conduct Disorder, are not caused by ADHD but occur in over half of the children who have true ADHD.

Finally the two ADHD parts and the comorbid conditions are influenced by a fourth part, the standard of parenting and support in the child's environment.

ADHD—the four parts

The first two parts of ADHD

Part 1 ADHD: hyperactive-impulsive behaviors (poor self-control of behavior).
Part 2 ADHD: attention deficit–learning problems (problems of executive control).
Note: Most ADHD children have a mix of both parts, though some can have one part in isolation (e.g., inattentive only).

The third part—comorbid conditions

■ Over half those with ADHD have an associated (comorbid) condition.

■ Between 40 percent and 60 percent have Oppositional Defiant Disorder and approximately 50 percent have a specific learning disability.

■ Other conditions include Conduct Disorder, Tic Disorder, poor coordination, depression, anxiety, Obsessive Compulsive Disorder, and Bipolar Disorder.

The fourth part—the child's living environment

■ Supportive parenting versus hostile, critical parenting.

■ Supportive schooling versus unaccepting education.

■ An extended stable family versus isolation and rejection.

True ADHD

Twenty years ago ADHD, or Hyperactivity as it was then known, was all about restless, busy behaviors—but now we realize that activity by itself is not the problem. The difficulties come from poor self-control of behavior and a deficit of attention.

Nowadays ADHD is accepted as these two parts, the hyperactive-impulsive behaviors (HI behaviors) and attention deficit–learning problems (problems of executive control). In 1994, when the American Psychiatric Association reviewed their criteria for diagnosis (DSM-IV), they recognized the importance of these two presentations.

They believed that almost all ADHD children show some degree of attention deficit–learning problems. In addition to this, the majority also showed the classic hyperactive-impulsive behaviors. A significant and probably underestimated number have only the deficit in attention, short-term memory, and learning (ADHD—predominantly inattentive).

ADHD (DSM-IV 1994)

- Attention Deficit Hyperactivity Disorder *combined* type (hyperactive–impulsive behaviors with difficulties of attention, learning, and executive control).

- Attention Deficit Hyperactivity Disorder *predominantly inattentive* type (predominant problems of attention, learning, and executive control).

- Attention Deficit Hyperactivity Disorder *predominantly hyperactive–impulsive* type (hyperactive, impulsive, poor self-control of behavior—Behavior Inhibition Disorder).

- Attention Deficit Hyperactivity Disorder *not otherwise specified* (a vague classification for those who don't quite fit).

Though the DSM-IV review committee stuck with the label Attention Deficit Hyperactivity Disorder (AD/HD), some panel members suggested two new terms. For the lack of self-control that causes the hyperactive-impulsive outbursts, they suggested the name Behavior Inhibition Disorder (BID). For the pure presentation of attention deficit–learning problems they suggested Attention Deficit Disorder (ADD). These terms were not accepted in 1994 but may well appear in the near future. In the meantime we are left with ADHD—predominantly hyperactive-impulsive, and ADHD—predominantly inattentive.

Hyperactive-impulsive behaviors (Behavior Inhibition Disorder)

There are differences in the sort of children who come to a pediatric clinic versus those who visit a psychiatry practice. Pediatricians see more of the mix of both the behavioral and inattention part of ADHD. Psychiatrists attract more of the hyperactive–impulsive behaviors, frequently associated with oppositional behavior or Conduct Disorder. This results in pediatricians and psychiatrists having a different view on what is the predominant problem in ADHD.

A child with hyperactive–impulsive behaviors intrudes into every aspect of our lives. Parents are amazed how their apparently intelligent child can do such stupid things. "I constantly worry what he is up to." "He doesn't seem to learn from his mistakes." "He doesn't seem to know when to back off." "He's eight years old and interrupts like a toddler." "He doesn't see how he's annoying other people." "He doesn't put the brakes on behavior." "He is funny the first time but just keeps going until everyone is sick of him."

These parents are talking about a problem of inadequate self-control of behavior (Behavior Inhibition Disorder) or more correctly, ADHD (hyperactive–impulsive). (For behaviors see Chapter 4, and also Appendix I, "The Criteria for Diagnosing ADHD (DSM-IV)".)

Some children have ADHD of the predominantly hyperactive-impulsive type, but the majority have a mix of these HI behaviors with attention deficit–learning problems.

Attention deficit—learning problems

Though it is the explosive, unthinking "HI behaviors" that may initially bring the ADHD child to pediatricians or psychiatrists for help, the problems of attention and academic underfunction may be much more damaging when viewed throughout a lifetime. Those who see attention deficit as an inability to concentrate have a very simplistic view of the situation. This weakness in executive control affects all aspects of classroom learning, productivity at work, and success in life.

Adults with attention deficit report difficulty getting started on a task, failing to focus on the important issues, problems with sustaining performance, finding it hard to pick up again after interruption, a hopeless short-term memory, switching off, reading but not retaining, difficulty holding several things in the mind at once, and being easily distracted. Every one of us suffers the occasional lapse in attention and learning, but in ADHD this causes clever children to underfunction in school and life. There are a number of ways of looking at the problems of executive control—one is given here and another version in Chapter 22.

Underfocus/overfocus

The inattentive part of ADHD is not simply a matter of flitting and lack of focus. The problems of attention are influenced by specific situations. The child may be inattentive at school, but give them a computer game or a goal to mind and they never miss a point. Some with ADHD get stuck on one idea; they can't take a step back and see the big picture. With them ADHD is not just "underattention," it is also "overattention." They can't let go of an idea and will pursue it past all reason.

This problem of overfocus and underfocus has frustrated psychiatrists as they try to use cognitive behavior therapy in the treatment of adults with ADHD. Here the therapist helps their patient take a step back from an unhealthy self-belief, regroup and recalibrate with some more positive attitudes. The results of this have been disappointing as those with ADHD find it hard to step back and let an idea go. When stimulant medication was given with cognitive behavior therapy, these adults were more flexible and therapy brought success.

By inattention we refer to a deficit in the ability to sustain, move, and appropriately direct focus. The stimulant drugs improve the ability to focus, disengage, and refocus.

Getting started and keeping going

The ADHD mind is bursting with bright ideas—the problem is putting them into action. Things generally go well in the early years of education, but this changes when self-motivation, time

management, and projects become important. The inattentive pro-
crastinates, fiddles, time-wastes, and makes any excuse to avoid
starting. His work output is uneven, with great bursts of enthusiasm followed by times of little action.

Many teenagers and adults are at their most productive with the
adrenaline rush of a last-minute deadline. Those who live with or
work with these people find this crisis-dependent productivity a
nerve-numbing experience. This mix of a slow start and uneven
output is an immense trial to teachers, parents, employers, and
those with ADHD.

A restless, circling brain

The inattentive becomes bored unless work is new, varied, and
closely supervised. There is great difficulty sustaining effort when
performing routine, monotonous tasks. Some adults and children
experience immense drowsiness as their interest fades. Pages of
print pass their eyes but nothing seems to register.

The inattentive finds it hard to regroup after interruptions. It is
not only outside events that steal their concentration—the restless,
constantly circling brain of ADHD is always scanning to find new
areas of focus. *Those with ADHD don't need others to distract them; they
distract themselves!*

This fast-moving, ever-circling brain gives the person with
ADHD an immense ability to create. Unfortunately the lack of
executive control can prevent this creativity being translated into
royalties.

Drifting and "spacing"

Some children with the "inattentive only" form of ADHD are
dreamy, drifty "space men." Their brains seem to move slowly,
but these children are often unnoticed at school as they behave
well and fail in silence. This dreamy form of ADHD is made much
worse by its strong association with specific learning disabilities,
particularly dyslexia. Teachers become exasperated as they try to
get through to these quiet unachievers.

There is some overlap and confusion when we talk of "inattentive
only." The DSM-IV criteria mention ADHD—predominantly inattentive, but this covers two groups. These are the "dreamy space men"
who are true inattentive only, and the predominantly inattentive

who are more animated and impulsive. They are different in their clinical presentation, but both have the same high incidence of associated specific learning disabilities.

This form of ADHD is currently creating great interest. It's probably much more common than we realize and may be a frequent cause of school failure in that gentle ADHD population—girls.

Retaining and remembering

One of the greatest frustrations to anyone with attention deficit is its effect on short-term memory. You remember the finest detail of the trip you took two years ago, but nothing of the instruction just given. Parents can't understand how a clever child can be so unaware of what has just been said and so forgetful.

We have seen wives of ADHD men arrange a hearing test, as they believe their loved ones must be deaf. Those who become high fliers need to be mothered by an organizing secretary, who acts as their "frontal lobe." They need to be provided with lists of instructions and memory jogs (see "Improving memory," in Chapter 12).

Educationalists have taken this one step further and now talk of "active working memory." This is what we need to hold several bits of information in our minds, while we add, subtract, and work out an answer. When active working memory is weak it affects areas such as mental arithmetic and reading comprehension. With reading, the child has forgotten what was at the top of the paragraph by the time they reach the bottom. Memorizing times tables, doing homework, and learning lists are all a hassle. As they close their books in the evening the information is in their head, but it evaporates before the test the next day.

No amount of aggravation by teachers, parents, or loved ones will change the "easy come, easy go" memory of ADHD. This is frustrating not only for parents and teachers but also for the ADHD student. They can put in so much effort and get so little reward.

In summary

The condition we call ADHD is made up of behavior problems (hyperactive–impulsive behaviors) and learning problems (attention deficit). The current understanding of ADHD suggests that the majority present with a mixture of hyperactive–impulsive behaviors combined with the learning problems. Though most ADHD children have this mixture, some will present with the learning problems in isolation (ADHD—predominantly inattentive). It is possible that this group of quiet unachievers accounts for much unrecognized school failure (particularly in compliant girls).

Now that we have a grip on the different components that make up true ADHD, let's introduce two additional factors to the equation: the comorbidities (Chapter 6) and the parenting environment (Chapter 7).

SIX

Associated Conditions— The Comorbidities

In medicine it is known that if one part of the body shows some difference in function, this greatly increases the chance of other differences occurring in that part. Take the example of a child with autism, which is a brain-based condition: autism rarely occurs in isolation—there is a 70 percent chance of the associated brain problem of intellectual disability and a 10 percent chance of epilepsy. Autism does not cause the intellectual disability or the epilepsy, but when one condition occurs, the others frequently coexist.

The presence of ADHD greatly increases the coexistence of associated or comorbid conditions. These include specific learning disabilities, Oppositional Defiant Disorder, Conduct Disorder, depression, tics, Tourette's syndrome, coordination problems, Obsessive Compulsive Disorder, and Bipolar–Manic Depressive Disorder. The ADHD does not cause the oppositional behavior, dyslexia, or the tics; they are just more likely to coexist.

As these associated problems occur in over half those who present with ADHD, this means that much of what is called ADHD is in fact a comorbid condition. It is important to recognize these common associations, as different treatments are needed for each problem.

Comorbidity and professional blindness

Over the years the understanding of ADHD has been obstructed by professionals who have looked at ADHD with tunnel vision. They believed that if a child had Oppositional Defiant Disorder this ruled out the diagnosis of ADHD—thus the treatment with stimulants was unethical. When dyslexia was diagnosed this was treated with remedial reading, without acknowledging problems of attention and behavior. Coordination problems were often treated with sensory motor integration therapy, the associated problems of behavior and school underfunction being missed. The correct treatment for a child does not have to be an either/or exercise. Two or more conditions can coexist and each must be taken seriously. This is where the modern "mixed bag" view of ADHD starts to become extremely complicated.

Specific learning disabilities

Approximately 50 percent of children with ADHD also suffer some specific weakness in learning. A specific learning disability implies that the child has a significant discrepancy between their tested intelligence and their performance in certain specific areas. The most frequent discrepancies are in reading, spelling, writing, language, and mathematics. (For more detailed information on reading problems see Chapters 22 and 23; for language problems see Chapters 22 and 24; for writing difficulties see Chapter 25.)

The child's ADHD does not cause the learning disabilities, though its presence makes remediation less successful. The treatment of ADHD with medication does not directly affect problems of learning, but medication can help the child to sit, settle down, concentrate, and be available to learn.

Parents are often unprepared for the slow, painful progress of treating a child with major dyslexia or Language Disorder. It is tempting to chase expensive and alternative cures in an attempt to speed things up. In the end most children with major reading problems do improve, but remain weak readers and spellers no matter how much pain we cause along the way.

We know that ADHD is a highly hereditable condition, and so too are most specific learning disabilities. The majority of children with a major reading problem have a close relative who reads and spells poorly. Parents whose children have a Language Disorder often say there is no family history of this, but when we try to unravel what the parents tell us, it seems that one of us has got a language problem.

Oppositional Defiant Disorder (ODD)

It is usually quoted that between 40 percent and 60 percent of ADHD children are oppositional. From our experience this seems a very high figure. But whatever the true percentage, Oppositional Defiant Disorder is certainly one of the most common comorbidities. ADHD children may be impulsive and unthinking, but following the event they are genuinely remorseful. This is not the case with Oppositional Defiant children, who may feel indignant and totally justified in the stand they took.

It is hard to know where oppositional behavior starts—normal toddlers are negative, but pathological defiance is unusual before the preschool years. The spectrum of ODD varies from a mildly oppositional attitude to a constant state of hostile defiance.

These children tend to say "no" on principle; they seek out the difficult path, challenge, refuse, and argue black is white. The most severe are vindictive, immensely annoying, and blame all others for their problems. They wait for their parents to draw the line so they can jump over it.

The hostile ODD child is "in your face" and seems to salute the world with a rude gesture. Children can have ODD without ADHD, but when ODD and ADHD combine this association of defiance and the explosive unthinking behavior of ADHD creates a volatile mixture.

Now, before you give up in despair and slit your wrists, there is some good news. If ODD children survive to adulthood, their future is generally favorable. Many give their parents a terrible time but are charming to other people ("outside angel–home devil"). At home, as children and teenagers, they seem to resent their parents, but in later life they mellow and most will regret the path they took—although by this time it's too late.

The origin of ODD seems to be largely biological (in the child's temperamental makeup). Some children are created with no potential to be oppositional no matter what troubles they meet. Others are made with a small seed of negativity, while a number of children are created to be very oppositional. How these small or large seeds develop is affected by parenting. Parents who force, confront, and are hostile in their relationships greatly increase the risk and extent of the ODD. Parents who accept, nurture, and steer toward the more peaceful path greatly lessen the impact of opposition.

One of the most common misunderstandings is the confusion between the generally unthinking behaviors of ADHD and the deliberately defiant features of ODD. Parents complain that the drugs

we prescribe for ADHD are not working. In fact the ADHD features have responded well but the comorbid behaviors of ODD remain. There is no drug treatment for ODD. The management involves a slow, behavioral approach which has limited success. Treating the associated ADHD makes the ODD child more focused and predictable. It is our experience that treating difficult young ADHD children at an early age greatly lessens the amount of opposition we see in later years. (See Appendix II, "The Criteria for Diagnosing Oppositional Defiant Disorder (DSM-IV)", and also "Oppositional Defiant Disorder—top tips for management" at the end of Chapter 10.)

Conduct Disorder (CD)

This is one comorbid behavior that no parent wants to see. The incidence in the North American ADHD population is close to 20 percent. The presence of Conduct Disorder with ADHD has a dramatic influence on outcome. Its features can be mild, moderate, or severe. Those with the most severe CD are destined for imprisonment, addiction, serious accidents, abuse, early death, or major social dysfunction.

The behaviors of CD include lying, cheating, stealing, threatening, cruelty, violating the rights of others, destruction of property, fire setting, and inflicting pain. It must be remembered that the unthinking ADHD child is quite capable of the occasional antisocial act, but after the event they understand what they have done and show remorse. Those with moderate or severe CD continue along the same path and show no moral regrets. There can be a malicious, even sadistic element to their behavior.

Conduct Disorder can occur in isolation, without being associated with ADHD, and in this form its onset is usually in adolescence. When CD is associated with ADHD it usually starts young, with a severe presentation of Oppositional Defiant Disorder before features of Conduct Disorder first come through between the ages of seven years and 10 years.

It is believed that the ADHD child who is free from Conduct Disorder at the age of 12 years is unlikely to develop the condition later on. This suggests there is a window of opportunity to change this catastrophic course, a child's future being won or lost in the early years. Though almost all ADHD children with Conduct Disorder also have severe features of Oppositional Defiant Disorder, the majority of children with ODD do not progress to develop Conduct Disorder.

The factors that increase the risk of Conduct Disorder are disharmony in the home, hostile–critical parenting, and probably the poor early treatment of ADHD.

There is a definite hereditary link in Conduct Disorder. This is of considerable concern as the children of such relationships commonly become available for adoption and fostering. Often an adoptive parent with all the best intentions will find themselves with an extremely difficult child. Fortunately, good early parenting lessens the potential impact of ADHD, oppositional behaviors, and conduct disorder.

If we believe the media, children with ADHD commonly present with uncontrollable criminal behavior. But children with ADHD do not deliberately destroy, abuse the rights of others, and inflict pain. These media beat-ups are describing Conduct Disorder. At this late stage, the treatment of associated ADHD is only addressing a small part of the total problem. (See Appendix III, "The Criteria for Diagnosing Conduct Disorder (DSM-IV)", and Appendix XVIII, "*TOUGH*LOVE.")

Depression

It is not uncommon for children or adults to be depressed, whether they have or do not have ADHD. Depression is rarely an issue before children start to compare and compete in grammar school. ADHD children yearn to behave, learn, and be accepted as others, just like their peers, but they simply don't know how to make this happen. It is normal for ADHD children to be disillusioned, but this does not make for a diagnosis of pathological depression.

The depressed child slips into a chronic state where they are moody, preoccupied, sad, and wish to withdraw. Some put a brave face on things, while others show their stress by becoming more irritable and annoying. The diagnosis is not easy to describe in words but parents should be concerned when they sense in their child a change of personality, a withdrawal from usual activities, a difficulty in close communication, a deeper state of sadness, or notice a decline in schoolwork. When depression and ADHD coexist, the depression should be treated as the first priority. In North America the new SSRI (selective serotonin reuptake inhibitor) antidepressants are sometimes prescribed in conjunction with stimulant medication. In other countries one of the older antidepressants, which also has an ADHD-improving effect, would usually be the first choice.

The anti-ADHD lobby groups (e.g. Citizens' Commission on Human Rights—Church of Scientology) frequently claim that stimulants cause ADHD children to become depressed. When stimulants are started in an excessive dose or the wrong preparation is prescribed, children may become teary, withdrawn, and "different." This is a short-term reaction to a trial of medication, which passes after four hours. There is a great difference between four hours of sadness and a chronic state of depression. Many ADHD children tell everyone that "the world sucks." This is their considered opinion; it's not a sign of depression. (See Appendix V, "The Criteria for Diagnosing Major Depressive and Manic Episodes, (Adult Criteria) (DSM-IV).")

Tics and Tourette's syndrome

Minor twitches and involuntary movements are common in the general population, but have a much higher incidence in those with ADHD. Tics refer to those involuntary twitches, usually around the eyes or face, but sometimes to a clearing of the throat, movement of the neck, or shrug of a shoulder. The most extreme form of tic disorder, Tourette's syndrome, involves throat noises, other major involuntary movements, and occasionally the uttering of inappropriate words. Tics and Tourette's are both comorbid conditions to ADHD.

The natural history of tics is for them to first appear when the child is around the ages of seven years to 10 years and to follow a course which comes and goes. As stimulant medication is first given around this age, it is easy to incorrectly believe that the drug has caused the tic.

Those who study tic disorder and Tourette's syndrome, state that the presence of tics rarely causes any significant problem in behavior, learning, or emotional well-being. The same cannot be said for the presence of ADHD, which can cause great disadvantage in all these areas. When a child with a tic is said to underfunction, it is usually the coexisting ADHD, not the tic, that is causing the difficulty. This is important to understand when planning treatment. Tics and Tourette's syndrome are no longer a contraindication to the use of stimulant medication. If ADHD is causing big problems, it needs to be treated. (See "Tics, Tourette's Syndrome and stimulant medication" at the end of Chapter 14, and Appendix IV, "The Criteria for Diagnosing Tic and Tourette's Disorder (DSM-IV).")

The clumsy child

Difficulties with coordination, motor planning, written work, and late neurological maturity are all commonly associated with ADHD. When ADHD and comorbid clumsiness coexist, some therapists see only the motor problems, calling this "the Clumsy Child Syndrome." Their intentions are good, but the child is only half helped if the problems of learning and behavior are misinterpreted. (For ways to improve coordination and writing see Chapter 25; see more on the coordination problem of ADHD in Chapter 4.)

Obsessive Compulsive Disorder (OCD)

There is a weak association between ADHD and the obsessive, almost ritualistic behaviors of OCD. This incidence is higher when the child with ADHD also has a tic disorder.

Those with OCD have an overfocus or unusual fixation. Things need to happen in a certain order—for example, there may be an obsession with hand washing, dirt on their clothes, or closing doors. This is different from the social aloofness and language problems that accompany the obsessions of autism. It is not the same as the "stuck" behaviors where many ADHD children pursue some trivial matter to death. These OCD children are upset at how the obsessions interfere in their lives, but they can't help themselves.

Occasionally stimulant medication produces the side effect of an almost obsessive overfocus. This is quickly reversed when the dose is reduced or a different preparation prescribed. Treatment of OCD should come from a specialist in psychiatry and will often involve one of the new SSRI antidepressants. These Prozac-like drugs help the OCD and some doctors give them in combination with stimulant medication when ADHD and OCD both need treatment.

Bipolar–Manic Depressive Disorder

If one looks at the biographies of Winston Churchill, his early home behaviors and school reports show classic ADHD. But it is also known that Churchill suffered depression, which was thought to be Bipolar Disorder.

Recent research shows a definite association between ADHD and Bipolar Disorder. (See Appendix XV, "Bipolar Disorder.") This is a very new and, as yet, not universally accepted view. The two conditions are quite separate, but their individual presentations can occur together. The presence of Bipolar Disorder gives ADHD a less favorable outcome, increasing the risk of foolish actions, social isolation, and addictive behavior, for example alcoholism.

Children with ADHD can be sparky, unthinking, and lose their temper, while children with Bipolar Disorder are said to present with major rage attacks. These are extreme, continue for a matter of hours, and are followed by a short period of quiet remorse. Children with Bipolar Disorder seem to have this highly volatile, short swing of mood, while adults have fluctuations of mood that last for days or weeks. The diagnosis and treatment of Bipolar Disorder are strictly for the psychiatrists. (See Appendix V, "The Criteria for Diagnosing Major Depressive and Manic Episodes, (Adult Criteria) (DSM-IV).")

Putting it all together

The condition we call ADHD is made up of various blends and severities of attention deficit–learning problems and hyperactive-impulsive behaviors. Over half of these ADHD children are further influenced by one or more of the associated comorbidities which cause additional psychiatric, neurological, and specific learning problems. The failure to see the association between ADHD and these comorbid conditions remains one of the most frequent causes of misunderstanding and incorrect treatment.

Finally, to add further confusion, these biologically based conditions are greatly influenced by the child's home and school environment. We are sure that supportive, accepting, nurturing parents give the best future to these children. Family disharmony, parental psychiatric disorders, and hostile–critical, coercive management all set children on a dangerous course. It would seem that the seeds that give the best and worst outcomes in ADHD are sown at a very early age. These environmental-parenting influences are now discussed in Chapter 7.

SEVEN

The Influence of Good and Bad Parenting

Until relatively recent times psychologists and psychiatrists believed that bad behavior was the result of family stress and poor parenting. When children presented with ADHD, all blame landed on the parents, without any mention of biology, brain, or the benefits of medication.

Over the years there has been a turnaround. And now, all but a small cluster of "psychodynamic dinosaurs" have seen the light. Modern research shows that ADHD is caused by a difference in brain function which can be successfully treated with medication.

This turnaround was achieved at a cost. In order to get the

parent-blamers to listen, it was necessary to overstress the importance of biology and brain chemicals. Now that pediatricians, psychiatrists, and parents are coexisting in peace, it's time to look at
parenting in a more balanced way. Certainly ADHD is driven by
brain chemicals, but parents are immensely influential in affecting
the outcome.

Parents—the ways we damage our children

No one is saying that these children are easy to live with—it's just
that in some ways we can boost their happiness and in others we
can drag them down. There is no doubt that hostile–critical parenting and major family disharmony are immensely destructive. These
factors, plus others in the list which follows, can turn a difficult but
loving four-year-old into an angry, defiant teenager with a ques-
tionable future.

Focus on failure

The problems that every adult meets in life are only as big as we
choose to see them. A tired, defeated parent might see their ADHD
child as 90 percent disobedient, difficult, and dumb, with only 10
percent of talent and charm. A stranger would be able to take a step
back from the front line and see the exact opposite. When a parent
is unhappy in their own life, unsupported and resentful, they often
perceive their children as much worse than they really are. If we incorrectly think a child is 90 percent difficult, our persistent put-
downs may turn this perception into reality.

Depressed parents

As a doctor, you quickly realize that life is no fairy tale. Parents we
meet struggle with illness, depression, alcoholic partners, and all
sorts of emotional difficulties. It is claimed that at least 10 percent
of the population will be significantly depressed at some time in
their lives. Depression eats away at our reserves, leaving us with no
charge in our emotional batteries. This robs a parent of drive, interest, direction, and the ability to give spontaneous warmth.

A depressed mother will have so little emotional energy that
those who depend on her will feel this flatness. With depression,

problems—whether big or little—become blurred and seem equally immense. There is a feeling of numbness which makes us overreact to unimportant issues, or we may totally withdraw and react to nothing. The management of an ADHD child requires a resourceful, clear-thinking mind, and this is not available in depression.

Depression is common in many parents. If it is present, it is made worse by having an ADHD child, who in turn is more difficult through having a depressed parent. Depression does not cause ADHD, but helping a depressed parent brings great benefit to the child, and all the family.

The first step is to recognize these feelings; the second is to seek help. For most, the modern treatment of depression is simple and effective. (See Appendix V, "The Criteria for Diagnosing Major Depressive and Manic Episodes, (Adult Criteria) (DSM-IV)".)

ADHD in the parent

If management of ADHD is going to work, there must be structure, organization, consistency, and a parent who thinks before she acts. The bad news is that ADHD is strongly hereditary and this frequently affects one parent. The good news is that the impulsive, disorganized parent is more often *not* the mother. Whether we like to admit it or not, mothers still provide structure and nurture in the homes of most of today's children.

Many ADHD adults have a warmth, energy, and Peter Pan spark that make them wonderful, creative parents. In others ADHD brings such disorganization, inconsistency, and impulsive outbursts that behavior management is a disaster.

A recent study by nutritionists showed that the concentration span of children who started school with a good breakfast was better than that of children who ate on the run. It is possible the lack of attention had little to do with diet, but came through the genes from parents who were too disorganized to prepare breakfast.

If you are a parent with ADHD, it is important to take a step back and see your vulnerabilities. Be obsessive about structure, routine, organization, and thinking before you blast the child with both barrels. We can't alter the attitude of our partner, but we can always smarten up our own act.

Family dysfunction

The evidence is inescapable—ADHD and Conduct Disorder are much more common where there is disharmony, dysfunction, and a split family. The analytical psychiatrists claim ADHD is caused by these dysfunctions, but the truth is much more complex.

We know that both ADHD and Conduct Disorder are often hereditary and also occur more often in males. The features of adult ADHD frequently include impulsive actions, intolerance, short-fused outbursts, and a blindness to the emotional needs of partners. These ADHD behaviors increase the risk of a failed relationship.

An ADHD child often inherits the disorder from a parent, and then the presence of that ADHD parent increases the risk of breakup and disharmony. The disharmony affects stability and consistency, which cause tension in the child's living environment. This increases the severity of the ADHD and damages the outcome for the child.

Adults with the mix of ADHD and Conduct Disorder often abuse drugs, have little consideration for the rights of others, and shoulder no responsibility. A common pattern for ADHD—Conduct Disordered men is to conceive, then leave. The mother is then stuck with the difficult child of a difficult man. A proportion of these children come up for foster care or adoption and this mix of heredity, frequently with an addict background, makes adoption risky.

But all disharmony is not due to parents with ADHD. In this country close to 50% of all relationships will break up before our children have left school. This must represent an immense amount of dispute, disagreement, and unhappiness in our homes.

There is no quick cure, but we must try to lessen the impact of fighting and parental disputes on all children, especially those with ADHD. Where possible, an amicable resolution to parent problems is always in the child's best interest. Anger with our partners may make us feel better but it does not suit children.

The emigrant lifestyle

Until recently it was thought that ADHD was much more common in the United States than in the United Kingdom. It seemed that all those restless creative genes had moved to the New World—but the low incidence of ADHD in Europe was a problem of professional misdiagnosis, not of emigration.

The genes of ADHD do predispose families to more restless, mobile, unsettled lifestyles. When I visit the remote mining towns of Australia I see many isolated mothers with challenging children. The busy menfolk love the 24-hour action of the mine—the mothers miss their friends, family, and the support of grandparents.

Even in the cities our ADHD families are more mobile, with frequent changes of home and school. It may be a necessity of life, but mothers and children cope best with a stable, long-term place to live and, where possible, a close extended family.

We don't want to encourage a boring, entrenched lifestyle, but much of the moving about in ADHD adults is ill-considered and unhelpful. Itchy feet may be a part of ADHD, but shooting ourselves in the foot is no remedy.

Hostile, forceful parenting

When we are given a difficult child there are two ways we can parent. We can accept, avoid escalation, support, and nurture or we can make no concessions, criticize, and apply ever-increasing force.

It requires immense patience to nurture the ADHD child but this brings benefits for esteem and ongoing relationships. Society expects parents to show they are in charge. If a child is difficult we are pressured to be tough and use whatever force it takes. But in ADHD force results in resentment, hostility, and a child who is angry with the world.

It is now believed that this hostile–critical start to life sows the seeds for much of the oppositional, Conduct Disordered behavior that is so destructive in adolescence. There is a message which keeps being repeated throughout this book—it is best to accept and nurture. In ADHD the alternative just does not work.

Parents—the way we nurture our children

It's a bit one-eyed to see parents as the only players in influencing a child's emotional health. Many other people play a part: teachers, friends, in-laws, schoolmates, even the soccer coach. Despite this, when it comes to the crunch, parents are the majority shareholders and we have the greatest influence over all that follows.

Accept and adapt

ADHD is real; it's in the child's brain, and in the short term the ADHD is not going to go away. Until this fact is accepted and allowances are made, you will get nowhere. Accepting and adapting our attitudes are the first steps in successful parenting.

Belonging

I recently attended a wedding held by a wonderful, warm Greek family. The bride had one pageboy, her three-year-old nephew, a bundle of immense mischief and energy. At the reception he pulled off her veil, hid under her dress, slid around the dance floor, pushed over the flower girls, and was into everything.

But this was no problem—everyone knew John, they diverted his excesses, protected his safety, and lovingly smiled at his immense exuberance. This boy belonged, he knew he was loved, accepted, and enjoyed by his family and their friends. This idea of belonging to an extended family or group of friends may seem old-fashioned and stuffy, but it is of immense importance to the emotional health of both adults and children.

A noncritical supporter

Children from one year to eight years are closely dependent on their parents, while after this age others exert their influence. It seems that children are at their best emotionally if able to talk and confide with an accepting adult. This can be mom, dad, aunts, grandparents, a teacher, or a friend. What they want is a supporter who believes in them.

A close grandparent can be a great ally. They are less rushed than parents and far enough from the front line of day-to-day discipline to be an impartial listener. Again, this is an old-fashioned idea, but a good grandparent can do more for an ADHD child than a whole convention full of counselors.

Knowing where you stand

It would be easy to misinterpret our nonconfronting approach as letting children get away with murder. Certainly we are not looking for fights, but a few clearly stated and firmly followed-through rules are essential.

Rules are not to be made in the heat of battle, they are laid down in a time of clear thought and calm. When a behavior happens, the rule is stated, the repercussions are outlined, then calmly followed through without debate (see Chapter 10). All human beings are at their emotional best when they operate within clearly defined limits and ADHD children are no exception. They need to know exactly where they stand.

Nurture

By this stage in the book our readers must be heavily overdosed on the word *nurture*. It keeps arising for a good reason—we believe it is vitally important. The child with ADHD can be immensely irritating, but most are sensitive and inwardly they wish to please. When they misbehave they don't need to be shot out of the water by the heavy artillery. Nice kids remain nice when accepted as they are, given realistic limits, guided, rewarded, enjoyed, and loved. They

don't want to be managed by force or fear; they need a parent who is a supporter, a believer, and a friend.

In summary

ADHD may be caused by an imbalance of brain chemicals, but the outcome is heavily influenced by us, the parents. We can meet fire with fire and escalate the situation to Bosnian-like proportions. This may give the superficial appearance of control, but compliance through fear wrecks relationships and robs children of love. Accepting, supporting, guiding, encouraging, and letting a lot of annoyances pass without a fight may seem like surrender, but when your child is at the age of 18 years, you will see we were right.

Psychiatry—the mind or the brain?

Modern psychiatrists are practical people who accept that both brain function and living environment affect a child's behavior. In the 1930s, 40s, and 50s there was immense interest in the mind, but not in the brain ("brainless psychiatry"). This was the era of analysts who interpreted all behavior in terms of present and past experiences.

Children with ADHD behavior were said to have had a depressed mother, faulty mother/child attachment, or unresolved emotional baggage from the mother's childhood. Treatment involved play therapy for the child and months of emotional exploration of the mother. Mothers were always the main target and it seemed fathers had done their bit at conception and after this had no real input.

In the 1950s the role of temperament and individuality was not accepted, but a breakthrough study in 1956 finally showed its importance. This was the New York Longitudinal Study, which followed 133 children from infancy to adulthood. Along the way the study showed the existence and persistence of a biological difference of behavior in all children. In the toddler years it appeared that approximately 40 percent of children were easygoing, 35 percent of average difficulty, 15 percent a moderate handful, and 10 percent a real challenge. This study of temperament has a great overlap with current research into ADHD, but at present researchers have not united to explore the common ground.

In North America in the late 1960s, individuality and brain differences were starting to be accepted, while in Australia and New Zealand this acceptance did not take off until the 1980s; in Europe (especially the UK) emphasis has been slow to move from "mind" to "brain."

In the early 1980s, Christopher Green and others were criticized for treating ADHD with stimulants. Psychologists and psychiatrists would give play therapy to the child and psychotherapy to the mother. They complained we were not addressing the deep psychological issues, and it was said that by removing the blame from the mothers we were colluding with them and preventing them from accepting their responsibility for the ADHD.

For those who have never lived through this era, it's hard to understand that it ever existed. This is now past history and we are all a lot wiser. Psychiatrists have become fascinated with brain function, heredity, brain chemicals, and the medical management of psychiatric conditions. New drugs have been developed which have revolutionized the treatment of depression, schizophrenia, and most major psychological difficulties. Psychiatrists have moved to a position that understands the importance of both "brain" and "mind."

EIGHT

ADHD—Making the Diagnosis

There is no one black-and-white test for ADHD. Anyone who sees the diagnosis in such simple terms has read too many books and worked with far too few children.

If this were an ideal world, each child would have intensive workups by psychologists, educators, behavioralists, occupational therapists, speech pathologists, and a pediatrician. But the world we work in often has such limited resources that we must be economical in assessment and concentrate our energies on providing proper treatment and long-term support.

If parents are concerned with the possibility of ADHD, they should first discuss this with the child's teacher. Referral may be made to the school counselor-psychologist and then possibly to a pediatrician, child psychiatrist, or psychologist.

The authors of this book use different methods of assessment, based on their research and practical experience. When Kit Chee assesses she uses formal questionnaires, detailed objective testing, and a carefully taken history. Chris Green relies more on the subtleties of history, the presentation of the child, and the reports of teachers. We believe that the children and parents in our care are equally well served by either of these approaches. It is the positive response to our intervention that is important, not the individual diagnostic method.

Diagnosis—the four steps

We see the diagnosis of ADHD as comprising four simple steps:

1. Look for alarm signals.

2. Exclude ADHD look-alikes.

3. Use some objective pointers toward diagnosis.

4. Take a detailed history tuned to the subtleties of ADHD.

I. Alarm signals

There are two main alarm signals that should always make one think of ADHD:

a *The child who significantly underfunctions at school, despite having a normal intellect and no major specific learning disabilities.*

b *The child who has an ADHD-like package of behavior problems which are considerably worse than would be expected for the standard of parenting and home environment.*

Underfunctions at school

Most parents seek our help after the start of school. The teacher is bewildered, as this child appears clever but is unable to deliver the goods. The teacher arranges for an educational psychologist (district school counselor) to test overall intellect and to exclude specific learning disabilities. The results show a degree of failure which is not in keeping with the intellect and specific learning abilities. ADHD must now be considered.

Unexpected behavior problems

At home the children in this family have equal love and discipline, yet this one child stands out as many times more difficult. The parents will be making heavy weather of management, due to a cluster of telltale ADHD behaviors. This child is significantly out of step with his peers and siblings.

Once alerted to the possibility of ADHD, it is time to move to the next step.

2. Exclude ADHD look-alikes

Many academic articles imply that ADHD is easily confused with a long list of look-alike behaviors. This may be true on paper, but in practice an experienced observer will quickly cut through any confusion. The most commonly quoted list of look-alikes includes the following.

The normal, active preschooler

The amount of activity, common sense, and intensity of behavior varies greatly in preschoolers. Some normally active children are called overactive, but they do not have ADHD. Their problem is a busy temperament which conflicts with the sometimes unreasonable expectations of their parents.

To diagnose ADHD in a preschooler, the behavior must be inappropriate even for this normally active and unthinking stage of development. In theory this look-alike behavior is easy to distinguish from ADHD, but in practice it can be quite difficult. When in doubt, we arrange a good preschool, give basic behavior suggestions, and see what happens over the next few months. Hopefully the diagnosis will then be clearer. In the majority of preschool-age children we diagnose, it is not the overactivity, but the explosive, intolerant behavior that forces us to start treatment.

Intellectual disability

Parents often confuse their child's intellectual disability with ADHD. If you have a five-year-old with the development of a two-and-a-half-year-old, you must expect the behavior to be active, inattentive, and unthinking—but this is not ADHD.

Children with developmental delay are at increased risk of also suffering from ADHD. When these two coexist, the behavior must be significantly out of step with the intellectual level, otherwise the diagnosis cannot be considered. Stimulant medication can be used in children with intellectual disability, but it has less chance of success.

The hearing-impaired child

Children with severe hearing loss can present with atypical behavior, but their behavior is more unresponsive and distant than that of ADHD children. Inattentive children don't listen and are often sent for hearing tests. Frequently, they are found to have a mild hearing loss caused by fluid in the middle ear (glue ear). This minor reduction in hearing does not cause ADHD, but it makes life much harder for the already inattentive child. If there is ever the slightest doubt about any child's hearing, this must be formally tested. It is not known why ADHD children and children with specific learning disabilities seem to have a higher incidence of glue ear.

Specific learning disabilities (SLD)

If children have a specific weakness in learning they become frustrated and lose concentration when the work becomes too hard. In these children the inattention occurs only when they are struggling with reading, mathematics, language, or whatever causes them stress. In ADHD the difficult behaviors and problems of persistence are present most of the time. In theory it should be easy to separate the behaviors of these two conditions, but as ADHD and SLD regularly coexist, it is not always that simple.

Autism—Asperger syndrome

This is said to be an ADHD look-alike, but it would be impossible for any experienced professional to confuse the two. Autistic children are aloof, have poor verbal and body language, and are somewhat obsessive. There is one subgroup of autism where children are extremely active (the "active but odd" subgroup). They are active but they are also extremely distant and detached. This aloofness with unusual language makes autism stand apart from ADHD. The treatment of ADHD rarely helps the active child with autism, though occasionally we have seen unexpected response to stimulant medication.

Epilepsy

Children with epilepsy are more likely to have an associated problem of ADHD. It is not the epilepsy which is causing this behavior, it is the child's brain difference, which shows itself in two symptoms: epilepsy and ADHD. Perfect control of the epilepsy rarely removes the associated problems of behavior.

Sometimes one of the anticonvulsant medications will exacerbate the ADHD behaviors. When in doubt, the dose or drug must be reviewed. Epilepsy or anticonvulsants are not a contraindication to the use of stimulant medication.

Depression

This is often said to mimic the behaviors of ADHD. In our experience depression in young children is quite rare and, when present, the child usually becomes withdrawn, rather than overactive and impulsive. Depression, however, can coexist with ADHD. Depression does not cause ADHD, but ADHD increases the risk of depression. Depression can result in a child who loses focus and direction but it does not cause the learning and behavior problems seen in ADHD. Depression mostly affects the ADHD adolescent who becomes demoralized by academic, emotional, and social problems. (See "Depression" in Chapter 6, "Associated Conditions—The Comorbidities.")

Brain injury

The child who has suffered some form of brain injury may present with behaviors which are difficult to distinguish from ADHD. Here the quality of the behaviors is generally different, with the child tending to be more restless, agitated, learning-disabled, and lacking in forethought and sense.

We often see children whose parents believe that a relatively minor illness or accident has resulted in the child acquiring ADHD. For a head injury to cause such behavior there would usually be a prolonged period of unconsciousness and weeks in a hospital. For a medical condition (e.g. meningitis or encephalitis) to cause these symptoms the child will generally have been critically ill.

When ADHD is the diagnosis, there will be a gradual onset. With a brain injury, there is a dramatic change in personality, learning, and behavior immediately following the traumatic event.

Behaviors that are caused by brain injury are managed in very much the same way as those of ADHD, though stimulant medication is less successful.

Family dysfunction

Though authors rarely consider this aspect at length, we find the unclear blend of inborn ADHD and the behaviors associated with a disturbed home environment to be the most difficult differential in diagnosis. Stress, inconsistency, and emotional disadvantage cause major problems of behavior in any child. These problems are usually different from pure ADHD, the children being more attention seeking, defiant, and unmanageable, though there is some overlap.

The confusion comes as the statistics show ADHD behavior to be more common in disadvantaged families. It is easy to blame it all on poor parenting, but it is not as simple as that. The adults in dysfunctional families sometimes slip to their disadvantaged situation through their academic underachievement and their impulsive, disorganized, socially inept behavior. The children of such relationships are then more likely to inherit the ADHD genes from one or both parents. Now we have a child with the predisposition to ADHD who will be made many times worse by the inconsistent management of a volatile home. The presence of family dysfunction does not exclude ADHD—the two can coexist. Often it is easier to treat ADHD than dysfunction.

3. Pointers toward diagnosis

Over the years researchers have worked hard to bring some science to the diagnosis of ADHD. Questionnaires have been created which allow teachers and parents to rate the behaviors. The American Psychiatric Association has come up with a list of diagnostic criteria.

Psychologists have developed tests and profiles that point to the presence of ADHD. Others have devised ways to measure attention and persistence. Recently, advanced electronics have allowed the analysis of brainwaves, which some believe to be helpful (Quantitative EEG–Brain Mapping).

Professionals may promote their way of assessing as the one and only method, but there remains no completely reliable test for ADHD. The methods currently available bring some objectivity into a very subjective area, but they are not foolproof and can be seen as nothing more than pointers toward a probable diagnosis of ADHD.

Questionnaires

Parents and teachers can complete questionnaires which score specific ADHD behaviors—the higher the score, the more likelihood of ADHD. Among those most commonly used are the Conners Teacher and Parent Rating Scales, the Achenbach Child Behavior Checklists, the Edelbrock Child Attention Problems Rating Scale, and the Barkley and DuPaul ADHD Rating Scale. These questionnaires allow for some objectivity, both in making the diagnosis and monitoring the effects of treatment. Though most of today's experts strongly recommend questionnaires, there are a few exceptions. Cynics such as Christopher Green feel that questionnaires are of most use to doctors who don't like talking to their patients. (See Appendix VI.)

The American Psychiatric Association diagnostic criteria (DSM-IV)

The DSM-IV (1994) guidelines give reasonably clear criteria for the diagnosis of ADHD. It is classified into three main types:

1. Attention Deficit Hyperactivity Disorder—with predominantly hyperactive-impulsive-type behavior (fidgety, restless, impulsive, impatient).

2. Attention Deficit Hyperactivity Disorders—with predominantly inattentive behavior (dreamy, nonlistening, easily distracted, inattentive, subtle learning problems).

3. Attention Deficit Hyperactivity Disorder—combined type— probably the most common presentation (inattentive and

hyperactive-impulsive behavior. (See Appendix I for list of criteria.)

Reality before science

For a child to have ADHD, by the DSM-IV criteria, they need to show six out of a list of nine behaviors. If they demonstrate six or more, it is ADHD, five or less and the diagnosis is in dispute. This seems so clear-cut, but it is not.

The child with four or five difficult behaviors may not fit the full criteria, but can still cause immense stress. The child with six behaviors may not come for treatment if the parents are saints and the school superb. A child from a dysfunctional home and unsupportive school may only have five features and receive treatment.

This subjective movement of the goalposts annoys the academics. Their problem is they can only see what they read in books, while we have to cope with the variables of real life. A condition may be caused by an imbalance of brain chemicals, but its impact is heavily influenced by strengths and weaknesses in the living environment.

Psychometric tests and profiles

All children who are believed to have ADHD should be given a standard intelligence test, followed by specialized assessments in reading, writing, spelling, math, and language. Unfortunately, as there are such limited resources, for many this remains an ideal, but not a reality.

If testing is done, the psychologist may comment that the child is restless, inattentive, and finds it hard to keep working at a task. But this is not always the case; some children with major ADHD can hold their concentration in this quiet one-to-one environment, but are unable to do so in a noisy classroom.

When a standard intelligence test is given this shows that intellectual slowness is not the cause of the poor behavior. The protocols used by most psychologists are made up of many subtests and ADHD children often produce a characteristic pattern of subscores. They are particularly weak in tasks that require sequencing ability and short-term memory.

When these subtests are analyzed, psychologists come up with the Kaufman factors, one of which reflects the child's freedom from distractibility. This is said to indicate the presence of ADHD, but though interesting, this is overrated and unreliable in diagnosis.

A new breed of psychologists, the neuropsychologists, look at more specialized functions of learning, in particular frontal lobe function. This part of the brain, which influences sense and the control of basic impulses, is often weak in those with ADHD. Neuropsychology can help pinpoint these problems, but at present it is more of academic interest than a precise pointer to ADHD. (See Appendices X and XI for descriptions of WISC-III, Kaufman factors, and neuropsychology tests.)

Tests of attention and persistence

These tests measure the main areas of weakness with ADHD (attention and persistence). They help make the diagnosis and then quantify the response to medication. These are some of the most useful tests available but they are still not foolproof.

The Paired Associate Learning Test

Here the psychologist verbally teaches a task, continually monitoring and scoring how well the information has been retained. This is a simple test of attention and memory, which requires no computer technology and is said to have reasonable accuracy. (See detailed description in Appendix VII.)

Continuous Performance Test (CPT)

This is a computer-driven test which requires the child to respond when an image appears on a screen. This has been well standardized and formally measures impulsivity and distractibility. The CPT is marketed under several brand names, for example Conners and TOVA. Despite some claims from those who collect the royalties, the CPT is not essential to the diagnosis or follow-up of the average child with ADHD. It is, however, of great advantage when the picture is predominantly of inattention or clouded by comorbid conditions. (See Appendix VII.)

Quantitative EEG (QEEG)

This technique, which is promoted under several trade names, for example Neurometrics, involves computer analysis of brainwave tracings. These are said to differentiate between pure ADHD, ADHD with associated specific learning disability, and the normal child. The tracings may also change when there is a response to medication.

Australian parents have good reason to be confused with these trade names. On expert advice, the minister of health recently removed the techniques from eligibility for Medicare rebate. At the same time newspapers claimed a new breakthrough in the diagnosis of ADHD, which was a similar technique under a different name.

This concept sounds exciting, but at present most view it as nothing more than an interesting research tool. (For details see Appendix VIII.)

4. Detailed history and observation

After seeing many ADHD children it becomes apparent that no two are exactly the same. Despite this, if one takes a careful history, there are usually telltale signs.

Frequent findings with ADHD children

- Many became toddler tornadoes the moment they got up on their feet.

- Some were busy preschoolers, a few were extremely volatile and roughed up other children.

- For many, the first school report used the words *disruptive* and *distractible*.

- There is a dramatic difference between the academic achievement in a one-to-one situation versus unsupervised study.

- Most are restless, and as you talk to them they fidget and their eyes flit.

- At home most hyperactive-impulsive ADHD children are insatiable, go on and on, and generate immense tension.

- Their behavior in a group is often embarrassing and when playing with one other child they are overpowering and bossy.

- Their impulsivity makes them both verbally and physically accident-prone.

- As you talk to the parents you quickly sense their frustration, stress, and confusion. (This is different from the feeling you get from the parents of a defiant, poorly managed child.)

- In the office young, impulsive, overactive children are easy to diagnose. The moment they walk in the door, the doctor will by reflex reach out to protect their property.

- In the office older children present less dramatically. Most, but not all, squirm, fidget, and fiddle. Their talk often gets side-tracked or they become lost in mid-sentence. Asking questions often gets the answer "Good." Their eyes and minds are all over the place.

- We estimate that over 90 percent of ADHD children can be identified by a properly tuned history. Sometimes ADHD will not be obvious in the doctor's office and then the diagnosis is made by listening carefully to the parents. When this happens, ADHD is diagnosed in the same way as many other medical conditions, for example, epilepsy; that is, by history. Doctors don't ask to see the epileptic fall to the floor and have a fit in front of them; they believe what parents tell them.

Those who present with pure inattention and subtle problems of learning are much more difficult to diagnose, and with them the tests and pointers are of special value. When major family dysfunction and the heavy behaviors of Oppositional Defiant Disorder or Conduct Disorder cloud the picture, diagnosis may become exceptionally hard. With experience it gets easier, but with these conditions it is never straightforward.

When it all seems too difficult, remember that we diagnose for one reason—so that we can help. If two months down the track a young life has had a major turnaround, we probably got it right!

Diagnosis by trial of medication

Diagnosis sometimes remains a matter of trial and error. At the present time it is seen as "politically incorrect" to suggest that diagnosis might be made by a trial of stimulant medication. This is despite unequivocal evidence that stimulants usually bring about a major turnaround in ADHD to a degree that is not found in any other conditions, or with placebos. I believe that a robust and sustained response to any treatment usually suggests we are on the right track. But this simplistic view would not be generally accepted for ADHD right now.

Conclusion

Sometimes too much science makes a simple job complicated. For instance, if our task was to tell the difference between a wild wolf and a friendly German shepherd, we could create a series of objective checklists, tests, and measurements. But even without these, few of us would be confused if one ran at us. As in most parts of medicine, the eye of the experienced beholder is more important than a laboratory load of tests.

With limited resources we must not fall into the trap of overdiagnosis and undertreatment. Diagnosis is only the start; it is what happens after that which really matters.

Summary: making the diagnosis

As we hear some colleagues talk on ADHD and specific learning disabilities (SLD), it seems that the diagnosis is impossible without a team of psychologists and a month of time. When resources are limited, anyone who teaches about ADHD must be clear as to what are the essentials for diagnosis and what are unreachable, impractical academic ideals.

With this in mind we put forward our three plans for assessment: the basic, the more objective, and the comprehensive. The quality of local resources, and the size of your wallet, will decide which you choose.

I. The basic method

Be alerted

■ Behavior out of step with parenting (fidgety, impulsive, insatiable, socially out of tune).

■ Underfunctions at school (disruptive, distractible, inattentive, poor memory, needs one-to-one supervision).

Exclude

- Obvious intellectual disability.
- Major family dysfunction.

Talk to school

- Is there any worry re intelligence?
- Is there any worry re SLD?
- What are the school's concerns?

Appointment with

- School psychologist, community health team, pediatrician, or child psychiatrist.
- These professionals will make the diagnosis having considered the above, which is then confirmed by parents' description and clinical presentation in the office.

Trial of stimulants

Monitored by:

- Feedback from school.
- Feedback from parents.

2. The more objective method

Be alerted

- Behavior out of step with parenting (fidgety, impulsive, insatiable, socially out of tune).
- Underfunctions at school (disruptive, distractible, inattentive, poor memory, needs one-to-one supervision).

Exclude

- Obvious intellectual disability.
- Major family dysfunction.

Talk to school

■ Is there any worry re intelligence?

■ Is there any worry re SLD?

■ What are the school's concerns?

Paperwork

■ Questionnaires completed by parents.

■ Questionnaires completed by school.

■ Formal report from school/preschool.

Educational psychologist (school counselor)

■ Basic tests of intellect.

■ Screening tests for SLD.

■ Classroom visit to observe.

Appointment with

■ Psychologist, pediatrician, or child psychiatrist.

■ These professionals will make the diagnosis having considered the above, which is then confirmed by parents' description and clinical presentation in the office.

Trial of stimulants

Monitored by:

■ Feedback from school.

■ Feedback from parents.

■ Repeat questionnaires.

3. The more comprehensive method

Be alerted

■ Behavior out of step with parenting (fidgety, impulsive, insatiable, socially out of tune).

- Underfunctions at school (disruptive, distractible, inattentive, poor memory, needs one-to-one supervision).

Exclude

- Obvious intellectual disability.
- Major family dysfunction.

Talk to school

- Is there any worry re intelligence?
- Is there any worry re SLD?
- What are the school's concerns?

Paperwork

- Questionnaires completed by parents.
- Questionnaires completed by school.
- Formal report from school/preschool.

Specialized tests

- Psychologist: detailed tests of general abilities and specific areas of learning.
- Educationalist: practical assessment of basic abilities in classroom learning.
- Pediatrician-Psychologist: Paired Associate Learning Test; Continuous Performance Type Test; QEEG (e.g. Neurometrics).

Appointment with

- Psychologist, community health team, pediatrician, or child psychiatrist.
- These professionals will make the diagnosis having considered the above, which is then confirmed by parents' description and clinical presentation in the office.

Trial of stimulants

Monitored by some of the following:

■ Questionnaires.

■ Paired Associate Learning Test.

■ QEEG.

■ Continuous Performance Test.

■ Feedback from school.

■ Feedback from parents.

NINE

The Stresses on Parents and Siblings

The difficulties experienced with ADHD are not the same for every family. These depend on the severity of the ADHD, whether the main features are behavior or learning problems, and the presence or absence of comorbid conditions such as Oppositional Defiant Disorder.

It would be safe to assume that a house charged with ADHD energy would not be a quiet place to relax. These children cause immense stress both to their parents and their siblings.

Stress-damaged parents

There must be supermen and wonderwomen out there who find ADHD easy, but so far we have not met them. The parents we deal with are tired, confused, and frequently full of self-doubts. Many have already had a real runaround. Often they have been told, "There's nothing wrong," "It's poor parenting," "You need to be stricter," "Did you suffer postnatal depression?", "Have you thought of a Parent Effectiveness Course?"

The number of experts who have to see a child before the correct diagnosis is made never ceases to amaze. Recently we saw an eight-year-old with classic ADHD. Over the previous two years the parents had sought help from one private and two school psychologists, an occupational therapist, a pediatrician, and two different child psychiatrists. An impressive list of learning, coordination, and emotional diagnoses had been made but none of them included ADHD. As this busy boy bounced into our waiting room, an elderly grandmother looked up and said, "He's got ADHD just like my grandson." She was right. It's a strange world where an insightful parent can see much more clearly than a college full of professionals.

Parents are irritated when experts criticize other experts, yet have little to offer themselves. They are angry when schools encourage some ill-proven test or therapy while making the parents feel guilty if they follow a properly researched treatment such as stimulant medication. Stressed parents have many unanswered questions and unresolved emotions.

It's my fault

As parents look at their friends, it seems they all have angelic, compliant children. With ADHD even the most knowledgeable, best-balanced parent will secretly believe that they are in some way to blame. This feeling is made worse by out-of-date community attitudes and the ignorant prejudices of powerful people in the media.

Then there are those interfering friends who question the diagnosis and tell the parents that the treatment is not safe. It upsets us to see good moms and dads blame themselves. We know these children are difficult, and would be many times worse if it weren't for these exceptional parents.

Disappointment, resentment, anger

By the time we see families they have done their best, but nothing they try seems to work. This leaves them feeling impotent and inadequate. Many are secretly disappointed that parenting has not lived up to expectations. Others are angry that one child has brought so much stress and disruption to what was once a hassle-free home. A few have an immense feeling of being trapped in a nightmare that just won't end.

Some mothers have supportive, heavily involved husbands and a good extended family; others carry all the worry and child care themselves. Often we meet mothers, now sole parents, left with the difficult child of a difficult man. Many look to us to work some miracle—they can't believe life was meant to be this difficult.

Dads appear better than moms

In most households it is still the mother who provides 90 percent of the care and parenting. But despite this, many fathers seem more in control than the mothers. It is not that mothers are poor parents, it's just that fathers tend to be firmer, louder, and make a greater impact as they are less often at home.

Children cause poor parenting

The parents we see start out with such high ideals, but after years of hitting their heads against a brick wall, they pull back on their discipline and go for the easier path. A professional, who knows nothing of their early struggle, sees the bad behavior and blames it on the apparent lack of firmness. They do not realize that discipline has moved this way as a result of the difficulty faced by the parents.

A group of researchers demonstrated this using video recordings to assess the quality of discipline. When the videos were analyzed the parents of ADHD children did not rate well. They were snappy, stressed, negative, and often inconsistent. On face value this proved that poor parenting caused the ADHD children to behave badly.

These children were then given their stimulant medication and refilmed. With the calmness brought to their child by medication, the parents were found to be in control and disciplining well. The parents were as competent as any other parents—it was the children who had changed. Many child-care experts have not yet grasped this fact. It is the behavior of an ADHD child that makes good parents appear poor, not poor parenting that creates the behavior of ADHD.

Some parents can't be helped

There is another side to this: some parents refuse to accept the nature of ADHD. As we talk they won't listen—they won't change and can't be helped. Usually there are three issues involved.

Treat all equally

Some mothers and fathers are quite angry when we suggest they treat the ADHD child in a different way from their siblings. "He's not going to change our life," "You can't tell us that one child should be treated differently," "If they are going to live in our house they will live by the same rules." With this attitude these parents make no allowances for ADHD—and so the child is always in trouble, home is unhappy, and this constant criticism erodes their esteem.

Looking for trouble

A country mother recently complained that the trip home from school was a time of great tension: "I stop to get the groceries, when I return to the car he has his brothers and sisters at each other's throats." We suggested she do her shopping on the way to pick up the children but this minor change in routine would not be considered.

Another mother complained of problems when she picked up her six-year-old after school. "He runs out, jumps around, gets into the car, climbs over the seats, toots the horn, and then we get into an impossible argument which leaves me in tears." We suggested she drive off as soon as this sparky child was released from school. "Are you telling me that I don't have the right to talk to my friends for as long as I wish? I am not going to be dictated to by a six-year-old."

Beat it out of them

If the child had a more obvious disability, it would be easier to accept. If they had been born with only one leg, we would not force them to run. If they were deaf, we would accept that no amount of shouting or beating would make them hear. Some parents refuse to recognize that ADHD is a genuine physical condition, then push, punish, and get nowhere.

Some fathers are just as uninsightful, inflexible, and impulsive as the children they produced. "I would never have been allowed to get away with this when I was a boy, I will knock it out of him." This heavy approach may achieve the impression of compliance, but don't be fooled. Obedience through fear robs the relationship of love and respect. You may appear to be winning now, but don't expect them to hang around when they grow up. If you want to be a lonely retiree who never sees your grandchildren, this is the course to take.

Siblings also suffer

I am sure some siblings wish they had been born an only child or possibly adopted out at birth. Despite this most brothers and sisters adapt, learning how to steer around explosions and avoid catching their brother's blame. There are a number of reasons for brothers and sisters to call this unfair.

Different rules for different people

"But, Mom, you would never let me get away with that." We hear this all the time, but if we don't have different rules and expectations, home will become a front-line war zone. Siblings must be told that their brother is a clever, creative kid, but he's lost the lever that applies the brakes to behavior. It's unfair, but whether you like it or not there are going to be different rules.

Invasion of space

"It's not fair, Mom, he's breaking my toys." Many ADHD children have fiddly fingers, an inquisitive mind, and no strong views on ownership. If you are going to live together for the next 10 years, there must be some firm rules about what can and cannot be touched. "Your brother's bedroom has been declared a total no-go area." "Upsetting your sister's homework will never be allowed." "If you as much as tap on her door or put your nose inside, a bolt of lightning will descend." Older brothers and sisters need their space, particularly when coming close to exam times. A door lock is not an unreasonable solution.

Taunts and tension

"Mom, he won't leave me alone." Siblings talk, play, and watch TV together, but the ADHD child intrudes like a fully charged detonator. They poke, tease, insult, and go on until even the cat and goldfish need therapy. Of course the siblings themselves are not without guilt. Some rise to great heights in their ability to stir up their brother with ADHD. This keeps the house in a constant state of red alert.

Parents must notice and praise when everyone is getting on together. If the conflict is plummeting out of control, it's time to separate the warring parties. In some families, nothing short of a general anesthetic will bring peaceful coexistence.

Siblings and school

"Do you know what your brother did in class today?" It's tough enough having a brother or sister who is full of energy, but their school behaviors are not your problem. Siblings must be taught to smile and sidestep such comments, but they still hurt.

Ruined for all of us

"Mom, it's not our fault, why do we have to go home early?" With any difficult child there must be limits to outside family activities. It's not fair for brothers and sisters but we can make it up to them. We may not always be able to do things as a family, but one parent can watch the sibling's soccer game, and take part in activities that would be impossible if the ADHD child was present.

Friends fed up

"Mom, he's annoying my friend." When friends come around to play there may be bossing, teasing, interfering, or hijacking the brother's or sister's friend for themselves. As social skills in ADHD are often weak, it's important to encourage the visits. Before the event set down some clear rules about what you expect and what you don't want. Give feedback when they play well, separate when they squabble, and keep ever-vigilant.

An uneven distribution of time

"Mom, you spend all your time doing things with John." An ADHD child consumes an immense amount of time and nervous energy. There are visits to doctors, therapists, and tutors, supervision of homework, and constantly keeping a lid on behavior. Certainly the distribution of time is unfair, but it's unavoidable. To allow the maximum amount of time with the siblings, make use of all resources, including fathers, grandparents, and friends.

Protecting siblings

- Have a few nonnegotiable rules about brother's and sister's space and property.

- Provide some secure places for storage.

- Make a rule that damage to others' property is repaired by a levy from pocket money.

- Enforce an absolute veto on any disturbance to homework or study.

- Allow older brothers and sisters to have a door lock.

- Separate squabbling siblings into different rooms.

- Have realistic limits on family excursions.

- Allocate one parent to be fully available for events such as the sibling's Saturday sport.

- Arrange overnight stays with family and friends, to share care.

In summary

No one said life was going to be easy, but even though siblings simmer, most families manage and still remain close. I recently reviewed a difficult boy whose teenage sisters wanted to attend the interview. They complained to their mom, "You don't tell Dr. Green the truth. The doctor doesn't know that our brother John is such a prize pain." We don't need a band of placard-waving siblings to protest outside our offices; we know how it feels.

TEN

The Top Tips for Better Behavior

Don't listen to any expert who believes that managing an impulsive, insatiable, immature child is easy. You can come up with the best behavior-modification plan ever devised, but it will never work as well as it does in the training manuals. ADHD children do not plan to behave badly; it just seems to happen, and after the event they feel true remorse. This regret is not present with Oppositional Defiant Disorder, where the hostile child deliberately oversteps the mark and gets pleasure from the pain they cause.

This chapter looks at the basic building blocks of better behavior in children with ADHD. Though the same techniques may be used with oppositional children, they are much less effective. Before we go any further it must be clearly stated that applying behavior techniques alone, without first refocusing the severe ADHD child using medication, will not produce miracles. Without medication, all we can expect is a percentage improvement and parents who are a little more in control.

Why usual methods fail

The techniques we use so successfully with other children don't work well in ADHD. For a behavior program to be effective, a child first needs to listen, plan ahead, remember, consider before they act, and be motivated by rewards. These are the weaknesses of ADHD, which explains why these children are so difficult to discipline. The ADHD child hears half the instruction and then forgets the rest. They don't see the sequence of events that is leading them into trouble, where action A leads to B, to C—and by E they are sliding into disaster.

The modern understanding of ADHD recognizes a weakness of frontal lobe function which causes poor control of unwise behavior. In ADHD, an idea hits the front of the mind and the child acts without thinking of the repercussions.

If lack of impulse control derails discipline, the situation is made worse by a poor response to reinforcement and reward. The average child will tidy their toys, be rewarded with a chocolate cookie, smile, and do it again. The ADHD child gets the cookie, complains it is not dark Vienna chocolate topped with sprinkles, then nags for another then another. These problems of planning ahead, acting without proper thought, and responding poorly to rewards make ADHD behavior hard to manage.

The building blocks to behavior management

When you follow parents through the ups and downs of many years, it seems some of our suggestions work and others are a waste of time. The best results come with clear communication, simple instructions, a small number of important rules, and rewards which are regular and repeated.

Most parents turn the corner when they realize it is best to back off and not go for the jugular over every trivial irritation. For many the miracle came with the introduction of medication which gave them a child who thought, listened, and was easier to reach. All parents feel stronger when they understand ADHD and realize they are not alone. But let's look at the full list of techniques that help produce better behavior.

Routine, structure, consistency

As human beings we are all happier when life is predictable and we know where we stand. This need for structure is many times more important in the ADHD child, who likes to have a fixed framework to direct his or her day. They wake at a certain time, put their paja-mas under their pillow, straighten the bedspread, get dressed, have breakfast, brush their teeth, feed the goldfish, and leave for school. If their equilibrium is thrown by anything different—a late night, a substitute teacher, visitors to the classroom, or a school excursion— this will set them off. If you want peace, keep to routine.

Get their attention

Whether you are training elephants in the circus, toddlers, or a child with ADHD, nothing will happen until you get their attention. Speak clearly, directly, and address them by name. Look them in the eye and show enthusiasm. With wriggly young children, hold their hands out in front or direct their face toward yours. In older children, approach from in front, and briefly touch to gain atten-tion—at this age firm holding is resented as it is an invasion of their space.

Once you have eye contact, give instructions, clearly, simply, and step-by-step. Mumbling, nagging, shouting, bombarding with words, and talking over the television will get you nowhere. If the child is not oppositional, ask for feedback to ensure the message has been taken on board. The secret to communication is eye contact, simple words, enthusiasm, and stepwise instruction.

Ignoring the unimportant

Parents can't help themselves—the child waves a fragment of red rag and they charge like a bull. If your plan is to avoid having your-self committed in the next few years, we urge you to ignore unimportant irritations. If they blow a raspberry, slurp their drink, or a pea falls to the floor, does it really matter? Successful parents realize the importance of taking a step back and engaging only in the big battles.

Know what triggers behavior

There are certain devastating events which are dynamite to discipline: children's parties, late nights, sickness, visitors, long car journeys, staying with relatives, and any change of routine. It's not always possible to avoid these, but anticipating does makes it easier to handle.

In-between times

Most ADHD children cope with the structure of the classroom and the hype of the playground, but they can't handle the gap between. They hit the playground like animals just released from captivity, and if trouble comes it is often in the first five minutes. When they return to class they are the last to calm themselves, settle down, and concentrate. Parents and teachers should know of this vulnerability and be on their guard in these "in-between times."

Medication increases focus

It's no secret that the authors of this book strongly support the use of stimulant medication in ADHD. Without it, the impulsive actions, lack of listening, and general disorganization of ADHD will sabotage the best behavioral program. Medication allows the child to self-monitor, plan their response, and be reached by reason. For most behavioral therapists, it is medication that turns a good program into one that is brilliant.

Too tough? Not tough enough?

We are strong believers in a gentle approach to ADHD, though at times we wonder if we are too permissive. On one hand we see parents who are uncompromising and tough, who have oppositional, resentful children. On the other are parents who are permissive and peace loving, who usually remain close to their less well-behaved children. We don't know the correct formula, but there must be some rules and firmness. Maybe the answer is 90 percent nurture and 10 percent toughness!

Children need rules

We don't want to run our homes like the Civil Service, every action governed by a hundred regulations, but there is room for a small, sensible framework of rules. These need to be drawn up in advance, created at a time of calm, not made in the heat of battle. They need to be simple, fair, few in number, and clearly understood.

"There will be no eating snacks just before your evening meal."
"You may bounce on the trampoline, not on your bed."
"You don't interrupt your sister while she is doing her homework."

Rules need to be enforced

When a rule is challenged, it must be clearly restated and then enforced. We must never be inflexible, but no amount of nagging or protest can change the referee's decisions. A rule is made, a child is reminded, action follows.

Avoid arguments

When they introduce arguing to the Olympics, ADHD children will scoop up all the medals. Arguing and debating with an ADHD child is a pointless pursuit—they are all words and no logic. Don't debate; you will never win and it shortens your life. State the rule and stand your ground.

"Can I have a cookie?"
"No, dinner is almost ready."
"But Grandma lets me have one."
"You know the rule!"

"Don't bounce on the bed."
"I'm only bobbing up and down."
"You know the rule!"

Avoid escalation

Some parents get so heated in their reaction they escalate every unimportant behavior. We know it can be irritating, but don't add fuel to the fire. Try to stay calm, use a matter-of-fact voice, and repeat the rule like a broken gramophone record.

"No cookies before dinner."
"But, Mom, I'm hungry."
"You know the rule."
"But that sucks."
"No cookies!"

"One, Two, Three Magic"

As adults we hate being cornered and confronted but, despite this, many of us give no leeway to our children. When confronted, most ADHD children refuse on principle. We tell them "Do it now" and they look at us as if we were impaired.

  Your grandmother had none of these problems; she asked politely, and if there was no sign of action, quietly counted to three. Counting is a well-tried, old technique, that gives that little bit of space needed to avoid reflex refusal. You state the rule, say "One," wait five seconds, "Two," wait five seconds, "Three," then act.

"No bouncing on the bed."
"I'm not bouncing."
"One." (wait five seconds)
"But, Mom."
"Two." (wait five seconds)
"Okay, I'll use the trampoline."

Parents in the North American support groups are particularly fond of the "One, Two, Three Magic" technique of U.S. psychologist Thomas Phelan, described in his book of the same name.

Separate the warring parties—time out

You can have your rules and your counting techniques, but there comes a point where things are heading seriously out of control.

Once behavior gets past a certain point, there is no place for reason—now you must back off and get some space.

Time out allows a deteriorating situation to be salvaged by briefly removing the child from all attention and audience. You can use a quiet corner, a time-out chair, sitting on a step, or a period of isolation in the bedroom. Have a simple name for this place, "the step," "the chair," "the room." The time period is approximately one minute for every year of life. With care, the technique can be used right up to the early teens.

When the time has been served, even if they are not openly repentant, they return to the real world. For time out to work it must be put in place without anger or debate, there must be no response to calling out, and once it's finished they restart with a completely clean slate.

"Don't annoy your sister when she is doing her homework."
"I'm not annoying her."
"You know the rule."
"She's annoying me."
"One." (wait five seconds)
"Two." (wait five seconds)
"Three." (wait five seconds)
"John, go to the chair now!"

A kitchen cooking timer allows parents to enforce time out without being questioned on how much time is left. Some parents don't put the *child* in time out, the adults take *themselves* to the backyard or even lock themselves in their bedroom. It may seem crazy but if it works, that's your business.

Have a backup plan

It's easy for experts like us, who write books, to talk about rules, counting, and time out. But real children look their parents in the eye and point-blank refuse. When this happens it's time to use the backup plan—parents must remain calm, use a monotonous voice, and give the child a choice.

"I want you to go to your room."
"No!"

"John, if you go now, when you come out you can watch *The Simpsons*. But if you choose not to go, there will be no television tonight."

A choice allows some room to maneuver and lessens the risk of re-flex refusal. Remember, we are talking about ADHD behaviors. Any technique will be much less effective with the negative hostility of Oppositional Defiant Disorder. (For top tips on ODD management, as suggested by the Australian psychologist Ian Wallace, see end of this chapter.)

Successful discipline

■ All the effective behavioral treatments for ADHD involve liv-ing by routine, rewarding the good, and taking a step back from confrontation.

■ Don't lock horns with an ADHD child and then increase the pressure. This produces a battle of wills, two angry parties, opposition, resentment, and damage to relationships.

■ Don't argue. Don't get heated. Don't escalate. Use a matter-of-fact, unemotional, controlled voice.

■ Give yourself room to maneuver:

* State the rule.
* Count to three.
* Use time out.
* Give choices.
* Don't force them into a cul-de-sac.

■ Remember, even the worst-behaved child is good 95 percent of the time. Reward this positive side; catch them being good!

■ In boxing, the victor is the one who uses the most force. In parenting, the winner is the one whose children still love them at the age of 18 years.

Encourage good behavior with rewards

The basic law of behavior modification states, "A behavior which pays off for the child will be repeated—a behavior that brings no advantage to the child will disappear." This means if we reward the right behavior, it should happen more frequently, while ignoring what's undesired means it should go away.

Unfortunately, it is just as easy to encourage the bad behavior as the good. A little child says "butt." We make a fuss and soon it's "butt," "butt," "butt!" As ADHD children quickly lose interest or up the ante, the secret of behavior modification is to reinforce with small, frequent rewards.

To encourage the best behavior we can use hard, soft, or cumulative rewards. A hard reward is something tangible such as money, food, or a special privilege. Soft rewards are praise, enthusiasm, or a show of parental pride. Cumulative refers to the collection of stars, stamps, or tokens, each given for a small period of good behavior, and eventually adding up to a major prize.

Hard and soft rewards lose their effect unless they are specific and regularly repeated. When a reward is used long-term, the payoff must vary, as this element of change prevents loss of interest or an increase in demands. Some ADHD behaviors respond best to ongoing rewards and for them we motivate with tokens and stars.

Token rewards

These are not unlike the frequent-flyer points used by airlines to encourage brand loyalty. For every desired behavior (flying Delta) you are given a small token of no individual value (frequent-flyer points). After two years of the desired behavior (loyalty to Delta) this adds up to a free trip to Disneyland.

A teacher can't expect the ADHD child to keep concentrating all day, but 10 minutes is achievable. Each short period on a task is rewarded by a mark or token (a check on a chart or a bead put in a cup). When 10 tokens have been collected they are traded for a worthwhile reward, for example getting out to play or 15 minutes on the computer.

While traveling long distance by car, the ADHD boy may annoy his sister. We can't expect six hours of perfect behavior, but each 15 minutes of peace can be rewarded by a token. When six are collected they stop at the next McDonald's. Token systems give rewards for good behavior; they do not fine the child for the bad.

One of our university colleagues has devised a simple system that gives and deducts points. At the start of the school day the child is given 10 tokens, just for being there and alive. For each good behavior the teacher adds two tokens and for the bad the teacher deducts one. No matter how disastrous the day the child always has the encouragement to come out on top.

Star systems

A star chart is a simple piece of paper with the days of the week down the left side and two or three target behaviors listed along the top. This system is only suited to a maximum of three easy-to-measure, specific behaviors, for example brushing teeth, feeding the cat, bringing home the lunch box. Each day when one of these is completed, a star is placed in the appropriate column. This draws attention to the target behavior and increases the chance of compliance. Be warned, a star system has limited benefits. It cannot be used in children under four years of age and you have two weeks to create change—after this they lose interest.

Motivate with privileges

In the older ADHD child privileges are an excellent form of motivation. A good burst of behavior might be recognized by a later bedtime, choosing dinner, ordering takeout, having a friend over to stay, or being excused from a usual household chore.

Withdrawal of privileges

Once we start taking away privileges we are moving from the positive part of discipline into the realms of punishment. For privilege withdrawal to be effective the privilege must be something the child depends on for pleasure, for example loss of television time.

When using this technique, don't get too heavy and don't prolong things. If the child perceives the punishment as unreasonable, they may overreact and behave many times worse. If it goes on too long, for example no TV for a month, they complain every day, leaving mom more punished than they are.

The usual loss of privilege involves missing half a favorite television program, no telephone tonight, or the bicycle locked up until the weekend. To be effective, keep it short, don't enter any debate, and choose something meaningful.

Punishment

This chapter is about molding behavior through encouragement, attention, and rewards, but there is still room for the limited use of punishment. Time out has already been mentioned. This both punishes and cools off by using a brief period away from attention and interest. It is a valuable technique which helps defuse the short-term crisis and avoids escalation.

Punishment must be treated with immense care as it is easy to get in much deeper than we wish. Children are confused when an unexpected punishment arrives out of the blue. They may misinterpret the sequence of events and only see their father's anger, "My dad went psycho and I was grounded for a week."

Some parents keep the pot boiling, constantly reminding the child of what they did yesterday. A marriage counselor would see this inability to forgive as a sure recipe for divorce. If we want to stay close in our relationship with our children, we must let past problems drop and hold no grudges.

The dangers of smacking

It is politically incorrect to condone the slightest smack, but in the real world it still happens. A smack may have some effect in the compliant angel, but so does everything else. In the difficult child, where nothing seems to work, smacking is unhelpful and dangerous.

The main dangers of smacking are escalation and resentment. You smack, the child looks defiant, you smack harder, they thumb their nose at you, and soon you are out of control. The more force you use, the more resentful they become. Resentment and hate do not make for happy relationships.

We always ask parents why they use such heavy discipline. *"It's the way I was brought up and it did me no harm."* "How close are you to your parents now?" *"I never see them, we have nothing in common!"* The case speaks for itself! We can't totally ban physical punishment but in ADHD it escalates, is ineffective, wrecks relationships, and can be downright dangerous.

Guidelines for punishment

■ Use punishment sparingly.

■ Give a clear warning.

■ Think before you act.

■ Communicate calmly.

■ Have a clear beginning and end.

■ Don't escalate.

■ Once finished, let the matter drop.

Last-straw explosions

ADHD children are constantly at their parents from dawn to dusk. It is all the little hassles that cause the stress, but one final straw breaks the camel's back. Good moms and dads give warnings and check behavior throughout the day; others do nothing until they can take no more, then explode. Many children are unaware why they are in such trouble and why their parents have gone ballistic.

Look at the start, not the end

One of our ADHD children was referred back with an urgent request for a brain scan. His school principal reported that this child had taken to beating his head against a wall and in this man's 20 years of teaching this implied either serious disturbance or brain damage.

On face value this was indeed bizarre behavior, but nobody had bothered to look at the events that led up to the incident. Our boy was playing happily, when he was deliberately picked on by a well-known school bully, who started to tease. With all the predictable overreaction of ADHD, he rose to the bait and soon was steaming. A teacher ran to the rescue, and threatened and blamed our innocent boy, which sent him over the top. The principal was summoned, who further fanned the flames—our patient became hysterical and beat his head against the wall.

As adults we are supposed to have more sense than children, but often we don't know when to take a step back. The head banging was not a sign of severe disturbance or brain damage; it was the end point of a sad sequence of events. Those who needed counseling were the bully who started it, the teacher who blamed, and the principal who lacked the insight to back off.

When analyzing behavior, always look at the beginning, not the end. A gentle puppy would never want to hurt its owner, but if frightened or cornered, it may bite. They are not to blame; it is those who upset them that deserve the punishment.

"I" statements—"you" statements

It is possible to say the same thing in two ways, each getting a different response. If I use an "I" statement, it transmits how "I" feel. If I use a "You" statement, it implies that "You" are being criticized. When an ADHD child annoys us it is the behavior we dislike, not the child. It may seem a trivial change, but where possible move from "You" to "I."

"You are always hurting your sister" becomes "I get upset when there's so much fighting." "You've ruined the outing for all of us" becomes "I am upset when we all have to come home early."

Feedback when good

On a bad day it may seem that nothing is going right, but even the worst child is in fact good 95 percent of the time. The secret of successful discipline is to notice, reinforce, and reward the good.

When things are going well, we must tell them so. "You were so good at the doctor's today." "You two are playing great." "It's nice to see such a tidy room." "I was proud of you at the party." Discipline is not punishment; we change behavior by encouraging the good. When you see it, praise it.

Discipline is a delicate balance of firmness and encouragement. It is not possible to overencourage, but it is easy to be too negative. When in doubt take the peaceful path; hold out the olive branch of nurture, not the stick of punishment. Don't get demoralized—if managing ADHD was all that easy, there would be no need for this book.

ADHD—top tips for behavioral management

(We asked Ian Wallace, Australia's best-known ADHD-specializing psychologist, to give his top suggestions for behavioral management.)

- **Avoid escalating the ADHD problem.** Avoid reasoning and lengthy debates. Act quickly. Don't talk too much. Use a firm, monotonous voice and speak in simple, brief sentences. Avoid emotional statements, harsh discipline, and criticism.

- **Develop rules and consistent structure.** ADHD children respond best when they understand the rules, know the limits, and expect consistent consequences. Stating prearranged rules helps parents keep out of irrational arguments.

- **Make them responsible for their own behavior.** Don't accept responsibility for your child's behavior and don't allow him to blame others. Make it your child's choice of behavior that leads to his choice of discipline or reward.

- **Have a prearranged discipline plan.** ADHD children behave better when they face the same system every day. With a plan, moms and dads are more likely to work together and less likely to act impulsively or irrationally.

- **Use immediate rewards and punishment.** Use quick, simple rewards or discipline that can be applied immediately. Don't give in. Delayed punishment does not work.

- **Balance out the positives and negatives.** Recognize the smallest gains and improvements. No child will improve through criticism.

- **Use a multimodal approach.** Most success comes from using a cluster of treatments. This includes medication, a behavior program, self-esteem building, remedial help, and good classroom management.

- **Work slowly and steadily.** Change will come, but don't expect too much too soon.

■ **Build on their strengths, creativity, and abilities.** These children have many unique talents. Foster their abilities and they will amaze you in later life.

Oppositional Defiant Disorder—top tips for management

Ian Wallace—psychologist (Sydney)

■ **Always avoid head-on confrontations.** ODD kids are looking for a victim. Avoid face-to-face battles. Use offhand tones, cool responses, and looking away, and give time for hostility to reduce.

■ **Sidestep impulsive rages.** ODD kids are impulsive and aggressive, so try to slow down, rather than stir up, the situation. Give them space by suggesting alternative options or just walk away for a moment. Let them feel they have a say; for example, "Well, there are two ways we can handle this, but you decide which is the best for you."

■ **Avoid arguing.** These kids have an interest in keeping their parents arguing. Allow them a few minutes of uninterrupted time to have their say. Listen attentively but set ground rules. They have the right to express themselves but this right is lost if they scream or become verbally abusive.

■ **Avoid Mexican standoffs.** Don't back the ODD child into a corner or leave them no way to save face. Don't moralize. Show other solutions that might work out for them. Always be prepared to give a little ground.

■ **Use distractibility to your advantage.** Jump positively on anything that is good—praise can divert from the main problem. Encourage any improvement but don't expect a total turnaround.

■ **Be on the same team.** If there are any gains, be in it with them; for example, "I'm really proud of you, we are working well as a team." Let them feel they are to some extent in control.

- ■ **Remember that they do care.** Don't be bluffed; ODD kids do care. Often they are too stubborn to admit they are wrong and that they need help.

- ■ **Help them to trust the world.** These ODD kids believe the world is as hostile as themselves. They need to see the world can treat them well. They enjoy 1:1 time, achievement, and leadership opportunities.

Ian Wallace is a consultant psychologist in Sydney, Australia. He is author of *You And Your ADD Child (Practical Behavioural Strategies)*, HarperCollins, Sydney, 1996.

ELEVEN

Practical Solutions to Common Behavior Problems

It would be an insult to parents to pretend that the lists in this chapter will miraculously cure all behavior problems. The suggestions are given for only one reason: to guide you in the right direction. Our aim is to give some simple pointers. Once you are standing at the battle front you will have to modify them as the events unfold.

Responding to ADHD behaviors

Pokes and teases his sister at mealtimes

Food is about nutrition, and mealtimes are for families to get together and communicate. Don't let squabbles and nitpicking cause stress—we want peace, not perfection. Have a few nonnegotiable rules and let the rest pass.

- "You can ramble on about any topic but you can't tease, insult, or abuse your sister."

- "You can wriggle, swing, and touch but there must be absolutely no contact with your sister or anything she owns."

- If the rule is broken, there is one warning, then action, as outlined in Chapter 10.

Eight years old and interrupts like a preschooler

Interrupting adults is a universal complaint. ADHD children are impulsive and forget if they don't tell you immediately. We must not block communication, but we should encourage them to wait.

- Give a gentle reminder: "Your turn in a minute, John."

- Keep repeating the rules of conversation, but don't become a negative nag.

- Allow the forgetful child to interrupt with a "cue word," which you pick up later. As you are talking they say "new teacher" and when appropriate you ask, "What's this about a new teacher?"

Surviving long car journeys

If your child fights, squabbles, and protests on the trip to the corner store, a 300-mile car trip could be a challenge. When long-distance travel ages parents and is a hazard to mental health, consider a quick air flight, a seat on a train, or simply stay home. Just because adults like to drive long distance doesn't mean it suits their children.

- Set down a few firm rules about teasing, poking, and annoying, in advance.

- Plan regular breaks, and inform them of the travel time.

- If the car tape player is to be used, allocate tape time in advance. An individual Walkman may help.

- Use a token system where short periods of peaceful travel are rewarded with a small token (a star, bead, etc.), which all adds up to a worthwhile reward (e.g. bonus spending money at the next stop).

■ Secure a large piece of luggage between the occupants of the backseat.

Bad language—bad attitude

A child who is impulsive and socially immature can be rude and inappropriate in what they say. Oppositional children are often hostile.

■ Words are often said for the reaction they get. Don't rise to the bait, make a clear statement that this is unacceptable, and don't escalate or debate.

■ In young children, explain the meaning of rude words; show the silliness of describing reproductive anatomy in public.

■ There is a difference between a five-year-old who copies without thought and the entrenched bad language of a 15-year-old. You can enforce some house rules in the adolescent, but the time to establish attitudes and language is much earlier on.

■ Notice and reinforce when they talk, relate, and respect in an appropriate way.

■ Children parrot the speech, abusive attitudes, and bad language of those they are close to. In the preschool years this comes from us, the parents.

■ When parenting has been hostile, negative, and verbally abusive since the early years, it is normal for the adolescent to treat their parents with the respect they deserve.

The bedroom is a mess

Order-loving mothers don't cope with a bomb-blast bedroom. The best chance of tidiness comes when parents start young. In the teenage years we can expect reasonable hygiene and occasional cleanups, but a spotless bedroom is a dream.

■ Regularly cull all excess junk, toys, and outgrown clothes.

■ Provide easy-access storage and hanging space.

■ With the young child, tidy the room together.

■ Use the "carrot" incentive: "You tidy this and I'll get your drink ready."

■ Have a preset inspection time each day.

■ A star chart helps focus attention on the clean room but it loses effect within a few weeks.

■ For each day of relative tidiness add a small productivity bonus to the pocket money.

■ By teen age we need to take a step back and ask whether it is worth driving a messy teenager out of your home for the sake of a clean bedroom.

Slow to get ready for school

There are two sorts of slow starters, those who switch off (dreamers-"spacers") and those who are out to annoy (foot draggers). The dreamers need to be organized, while the foot draggers get two or three reminders and then if they choose to be late this is between them and the school principal.

Dreamers

■ With dreamy children pack their school bag the night before and set out their clothes in preparation.

■ Keep reminding, checking, and encouraging progress.

■ Reward results, don't get angry, don't despair.

Foot draggers

■ Foot draggers need to know the rules.

■ There is one wake-up call, a five-minute reminder, then a statement when it is 10 minutes before the school bus departs.

■ Set a cooking timer which gives a warning; this avoids nagging.

- Eating breakfast on the run is unsatisfactory but it's better than conflict.

- If they choose to be late, don't break the speed limits getting them there.

- The consequence of this is between them and their school.

- Don't allow a dawdling child to ruin the rest of your day.

Uses ADHD as an excuse

Most children receive an emotional boost when they realize they are not dumb, but have ADHD. A few use the diagnosis in the worst possible way, informing their teacher that they can't be expected to work hard because they have a disorder. The diagnosis of ADHD must never be allowed to justify laziness or lack of effort.

- The ADHD child may need extra time to finish work, but it must still be completed.

- The ADHD child with specific learning disability may be eligible for a reader, a scribe, or extra time in examinations, but they still have to know their work.

- ADHD is an explanation; it must never be used as an excuse.

Breaks his sister's property

If a child has an inquisitive mind, fiddly fingers, and doesn't think ahead, things will get broken.

- Have a small number of rules about what can and what cannot be touched.

- Notice when they show care and respect for other people's property.

- Distinguish between the occasional unthinking act and damage which follows deliberately disregarding a warning.

- Instruct siblings to keep their treasures secure and make this a no-go area for their ADHD brothers.

■ Breakages can be replaced using a small levy on the pocket money, which is deducted at source. Don't set up an impossibly harsh repayment system as this causes resentment and hostility.

Breaks in unthinking rage

The hyperactive, impulsive child can have a remarkably short fuse. When things go badly they overreact, even destroying their own treasures. After it's happened they see their stupidity, which makes them twice as upset.

■ The angriest human beings are those who are angry at their own silliness.

■ Don't nag as this adds insult to injury.

■ If they break something important to them—for example an almost completed model airplane—support, don't criticize.

■ Don't rub salt in the wound—even if they say they don't care, they are hurting.

Lies—bending the truth

Everyone knows that lying is a sin, while bending the truth is a requirement of success in public life or politics. There is a difference between the occasional untruth of the young and the pathological planned deceit of an out-of-control adolescent.

■ In the younger child, don't overreact; calmly say that you do not think it is true.

■ Don't debate; quietly state your opinion.

■ Make sure that honesty pays off—they should receive less punishment for owning up than for denying fault.

■ If you encourage openness when they are young, they should still confide in you in their tempestuous teens.

■ It is unfair to expect our children to be more truthful than the adults they live with.

Dangerous bike riding

A bicycle gives a great outlet for the pent-up energy of the ADHD child. Unfortunately, hyperactive, impulsive children can be a danger on the roads. We don't want to rob them of this important activity, but we have to keep them safe.

- Have clear rules about helmets, stopping at intersections, crossing main roads, and what areas are off-limits.

- Have rules about care of the bike, locking, and putting it away at night.

- Notice and reinforce safe riding.

- Maintain some supervision when they are challenging their friends on jumps, ramps, and riding through the air.

- When rules are disregarded, lock up the bicycle for a week and don't debate or argue your actions.

- If you think bicycles are a worry, wait until they start driving your car!

Birthday parties

One of the best measures of successful treatment is an increase in the number of invitations to children's parties. Often the hype and energy of so many children send the busy child ballistic.

- Prepare properly and arrive unstressed.

- Ensure medication has been given and will be in balance during the party hours.

- Give an additional dose of medication if this is appropriate.

- If worried about behavior, go a little late and pick up early.

- With younger children, stay and help supervise.

- When organizing your own child's party ensure you have enough adult help on hand.

■ Think of inviting a favorite teacher from school, as this provides a form of "police presence."

Socially out of tune

Some ADHD children can be such charmers, but others are socially clumsy, and irritate. They push in, overpower, invade space, and the more they try, the worse it gets.

■ Reinforce when they play well and interact appropriately.

■ Give a brief reminder when their actions are upsetting others.

■ Don't become negative or constantly criticize.

■ Discreetly ask them how it would feel if they were in the other person's place.

■ Social-skills training programs seem essential for every ADHD child, but the results appear more successful in the therapy room than in the outside world.

■ The development of social skills comes gradually with age and maturity.

Homework hassles

If the day at school has been a struggle, the last thing you want is more schoolwork at home. The attitude to homework varies greatly from child to child, but the secret is to get it right in the early school years, establish the homework habit, and be an involved parent.

■ Have a fixed homework time which allows some freedom to relax after school but is not late evening, when they are overtired.

■ Have a special homework place, almost like a shrine, which helps the human concentrate on a higher plane.

■ Have a contract which allocates a certain amount of full-focus work, followed by a break, then another period of work.

■ If after an appropriate amount of effort the work is still unfinished, leave it there.

- ■ Help, supervise, check, and be involved from the early years.

- ■ Use reminders to make sure the right books come home and the requirements are understood.

- ■ With school projects and high-school study, parents still need to be involved, particularly to get them started.

TWELVE

Improving School Performance—Tips for Parents and Teachers

Trying to teach an impulsive, inattentive child is never easy. Even with the best intervention available they will always have more talent and creativity than they are able to demonstrate in the examination hall. There are no simple solutions, but most success comes with teaching in small steps, and with variety, structure, and tricks to help short-term memory.

Practical classroom suggestions

Which class?

The ADHD child thrives on calm, consistency, and one-to-one encouragement. If they were royalty they would have a full-time personal tutor, but in the real world they will be taught in the same room as 30 others. When choosing a class, aim for the traditional closed-plan style. Avoid the composite classes where more than one year's grade are taught together—unless there is some exceptional draw card, such as a high teacher-to-pupil ratio.

These children do not cope with disruption and must be protected from teachers with an unreliable attendance record or those planning long-term leave. In small schools, the challenging children are often placed in the class taken by the school principal. This may be the most tolerant and experienced teacher in school, but the ADHD child is unsettled by all the administrative interruptions. When choosing a class we aim for the minimum of distraction, but even if placed in a soundproof cell, these children are still capable of distracting themselves.

Choosing the right teacher

For the ADHD child, success at school varies greatly from year to year. It is not that these children change, it is just that some years the pupil and teacher hit it off and some years they don't. There are still teachers who believe the ADHD child can be cured with heavy discipline. Others are almost as impulsive and inflexible as the child they are trying to help. When the ADHD child is placed with an inflexible, uninsightful teacher, the adult stands on their pride and may escalate a trivial behavior to the point of school suspension. The ideal teacher is firm, flexible, and knows when to back off.

All human beings like to be welcomed each day with enthusiasm and eye contact. We listen best to animated people who vary their voices and make each individual feel he or she is the one that matters. ADHD children need to know they are accepted and appreciated, but at the same time the teacher is definitely in charge.

Sensible seating

It is tempting to hide the disruptive child as far away from the rest of the class as possible. But if he is going to learn, the child needs to be near the front, preferably sandwiched between his two most placid classmates. He should be facing the teacher, eye to eye. Instructions should be given from in front of the child as he can lose direction when twisting to the side or back. Some companies who specialize in the training of business executives believe the U-shape seating plan gives best results, though space and department policy may not make this an option.

Order and organization

ADHD children need to learn how to prioritize and organize or they will always underachieve. Teachers as well as parents can help them with rules, routine, lists, and structure.

Rules

ADHD children must know what is expected and where they stand. There should be a small number of clearly stated rules and regular reminders. At the start of each school day the rules about calling out in class, disturbing others, and leaving your seat are mentioned to all students. Special rules for ADHD children are discussed with them in private.

Routine

ADHD children require routine and cope poorly with unexpected surprises. They must know the plan at the start of each school day and be aware of what is going to happen next. When moving from one activity to another, they need to be allowed to wind down, then must be picked up again on the other side.

Lists

These are the lifesavers for older children and adults. They list jobs for the day, homework, and the equipment they need. Ticking off the completed tasks provides structure and gives a feeling of achievement.

Planning and self-monitoring

Sometime after the age of eight years, children can be taught to check and plan. At bedtime they are encouraged to consider the next day's activities, get their books ready, pack their sports clothes, and think ahead. At the end of school they stop for a minute and ask three questions, "What homework do I have?", "What books do I need?", and "What messages do I bring home?" After their swimming lesson they ask, "Do I have my swimsuit?", "my towel?", "my goggles?", and "my bus pass?" It's slow and frustrating but teaching the child to self-monitor will eventually pay off.

Teaching about sequence

Many ADHD children fight to keep their speech, thought, and schoolwork in sequence. If they will accept adult correction, help them organize their thoughts. The young child rushes in with some unintelligible story about a dog. Slow them down and say "What dog?", "Where was the dog?", "What did the dog do?" When reading a story stop at the end of a page and ask, "What is going to happen next?", "What led to this problem?" As they are settling down for the night get them to talk through the sequence of some day-to-day activity, for example setting the dinner table or fixing a puncture on their bike.

Self-talk

Bomb-disposal experts are more reliable when they talk themselves trough the correct sequence of cutting the wires. Pilots run through a checklist prior to takeoff. Talking aloud is not welcomed by teachers, but for some teenagers and adults it greatly improves accuracy.

A framework

When a child is forgetful and disorganized they need to work from a framework. "What is the topic of this project?" "What are the major headings?" "What order do they come in?" "What information comes under each heading?" "Is there an imbalance of information in any section?" "Have I missed anything?"

Breaking into chunks

When the whole task seems impossibly big, it must be broken into a sequence of steps or small parts. A "do" list is made: one piece is tackled first, then another, then another.

An overview

If children start with an overview in their heads, the fine detail is easier to handle. For example, they have been given a novel to read for their high-school exam. If the weak reader has a summary of the characters and the plot before starting the novel, then the fine print will fit onto this framework.

Time allocation

ADHD children have difficulty managing time. In an exam they allocate half the time to a quarter of the questions. When doing homework, they spend an hour coloring a picture and leave little time for the writing. From the primary-school years on, prioritizing and time allocation are techniques that must be taught.

Holding attention

The greatest challenge for any teacher is to hold the ADHD child's attention without humiliating them in front of their friends. Attention is held with cue words, enthusiasm, variety, and with brief, stepwise instructions.

Cue words

When the class is drifting the clever teacher uses words such as "ready," "wait for it," "this is the interesting bit," "now, here we go!"

Animated—enthusiastic

If teaching is presented in a bored, unexcited voice, the message is unlikely to get past the left earlobe. The first step in communication is to gain eye contact and attention by using an enthusiastic, firm, businesslike tone. The animated teacher uses body language and their eyes, and pauses or talks softly to draw the children in.

Be brief

Instructions need to be short and to the point. Don't hide important messages in a mass of unnecessary words. Tell the child what you wish them to do, not what you do not want them to do.

Stepwise instructions

Long lists of instructions do not suit the ADHD child. They have memory lapses, and forget the order, and this results in a shambles. In the early school years work should be presented in a series of simple steps. "Take a clean page of paper." "Now take your ruler."

"Put the ruler on the lefthand side." "Draw a line down the page." "Now take your pen . . ."

Variety

Boredom is a big problem in ADHD and variation helps this loss of interest. Clever teachers change their tone of voice and the speed of presentation, or stop unexpectedly. The child is asked to answer questions or to play teacher and teach the lesson back to the class. Pictures, diagrams, tapes, and models all give variety and help reinforce listening. Some teachers provide a clipboard to allow the ADHD child to keep their work in front of them, no matter how much they move or wriggle around. Some even allocate seats in different parts of the class, and when getting bored, the child gives a signal and they move to the reserve position.

Feedback

Because a child has been told, it does not mean he understands. Teachers must keep checking that messages are received and parents must encourage the ADHD child to ask when he is lost.

Improving memory

Visual cues

Those who live with ADHD children or adults cannot believe how they forget so quickly. But we can improve memory using all sorts of clues, lists, and memory jogs. Verbal information is often lost, but when a verbal is tagged to a visual cue, it may be held. In the early school years we learn our alphabet with an "a" beside the picture of an "apple." We remember the states of the Union by visualizing a map. Teachers can tag bits of information to a color, for example all the place-names of a project in blue and people's names in red. Visual cues are not confined to school—we may not remember the floor in the parking lot but we know it was the yellow level.

Key words and lists

Key words are used to draw the child's attention to an idea, in the hope it will jog his or her memory. Every mother uses this—her notes say "dentist," "meat," "pay bill." Children can use key words to transform a lecture or chapter into a list of key facts, for example: Captain Cook—*Endeavour*—UK Aug. 1768—Tahiti—Great Southern Continent—NZ Oct. 69 to April 70—Botany Bay 29 April 1770—Hits reef—Batavia—Fever kills crew—Home June 1771.

Association

We often associate a piece of information with a certain picture or a setting. If we leave the ironing to go and get something, then forget what it was, if we think back to ironing, we may remember. When we are introduced to a group of people the names may be easier to remember if tagged to another image, for example Hillary—"The First Lady;" Wendy—"Peter Pan's friend;" Greg—"the golfer."

Rhymes and mnemonics

In my medical training it was compulsory to learn the names and relative position of every artery, nerve, vein, and muscle in the entire body. For me this was made possible with numerous memory jogs, for example in the groin there is a major artery, vein, and nerve, but which one is in which position? We remembered "Motor VAN": starting from the middle (M) there was a vein (V), an artery (A), and then a nerve (N).

As adults we remember "thirty days has September, April, June, and November." We know "i" before "e" except after "c." The colors of the rainbow are red, orange, yellow, green, blue, indigo, and violet: "ROYGBIV."

Children and teachers can invent their own reminders. If you have difficulty knowing whether you spell "apparent" as *aparant* or *apparent*, remember "a two-parent family" (two "ps"—"pparent"). When confused whether to use the word *principle* or *principal*, we remember it is "our 'pal' the principal." Many ADHD children never master the difficult parts of the times tables, for example 7 times 9, but some nonsense rhyme will jog them along—"seven times nine on a sick old tree, seven times nine is sixty-three."

Memory jogs

Children can use the reminders that keep forgetful adults on track: writing on a hand, notes on a scrap of paper, knots in a handkerchief, an elastic band around the wrist, a watch on the wrong hand. Then there are gadgets such as a watch alarm, an electronic organizer, and memo takers.

Vulnerable times

Those who teach ADHD children don't need a crystal ball to predict the problem areas. These children call out in class, touch and tap, overreact to teasing, and don't cope with changes.

Calling out in class

Most ADHD children are known for their call-outs and "smart ass" comments. This is all part of their impulsive, immature, "poor brakes" behavior. They will never be the easiest child in the class, but there are some ways to help.

Firstly, if the child is on medication, ensure the levels are correctly balanced, as impulsive incidents increase when drugs drop off. These children must be cautioned for their call-outs, but not ridiculed in front of their classmates. The whole class must be constantly reminded of the rules. If the message is not taken on board, the ADHD child is addressed alone and informed of the expectations, and if call-outs continue they must know what will happen.

When this behavior occurs the teacher makes a clear signal by using strong eye contact ("the look"), a special word, or secret gesture. Tokens can be given for each 10 to 20 minutes of self-control, which eventually add up to a special privilege. Sometimes a deduction system is equally effective. Here the child starts with "four lives," and if one remains at the end of class they leave with all their friends. If the lives have been spent they stay back for some minutes. With each interruption the teacher signals the loss of a life, using "the look" and tearing off one of four tags. Fortunately, calling out decreases at the end of the primary-school years but is often replaced by smart comments and by taunting teachers.

Touching and tapping

You can put a total ban on all clicking pens, but these children will still find something to tap, touch, or jiggle. Fiddly fingers are so much a part of the child's makeup, wise teachers accept the inevitable and teach them to jiggle quietly. Others try to divert using a squeezy worry ball or something quiet to twiddle. Some adults are no better, they tap their fingers, chew gum, smoke, bite their nails, and jaw-clench, but at this age it seems to be socially acceptable.

Changes—in-between times

Children with ADHD are not just overactive; they are overactive at the wrong times. They come in from the playground airborne, settle down slowly, then wind up when they move again. It is this change from a calm, controlled environment to free play that causes the stress. After a break the focus should be gradually increased with some general instruction, and when settled, the child can move to the more complex work. There should be a warning five minutes before the end of class, allowing a gradual wind-down time. Concerts and school excursions can be an immense challenge due to the general level of hype and the loss of routine. There are no sure remedies but if we are prepared for these vulnerable times we can be on our guard.

Overreacting to teasing

We often see gentle, sensitive children who are labeled "aggressive." They are not deliberately nasty; their problem is overreaction to taunts and teasing. These children are sought out by school bullies, who stir them up for their own sick needs.

Distraught parents often phone to say their child has been suspended. They tell of a predictable sequence of events. The ADHD child is happy and minding his own business, he is teased, he reacts, the bully enjoys the reaction and teases more, the ADHD child overreacts, the teacher makes a clumsy intervention, the blowup escalates, and the innocent child is suspended for three days.

Teachers need to be aware of this vulnerability of ADHD and soothe, not inflame. They need to look at the events at the start of play, rather than the final scene. Those who tease and bully are aggressive and should be punished appropriately. In the junior-high-school years ADHD children must be instructed to hold fire and talk to the supervising teacher. We can suggest they count to 10 and turn the other cheek, but even intelligent adults find this difficult. By the high-school years, the explosive edge has started to mellow and now we can role-play various verbal responses to protect against taunts. The bully might be told, "You must be having a particularly bad day," or "You seem to have some sort of problem."

Other points

■ **Communicate with the school** Parents often become disheartened, and because of this may suffer a severe dose of "school refusal." To avoid the stress, they avoid parent activities and keep away as much as possible. It's important for parents to show they are genuinely interested. We must keep the lines of communication open, try to talk to the teacher at least every two weeks, and if necessary have a message book operating between school and home. Don't demand and criticize, as this puts teachers off—ask how you can help.

■ **Tell when you don't understand** When the ADHD child loses the plot he falls behind and is often called lazy. This might not have happened if the child had admitted his difficulty early on. Teachers are approachable people and children must be encouraged to tell them when they don't understand.

■ **Messages between school and home** It would be more reliable to send a message by pigeon than by most of the children in our care. If it's important, attach it to some vital piece of equipment; for example it could be taped to the lunch box, clipped to the homework books, or attached to the papers for the first lesson.

■ **A poor reaction to praise** It is a sin to be vain, but despite this most human beings love to hear praise. There are, however, some children who misbehave, argue, or go silly with general praise. You tell them they are doing well—"No, I am not." You tell them their work is good—"It stinks." This can usually be avoided if we keep praise specific. Instead of "Your written work is good," say "Your letters are so much clearer." Instead of "You have written a really good story," say "I like the characters in this story."

■ **Show evidence of improvement** These children can be pretty negative and don't believe our reassurance. When they are unconvinced by words, don't argue; just show the evidence. "This was your written work first term—look at it now." "This is the sort of math you were doing last year—look at it now."

■ **Teaching exam techniques** By the high-school years many ADHD children have developed the drive and determination to really succeed. Despite this most will underperform in their exams. Questions are misread, time is allocated unwisely, and they are disadvantaged by poor writing and unreliable spelling. Schools are often surprised at the amount of hidden talent when they test the ADHD child by oral exam or allow a scribe to do their writing. It's not good enough to teach ADHD (or ADHD–dyslexic) children information—they need to be shown how to study, take notes, summarize, highlight, read questions carefully, structure answers, correctly allocate time, and doubly check important instructions.

■ **To repeat or not?** ADHD children may be up to standard level in learning, but out of their depth emotionally. As their brains mature, many of the problems of attention, behavior, and learning get easier and for this reason it is better to take school at a somewhat slower pace. If a preschool director recommends staying back a year parents should listen. Once in school, holding back in the first or second year occasionally brings some emotional benefit. Many experts dislike repeating, and say it is remedial help, rather than repetition, that is needed.

■ **How much remedial help?** With ADHD so intertwined with specific learning disabilities, many children need extra help with reading, writing, mathematics, and language. In an ideal world the school system would be adequately funded to provide small classes and all the required remedial workers. But times are tough and a lot of help must now come from parents, perceptive principals, and class teachers.

Private tutors can increase academic confidence in a child but if they do too much it is a turnoff. Remember, these problem areas will cause pain, and after a difficult day at school children don't need their noses wiped in further failure. It's unhealthy to spend too much time focusing on areas of weakness—we need a balance between extra help and success in outside interests.

■ **Homework** This is mostly the school's problem and must not be allowed to ruin parent/child relationships. Homework will never happen unless we have the right books and know what has to be done. Before leaving school devise some sort of memory jog, for example a note clipped to the bus pass to remind, "What is my homework?", "Have I got the books?" Some parents have a second set of books at home and others use a homework communication book between home and teacher. Jointly decide on the best time slot for high-concentration homework, for example half an hour after arriving home. Create a constant area for homework with good light, no television, and their gear easily available. If the child is on medication, homework is easier when the stimulant levels remain active in the late afternoon. Devise the length that best suits your child, probably half an hour of full-on work followed by a short break, then another half hour. A child's enthusiasm is greatly influenced by the interest and support parents give from an early age. Help, encouragement, checking, being available, and discussion all give the best results. Any child who has done her best for the full time allocation should be praised for what she has done, not punished for the bits that are incomplete.

■ **Special allowances are available** Children with ADHD have no problem of ability, their difficulty is output. They also have an extremely high risk of associated specific learning disabilities; when ADHD and SLD present together, the child may be eligible for special accommodation of their problems. When it comes to exams, some children may be allowed extra time or allocated a reader or scribe. Some increase their classroom accuracy and output with computers, while others may tape-record information. When dyslexia blocks reading for pleasure, children may still enjoy literature by using talking books made available through their local library.

Summary: Improving school performance

The right teacher

- ■ Enthusiastic, interested.

- ■ Firm but flexible.

- ■ Avoids escalation, knows when to back off.

- ■ A good attendance record.

- ■ Welcoming, supportive.

Sensible seating

- Near the front.
- Sandwiched between two quiet children.
- Eye to eye with the teacher.
- Receives all instructions from directly in front.
- Write on a clipboard.

Organizing the disorganized

- Keep to routine.
- Have class and individual rules.
- Teach list making.
- Teach self-monitoring.
- Teach order and sequence.
- Encourage self-talk.
- Teach breaking big projects into chunks.
- Provide framework and overview before fine detail.
- Teach time allocation.

Increasing attention

- Animated, enthusiastic teaching style.
- Cue words to alert attention.
- Be brief and to the point.
- Instruct in simple steps.
- Vary voice, tone, volume, and teaching methods.
- Ask questions and get feedback.

Improving memory

- Tag verbal information to a visual clue.

- List key words to jog memory.

- Associate new information with something already known.

- Use mnemonics.

- Use memory jogs, for example knot in handkerchief, watch on wrong wrist.

Be alert to ADHD vulnerabilities

- Calls out, makes smart comments.

- Touches, taps, fidgets, and fiddles.

- Copes badly with transitions.

- Overreacts to playground teasing.

- Is slow to copy down information.

- Forgets homework books.

- Forgets messages for home.

- Has difficulty starting projects.

- Needs tight structure for homework.

- Is easily led, quickly blamed.

- Gets lost, falls behind, loses interest.

- May show dramatic deterioration of behavior and learning as medication levels drop off.

THIRTEEN
Other Therapies and Diet

The last 20 years has been an interesting time. First, we heard that ADHD would disappear when lead was removed from gasoline. Then we digressed into diet, vitamin B₆, zinc, multi-vitamins, and, more recently, evening-primrose oil, tuna fish oil, and various plant extracts. Tinted lenses and eye exercises were promoted for dyslexia. Sensory integration therapy was said to help the learning disabled; motor programs came and went.

Psychiatrists tried to understand the thinking of ADHD children through play, while their parents had their emotions analyzed in long-term talking therapy. Along the way there have been a number of psychological treatments that were sound in theory but decidedly disappointing in their results.

Meanwhile, the media has feasted on farfetched, often wacky claims, and professionals with a particular ax to grind have often criticized those with a more up-to-date overview. It is no wonder that parents are confused.

Let's look at some of these much-promoted forms of therapy. Which of these help in theory, which help in practice, and which don't help at all?

Cognitive behavior therapy

In this technique the psychologist gets a child to talk their way through what is happening around them, and then to be more reasoned and reflective in the way they respond to a situation. The hope is that cognitively trained children will then teach themselves to step back a pace, and self-regulate their behavior. This seems a sensible form of treatment for every child with ADHD, but unfortunately the results have been very disappointing.

The young ADHD child is far too impulsive to think through a situation before he reacts, and older children are not much better. The technique has been found helpful in adults with ADHD, but only when they are first focused with stimulant medication.

Social-skills training

ADHD children appear unaware of how their behavior bothers other people. They are greatly disadvantaged by being socially out of tune, and when the technique of social-skills training arrived, we saw this as an exciting innovation.

In this program, children are taught in groups to think how their words and behaviors affect those around them. If they interact well, this good behavior is reinforced; when they behave badly, they are asked to reflect on how this affects others.

Social-skills training seems essential for every child with ADHD but, unfortunately, the results have been far from good. Research shows that social skills can be taught in the therapy room but the benefits have little flow onto the outside world.

Sensory integration

In the early 1970s an American therapist, Jean Ayres, popularized the idea of sensory integration. Her main interest was the learning disabilities which are often part of ADHD. Her techniques involve movement, swinging, spinning, and balance. These actions were thought to help brain maturation, which has a flow on to academic and other abilities.

There are still a number of centers which promote variations of Ayres's work, but we do not recommend these theories to patients in our care. The results of recent studies show the therapeutic effect of sensory integration to have little advantage over simpler traditional interventions. (See "Controversial therapies for ADHD," in Appendix XV.)

Occupational therapy

Most ADHD children have terrible handwriting. This can be helped by a good occupational therapist, who will work on the pen grip, organization of the letters, and the flow from word to word. Stimulant medication is often used in conjunction with occupational therapy, as this also helps with both neatness and accuracy.

Many ADHD children have poor motor planning and coordination, which leaves them unable to tie shoelaces, throw straight, catch a ball, or move smoothly. A short period with an enthusiastic therapist can help a child to make the best of what they have got and at the same time give a great boost to self-confidence. Occupational therapy can bring about a percentage improvement, but it will never turn the child with two left feet into a world-class athlete or graceful dancer (see Chapter 25, "Hints to Help Handwriting and Coordination.")

The talking cures

In the early 1980s North America was years ahead of the rest of the world in its understanding of ADHD. In Australia and Europe child psychiatrists were more interested in the environmental-analytical, rather than the biological-behavioral approach. Certainly, in Sydney and Melbourne, many colleagues believed that ADHD behaviors came from unresolved feelings, dysfunctions, and past events in the parents' lives. Often parents were taken into long-term therapy, to talk through their perceived problems, while some children were engaged through play.

These ideas were 20 years behind the more pragmatic, eclectic views of the U.S. These entrenched attitudes were challenged by Dr. Christopher Green and others, who saw ADHD as an inherited, biological problem which was not caused by poor parenting.

For our sins, we were accused of colluding with parents to prevent them from facing up to their role in causing the condition. There was even greater uproar when these "parent problems" were treated with stimulant medication.

Though there are still some influential "mind therapists" who continue to be uncomfortable with the view that parents are not to blame and ADHD is a result of a brain dysfunction, they are now in a shrinking minority.

Today most child psychiatrists and psychologists see play therapy with an inattentive, unthinking child, to be of little value. Certainly the "talking cures" have a place in managing the emotional problems of some parents, but not in treating ADHD. Formal family therapy is generally unhelpful, though clever psychiatrists use a less structured approach to help all members of a family work together to support their ADHD brother or sister.

Today's psychiatrists have a major role to play, in making the diagnosis, implementing behavioral programs, supporting parents, and prescribing medication.

Developmental optometry—eye exercises

When vision and eye movements are tested in great detail, many normal adults and children will appear to have some minor difference. Those who specialize in this developmental testing believe that these subtle problems of eye function are in some way linked to learning difficulties.

Some of the ADHD children in our care who are weak readers have been sent by their schools to developmental optometrists. Parents often return to our clinic angry that our hospital eye specialists failed to diagnose some significant defect. Many of these children are prescribed eye exercises or given low-strength lenses. In our experience, few persist with these for more than a matter of months.

The American Academy of Pediatrics and the Australian College of Paediatrics have put out policy statements on vision and learning. In essence, they believe that for most children such treatments are of minimal or no benefit. (See "Controversial therapies for ADHD," in Appendix XV.)

Tinted lenses

In the mid 1980s a Californian, Helen Irlen, patented certain lens tints which she claimed helped the reading-disabled. Our media responded enthusiastically with stories on *60 Minutes* and in major magazines. Few studies seem to have shown the success that was initially claimed. The very best results suggest that there is a small subgroup who might be helped, but in general the evidence seems unimpressive. (See "Tinted lenses," in Appendix XV.)

Multivitamins and zinc

In the early 1980s it was said that vitamin B_6 benefited both inattentive and learning-disabled children. Then zinc was claimed to help in ADHD and autism. Now multivitamins have become popular.

There is no reputable research to show that any of these remedies has a significant effect on either ADHD or its associated learning disabilities. Extra vitamins most certainly have a place in malabsorption and famine relief, but not in learning and behavior.

Natural Medicines

There is a great fascination with natural therapies and plant extracts in the treatment of ADHD. We are not tunnel-vision, "drugs only" doctors; all we ask is honesty. Before Ritalin was allowed on the market there were years of development, double-blind studies, and careful research. In the 40 years since this license was granted it has been studied extensively.

The same restrictions do not apply to a natural product. Many arrive on the market with little reputable evidence of effect and no guarantee of long-term safety. It is not the natural therapies we dislike, it is the unjust claims that a relatively unproven natural substance is as effective as and safer than a drug which has been thoroughly researched.

Natural remedies are known to have a significant number of side effects. Being natural does not mean that a product is safe—opium, snake venom, and tobacco are very natural. Over the years double-blind, controlled studies have shown that stimulants are effective in over 80 percent of children with ADHD. With these figures it is hard to understand why parents seek out remedies that are untried and unproven.

Neuron entrapment—biofeedback—sugar

We often see children who have attended alternative practitioners for cranial manipulation and realignment of the neck. The parents tell us that their child had impaired blood flow to the base of the brain or entrapment of a nerve inside the skull. Neurologists are 100 percent certain there is no validity to these claims. If gentle pressure to the neck and skull can realign parts of the brain, our football heroes must lose a lot of learning every week.

Biofeedback is one of the newer techniques being promoted. The child watches a computer screen which shows a tracing of their brainwave activity. By modifying their way of working, they then change the tracing, the theory being that you can retrain through feedback. To be effective, many treatments are needed, which are not without cost. This is not a technique we recommend in our practice.

Sugar is again under assault. One presumes it is part of our puritan upbringing, where anything which gives pleasure is probably evil. Parents often claim that replacing sugar with honey leads to better behavior but this has been well researched and proven to be completely untrue. Honey is sugar which has been recycled through a bee, with a number of nature's preservatives and pollutants added along the way. There is no doubt that sugar rots children's teeth and makes them fat, but carefully conducted trials have shown it has no effect on learning or behavior.

The Feingold Diet

In 1973, Dr. Ben Feingold, a former professor of allergy in San Francisco, suggested a relationship between diet and what was then known as Hyperactivity. He went to the media with his startling but unproven theory, claiming that many artificial food additives, as well as some quite natural substances, were affecting the behavior of our children. Specifically, he claimed that the reported rates of Hyperactivity were increasing in proportion to the number of additives which legally pollute food. He told the press that his special diet could improve the behavior in 50 percent of these hyped-up little people. These claims had great repercussions as they were published in newspapers all around the world. The American government was obliged to set up committees and organize research projects to investigate the claims.

In the next decade, parents saw diet as the cornerstone of Hyperactivity. Parent support groups were established that became so obsessed with food that stimulant medication and other treatments were largely ignored.

Many parents still misunderstand what is meant by the Feingold Diet. It is not only about giving up chocolate, cola drinks, flavorings, and colorings. It is also about avoiding nature's preservatives, for example, the natural salicylates which occur in foods such as strawberries, tomatoes, oranges, and pineapples. Hidden preservatives can also be a problem, as in sausages, salami, and some "extremely dead" dried meats. A few children even react to toothpaste and honey, or—when they come in contact with it—perfume and dishwashing liquid.

The original Feingold Diet did have some inconsistencies. Pineapple juice was suggested as one of the safe drinks, when it is now known to be high in natural preservatives.

Exclusion diets

Today much more reliable diets are available. These diets start by excluding all potentially harmful foods, placing the child and her family on a diet of water, pear juice, preservative-free bread, and unseasoned meats. Natural sugar syrup has never been implicated in bad behavior, so this is used in place of jams and spreads.

This strict diet is kept going for a number of weeks and if there is no significant improvement, it is stopped. If the diet helps, the dietitian will gradually introduce other groups of food until those that are causing the harm have been clearly isolated. Finally, an individual diet is suggested which avoids the troublesome foods.

Note: All exclusion diets should be implemented and supervised by a dietitian or doctor specializing in this area. (See Appendix XIII, "Food Intolerance—Treatment Through Diet.")

Research into diet

Following Feingold's claims, an American congressional commission looked at the question of additives and encouraged research trials. Feingold had claimed that 50 percent of children with behavioral problems would be helped by the diet. The question was whether this figure was correct and how much of this was a placebo effect. "Placebo" is the term used to describe an inert substance that is given to a patient instead of an active treatment (e.g., a patient believes they have been given an aspirin when instead they have received a sugar tablet). Studies show that one third of people will believe that this nontreatment has made them feel somewhat better.

To combat the placebo effect, trials on diet had to be conducted "completely blind." That is, parents and others who observed the behaviors could not know if the children were on or off the diet. Many methods were used, including a sort of "meals on wheels" where all food was delivered from outside the trial group's homes.

When 50 percent who claimed to be helped by diet were challenged blindly with additives, only one in 10 showed any change in their behavior. Most of the initial studies showed this 1-in-10 result. This represents 5 percent of Feingold's initial claim of improvement in 50 percent of the children.

Since that time there have been several studies which have reported a more impressive response (up to 60 percent), but in most, the 5 percent figure still stands. (See "Allergy, food additives, and hyperactivity," in Appendix XV.)

Diet not specific for ADHD

If diet affects behavior, it does so in children whether they do or do not have ADHD. It now seems that when diet works, its main effect is on activity and irritability. There is little evidence that diet significantly alters the inattention, impulsivity, and insatiability that are so troublesome in ADHD.

The current view is that diet does affect some children, but a change in diet makes little difference to the trio of behaviors that causes most of the bother in ADHD.

Our experience with diet

A number of parents in our practice certainly see changes with diet, but these are only with one or two clearly identified foods. Chocolate, cola, some flavor additives, strawberries, and some artificial colorings would be among the more common examples. It must be emphasized that this is a minority, and what's more, the parents are usually quite clear as to the offending food, so they avoid it. If there has been no obvious reaction to any one food, it is our experience that a strict exclusion diet will rarely bring any benefits.

We must state that some colleagues, whom we greatly respect, strongly support diet and claim good results. They believe diet is particularly useful in the preschool child with ADHD. They feel that those of us who have less success do not follow the diet with sufficient dedication. We have no monopoly on opinion; parents must follow the path that shows them any significant success. (For details of ADHD diets see Appendix XIII.)

Conclusion

It is tough for today's parents. Services to diagnose and treat ADHD are often underfunded and overloaded. Finally, when treatment is provided, many children move ahead with painfully slow progress. While this happens frustrated parents grasp at any outside chance of help.

Diet has a smaller part to play in the treatment of ADHD than popular mythology might suggest. Diet never causes ADHD, though in a minority of ADHD and non-ADHD children, certain foodstuffs may make their behavior more active and possibly more irritable. There seems to be little evidence that diet directly affects attention, impulsivity, or insatiability. Sugar has not been shown to cause bad behavior. If parents wish to try a diet, they have our full support. But we suggest that they do it properly, under the supervision of a knowledgeable doctor or dietitian.

Parents should never be prevented from following any remedy they choose. All we ask is that the well-researched, proven treatments are used first, before resorting to those of debatable benefit.

FOURTEEN

Medication—The Facts

We make no apology for our enthusiasm for the use of methylphenidate (Ritalin) and dextroamphetamine (Dexedrine) in the treatment of children with ADHD. The body of evidence is now so great that no reputable research center questions the benefit and safety of these stimulant medications. We realize there are still antidrug activists who claim medication is unhelpful and dangerous. As educated adults we recognize that the world is full of influential people who mislead through deliberate intent or through ignorance.

A whole generation of Japanese were taught that their armies were not the aggressor in the 1940s. Leaders can make claims and people can believe blindly, but those who were at Pearl Harbor, Singapore, or on the Burma railway know the truth. There may be people who dispute the facts about stimulant medication but the benefits are now so clearly documented, it is no longer worth debating the point. (See Appendices XV and XVI for reviews of the research.)

Medication is discussed over the next four chapters. Firstly, in this chapter, we look at the benefits and potential side effects of these treatments. Then we address the issues of prescribing and troubleshooting the stimulants (Chapter 15). Next we look at the second-line, nonstimulant drugs (Chapter 16). Finally, we have put together a list of every possible question on the subject of medication (Chapter 17).

The medications

The drugs methylphenidate (Ritalin), dextroamphetamine sulfate (Dexedrine), and pemoline (Cylert) are the most commonly used and most effective preparations for the treatment of ADHD. When they fail to bring a satisfactory response, the second-line drugs are used: imipramine (Tofranil), desipramine (Norpramin), clonidine (Catapres), and in the near future, moclobemide (Aurorix).

Of these alternative drugs, clonidine is indicated when a child's activity and impulsivity are still causing problems despite the use of stimulant medication. Clonidine is also used when there are major difficulties with settling down to sleep. As clonidine appears to have little benefit in increasing attention, it is used in combination with methylphenidate or dextroamphetamine. Imipramine, desipramine, and the new preparation moclobemide have some effect on attention but their main benefits are to behavior and mood. (See Chapter 16, "Medication—The Nonstimulants.")

The stimulants

It seems a piece of faulty logic to give a stimulant medication to a child who is already overstimulated, but this is just what they need. The stimulants, or more correctly the psychostimulants, are believed to work by increasing the neurotransmitter chemicals dopamine and noradrenaline in certain parts of the brain. (See discussion of neurotransmitters in Chapter 3.)

These medications are not sedatives—they do not dull a child's faculties. Stimulants enhance and normalize the slight chemical imbalance of ADHD. This allows the child to make use of his natural abilities to select, focus, shut out distraction, and think before he acts.

The use of stimulant medications for treating ADHD is not new. They were first shown to be effective in 1937, but were not widely used until the late 1950s when methylphenidate (Ritalin) was first introduced. In the last half century many parents have been frightened off stimulants by a media that branded them unsafe and controversial. The grounds for these antidrug opinions never came from any scientific source. They originated from sensation-seeking journalists who were fed inaccurate information by pressure groups such as the Citizens' Commission on Human Rights (CCHR), a part of the Church of Scientology. The late 1980s was the worst time for this campaign of misinformation, but as we write, this message is still being promoted in leaflets and "letters to the editor." It is important for parents to distinguish genuine controversy from a hatchet job that serves its own biased agenda (See discussion of CCHR in Chapter 2).

Ritalin and dextroamphetamine—not quite the same

At present the two most effective stimulant preparations are methylphenidate (Ritalin) and dextroamphetamine. It is said that these drugs are similar in effect, but in our clinical trials more than half the subjects will respond better to one medication than the other. If one preparation is ineffective or causes upset, the other should always be tried. Ideally both should be trialed in every child, to ensure they are getting the medication that best suits their individual needs.

In theory dextroamphetamine remains active slightly longer than Ritalin, but in many children it is hard to see much difference. One 10 mg tablet of Ritalin is said to equal one 5 mg tablet of dextroamphetamine.

We now believe that more frequent doses of a short-acting preparation or a mix of long and short will give the best levels for learning and behavior.

Second-line stimulants

Pemoline (Cylert) is a long-acting nonamphetamine stimulant whose benefits are close but not equal to those of Ritalin and dextroamphetamine. It is prescribed when the effect of the stimulants is inadequate. Pemoline has no "street value," which makes it the preferred treatment when alcohol or drug addiction coexist with ADHD. Pemoline is a long-acting drug which can affect liver function.

Adderall (a combination of four salts of amphetamine) has recently been reintroduced into the American market. Though some claim this is almost equal to the first-line stimulants, no one suggests it is superior in effect. Adderall has the advantage of a longer period of activity than Ritalin or dextroamphetamine.

Stimulants—absorption and action

Note: The word "stimulants" in these chapters refers specifically to methylphenidate and dextroamphetamine prescribed in their standard (non-long-acting) forms.

The stimulants are in many ways similar to the Ventolin inhaler used in asthma. With Ventolin, you take a couple of puffs, which kick in after a quarter to half an hour, and in three to five hours the effect is starting to wane. Stimulants are absorbed quickly even on a full stomach and reach a fairly constant level in the blood. To exert their effect on the neurotransmitters, they must cross the blood-brain barrier, a process that varies greatly from child to child. This variability in the amount that moves from blood to brain makes the measurement of blood levels unhelpful in judging the response. It also shows the foolishness of calculating dose by body weight.

Stimulants start to work in about half an hour, though this varies greatly. The peak effect on behavioral learning starts to drop after three to five hours, with dextroamphetamine usually lasting slightly longer. Half of the dose of Ritalin has left the body at the time it loses effect, between three and a half and five and a half hours. This means that approximately half the original level remains at the time that the next tablet is given. This is why we give most medication early in the morning and smaller doses as the day progresses, for example one tablet at breakfast, three-quarters of a tablet at midday, and half a tablet at 3:30 P.M. By 12 hours, almost all the Ritalin has left the body, dextroamphetamine lasting somewhat longer. The length of action or stimulant dosage is not influenced by other common medications, for example antibiotics, Tylenol, or antiepileptics.

Medication in ADHD—a quick guide

The stimulants

■ Ritalin (methylphenidate), 5 mg, 10 mg, 20 mg tablets. (Also Ritalin sustained release 20 mg tablet)

■ Dexedrine (dextroamphetamine sulfate), 5 mg tablet. (Also Dexedrine Spansules 5 mg, 10 mg, and 15 mg capsules)

The second-line stimulants

■ Catapres (clonidine): Helps activity and impulsivity but not attention. Also used for sleep problems.

■ Tofranil (imipramine): Helps the ADHD behaviors and has some effect on inattention.

■ Nonpranun (desipramine): Helps the ADHD behaviors and has some effect on inattention.

■ Cylert (pemoline): A nonamphetamine stimulant. Helps inattention and ADHD behaviors. A second-line treatment.

■ Adderall: A combination of amphetamine salts. Apparently no better than other stimulants, though longer-acting.

Proven short-term benefits

The action of stimulants has been studied extensively, most researchers reporting improvements in 70 percent to 90 percent of children with ADHD. These are by far the most successful drugs used in child psychiatry and also the safest. In 1980 one researcher reported a high placebo rate, where an inactive tablet was shown to bring some benefits to behavior and learning. This result has not been found by other researchers, who now describe a remarkably low placebo effect. The success of stimulants is not the figment of anyone's imagination.

Stimulants reduce restlessness, keep the child focused on a task, improve classroom productivity, and increase self-monitoring and accuracy. Children are less impulsive and disruptive, and they learn when to back off. Written work is neater and speech that once wandered may come back on track. Interactions improve between children, parents, teachers, and peers. Parents tell us they have a child who listens, takes instructions on board, and can now accept reason.

Stimulants do not increase intelligence, though psychology tests may now be easier to administer. Specific learning disabilities, for example dyslexia, are not directly improved by stimulants, but once the dyslexic child starts to concentrate, the benefits of re-mediation increase. Stimulants do not increase the child's natural abilities; they just allow him to make the most of what he's got. Stimulants do not treat the behaviors of Oppositional Defiant Disorder or Conduct Disorder, though curbing the impulsivity of ADHD may make these children safer and more predictable.

Unproven long-term benefits

It has been shown conclusively that stimulants work in the short term; however, long-term gains are presumed but not proven. Most of the old studies did not distinguish between pure ADHD and ADHD with Conduct Disorder, this latter combination having a poor outcome, whether treated with medication or not. To resolve this we need objective, long-term studies, where some children with pure ADHD are treated and others left to fail, but nowadays this might be viewed as unethical.

There is no doubt that the ADHD child treated with stimulants is better today, tomorrow, next week, next month, and next year. In this period we know they are closer to their parents, happier in life, achieve at school, and have more friends. It is our belief that if we get the short term right, this will follow through to the long term.

A particular bit of research suggests that we are on the right track. When one group of U.S. high-school children with ADHD was treated with medication and one was not, those untreated had a higher dropout rate and an increased risk of substance abuse. It would appear that if stimulants allow a child to maintain relation-ships, self-esteem, and the will to learn, this may lessen the risk of dropping out and addiction.

Eventually long-term results will show that with medication there is less nagging, negativity, and anger. When happier, less negative parents have a more responsive, rewarding child, this must provide a "win-win" situation for all the players. To be fair to stimulants, none of the alternative treatments, such as behavioral programs, diet, remedial education, and psychiatric intervention, has itself been proven in the long term.

Do ADHD children become addicted?

The word *amphetamine* causes anxiety about addiction. Though stimulants have been used in ADHD children for over half a century, there is no evidence of addiction, dependency, or an increased risk of later substance abuse. Children, adolescents, and even adults with ADHD live their lives with circling, muddled minds. When medication is effective they become more clear thinking and focused. Humans take addictive drugs to escape the world, not to become fully focused on reality.

Stimulants do not cure ADHD

The problems of ADHD generally lessen with age and maturity. While this is happening, stimulants help the children make the most of their abilities and stop them drifting from the straight and narrow. Our aim is to protect the children's esteem, their will to learn, and family relationships, until maturity brings some sort of natural resolution. If we keep children emotionally and educationally intact, they can eventually use their considerable abilities. If we lose the plot in the early years, the improvement that comes with maturity has no foundation to build on.

When to try stimulants

For years it has been policy to start with a behavior program, and after some time to consider medication. This policy viewed stimulants as the backstop, to be used when all else had failed. Current teaching does not agree—we now focus the child with medication and once we have a receptive subject, other treatments are introduced. Nowadays most children with major ADHD will be trialed on stimulants in the first few visits to their pediatrician. If you can reach (with stimulants), then you are able to teach (with behavior programs, therapy, and schooling).

As we write, a major U.S. multicenter study is researching the relative values of the different ADHD treatments. Centers around the country are comparing the effects of certain treatments given alone or in combination. The study is far from finished, but rumors suggest that treatments that don't first prime with medication may be relatively unsuccessful.

What age can we treat?

Though most children treated with stimulants are of school age, there is no reason why medication cannot be used with the three-to-five-year-olds as well as with the late teens and adults. We think carefully before prescribing in four-year-olds, but see great successes. In our practice the three-to-four-year-olds are treated only when the problems are causing great difficulty. Between two and a half and three years a very small number of extreme children may be carefully assessed and successfully treated with stimulant medication.

If the stimulants are tried and found ineffective in the under-fives, they are worth reintroducing at an older age, as there may now be a positive response. In the mid 1980s high-school children were often taken off their medication in their early teens, which resulted in needless underachievement. Many children with ADHD will now continue to take medication through their school years and into college-level studies. With the modern understanding of adult ADHD, some will continue into adulthood.

Possible side effects

Withdrawn, teary, upset

When starting medication a few children may become withdrawn, teary, upset, irritable, and unhappy. Some are angry but don't know why. These side effects occur only when introducing medicine or increasing the dose, and once the levels are fine-tuned they will not reappear. We find that approximately one in 10 children will suffer some of these problems as we trial both Ritalin and dextroamphetamine, but these side effects are short-lived, passing after four hours as the levels fall. If the stimulants are introduced gradually, the risk of this problem is greatly reduced. When it does occur the dose should be lowered or the other preparation given. Any child who appears doped, dazed, unhappy, or "different" on medication is being incorrectly treated. If there is the slightest concern about any unwanted effect, the medicine should be stopped and the prescribing doctor contacted. We are in the business of helping, not harming children.

Appetite reduction

Many parents mention that appetite is reduced, but very few find it a major problem. Medication should be given with meals to allow the food to arrive in the stomach before the drug deadens appetite. The afternoon dose can be lowered or suspended, which allows catch-up nutrition in the evening. Appetizing food, for example flavored milk or yogurt, can be offered at times of low appetite, particularly during school hours when learning takes priority ahead of food intake. Substantial snacks are offered after school, and supper is given before bed. High-energy supplements can be bought from the local supermarket, for example Ensure. If appetite suppression is a major problem on one drug, the other preparations may be offered. In rare cases stimulants are suspended and a second-line treatment is prescribed. With food intake, it's important to get our priorities straight. Do we want a trim child who relates and achieves or a chubby kid with little education and a bad attitude?

Tics and Tourette's syndrome

Involuntary movements are frequently associated with ADHD. Though they are not caused by stimulants, tics occasionally surface or appear to become worse during treatment. (See statement on tics at the end of this chapter.)

Sleep problems

Many ADHD children find it difficult to settle down at night, a problem usually existing long before medication was prescribed. In most ADHD children medication makes little difference to sleep. Where stimulants damage a previously good sleep pattern, the afternoon dose should be reduced or suspended and occasionally the midday dose given earlier. When sleep problems are causing great hardship the drug clonidine may be given at night. A few ADHD children (maybe 1 in 10) settle better if they are given a bedtime dose of stimulant. If this works, it focuses their restless minds, almost like counting sheep or meditating.

Rebound behavior

A few children rebound into a brief patch of much worse behavior as the drug wears off. This hits after three and a half to four and a half hours and can last for up to an hour. Rebound is avoided by increasing the previous dose or giving another dose just before the wear-off time or adding a slow-release preparation.

Growth retardation

In the early 1980s it was believed that long-term, high-dose, uninterrupted treatment reduced a child's final measurement of height. For this to happen the dose needed to be considerable and it appeared that the degree of height reduction was unlikely to be greater than one or two centimeters. Parents of extremely difficult children were in no doubt that the risk of losing a centimeter in height was a small price to pay for school achievement and family harmony. The current literature largely discards the concerns over growth retardation caused by stimulants. There is some evidence that those with ADHD or Anxiety Disorder may have a slightly decreased growth rate, and if this is true, growth retardation may be due to ADHD, not medication. We still measure height and weight and maintain our children on the lowest dose that gives the maximum effect. Drug holidays are no longer recommended.

Headache—stomachache

A number of children feel slight nausea due to the appetite suppression of stimulants. This is rarely a problem and can be addressed by giving the medication with food, lowering the dose, or changing to the other preparation. Very occasionally frank abdominal pain is experienced, sometimes persisting as the dose is lowered and forcing medicine to be suspended. Headache is a rare side effect. It must not be mistaken for the tension headache experienced by many ADHD children due to the stresses of school. Where stimulants cause significant headaches the dose is lowered and the other preparation tried.

Edgy—ill at ease

Some adults and children respond well to the stimulants but feel on edge and not at peace with the world. Doctors must specifically ask how their patients feel, and change, reduce, or add as needed.

Overfocus

The benefit of stimulants is their ability to focus the inattentive child—and sometimes they do their job too well. Occasionally children become "spaced out," slow moving, or almost obsessive. When this happens the dose must be reduced and if any concerns remain, the prescribing doctor should be contacted. (See Appendix XII, "The Stimulants—Small-Print Side Effects," for more detailed information.)

Stimulants—the final word

The drugs Ritalin and dextroamphetamine have been extensively studied. At least 80 percent of school-age ADHD children will show benefits of treatment in the short term. Although we presume these will continue in the long term, at the time of writing this is not proven. These drugs are not sedatives; they enhance and normalize the inattentive child's natural abilities. Stimulants help the child focus, reflect, and achieve academically, socially, and behaviorally.

Some people still state that there is controversy regarding the use of these drugs, but these are now accepted as the single most effective form of therapy. Any professional who questions the use of stimulants in ADHD must be viewed as out of touch with modern research literature. It is important not to confuse the word *controversy* with the word *ignorance*!

Stimulants

- Not new, have been used for over half a century.
- These are not sedatives.
- Stimulants enhance and normalize brain function.

- Help focus attention and allow children to think before they act.

- Help children listen, understand, and learn.

- Effective in over 80 percent of children with ADHD.

- Proven short-term benefits, long-term presumed but not proven.

- Stimulants do not cure ADHD.

- Addiction is not a problem in ADHD. Stimulants bring the child into clear-thinking reality.

- Appetite reduction and sleep problems can occur, but are easily corrected.

- Emotional upset, tears, and withdrawn behavior can happen if the dose is too high or the wrong preparation is used.

- These drugs are short acting: they start working in a quarter to half an hour and wear off in three to five hours. Slow-release preparations are available for both Ritalin (SR) and Dexedrine (spansules).

- Behavior sometimes rebounds as the drug starts to wear off.

- One (10 mg) Ritalin tablet is almost equal to one (5 mg) dextroamphetamine tablet.

- Many children will respond better to one preparation than the other. In our practice both are usually trialed.

- If side effects are troublesome on one drug, try the other.

- Stimulants are the single most effective form of therapy in ADHD.

- Stimulants help the dyslexic-ADHD child attend, but don't directly affect reading.

- Stimulants help the ADHD-ODD child be less impulsive, but don't improve oppositional behavior.

- Behavior modification and educational interventions are important, but usually do better in conjunction with stimulants.

- A lot of misinformation has appeared in the media concerning these medications.

- It is parents—not doctors, psychologists, or educationalists—who decide if medication will be started, continued, or suspended.

- Medication will continue for as long as parents and teachers see significant benefits. This may be six months, six years, or even into adulthood.

Tics, Tourette's syndrome, and stimulant medication

A tic is a repeated involuntary movement, most commonly of the eyelids or face, but may also involve throat clearing, grunting, or shrugging a shoulder. Tics occur in 5 percent to 10 percent of the general child population at some time. Though tics are common in all children and adults, they are many times more likely in those with ADHD.

The most severe presentation of Tic Disorder is called Tourette's syndrome. It involves throat clearing, grunting, or even uncontrolled use of words as well as two or more types of major motor tics. (See Appendix IV, "The Criteria for Diagnosing Tic and Tourette's Disorder (DSM-IV).") By definition, Tourette's syndrome is diagnosed only when the symptoms have been present for at least one year and cause significant problems. The incidence of Tourette's syndrome in the general population is approximately one in 2,000, and one-half of those affected also have ADHD. Our interest in the association of Tic Disorder and ADHD arises from the claim that stimulant medication increases the risk of tics and in some cases locks in the tic for life.

The natural history of tics

A recent study, sponsored by the Tourette Society and the U.S. National Institute of Mental Health, focused on all children attending one clinic (T. Spencer). Tics were noted in 20 percent of children presenting with ADHD, while 89 percent of those presenting with tics were shown to have ADHD. The usual onset of ADHD symptoms was found to be just before the third birthday, while tics tended to appear around the age of seven years to 10 years.

The usual presentation of tics was to come and go for no good reason. As most ADHD children start stimulant medication between the age of five years and 10 years, the appearance of tics and the start of medication may coincide. As the tics tend to wax and wane they may either increase or decrease with the introduction of medication. If they increase, it is easy to blame this on the commencement of medication.

Tics or ADHD—which needs treatment?

Another study (T. Spencer) looked at two groups of children: one of these had ADHD alone and the other ADHD and tics. Detailed analysis of both groups found that they were equally affected by learning problems and behavioral difficulties, whether tics were or were not present. The only difference was a slightly increased risk of Obsessive Compulsive Disorder in those who had both tics and ADHD.

From this it would appear that tics in isolation do not usually cause behavior, learning, or other difficulties. Tics in association with ADHD do cause problems, due to the educational, social, and psychiatric complications of ADHD. When ADHD and tics coexist, the ADHD must be taken seriously.

Legal concerns

As doctors we are wary of ambulance-chasing lawyers who claim black is white if shown the slightest tone of gray. Over the years great care has been taken to ensure parents are fully informed of the true nature of tics and the small but possible risk of stimulants. A potential court case might claim that tics or Tourette's syndrome would not have occurred without the introduction of stimulants and that a minor tic that became locked in would have remained trivial except for the doctor's prescription of the drug.

Despite worries in the last decade most guidelines now state that stimulants are not contraindicated in Tic Disorder or Tourette's syndrome. One study even suggested that tics might reduce with the introduction of stimulants. It is possible that a potential tic may have come to the surface, or that Tourette's syndrome that was about to present made an earlier appearance, due to the prescription of medication. Current opinion states that stimulants do not cause tics or Tourette's syndrome and do not seem to lock in tics that were otherwise going to be unimportant.

Treatment of ADHD occurring with tics

The most effective drug to treat tics and Tourette's syndrome is one of the neuroleptic preparations, for example haloperidol (Haldol). This decreases the levels of the neurotransmitter dopamine. The best treatment for ADHD is one of the stimulant preparations which increase the neurotransmitter dopamine. This creates a dilemma for treatment. With this confusion we must be clear what is causing the major problem—is it ADHD or tics? In the great majority of cases it is the ADHD which disrupts the quality of life, not the tics.

In our practice, when tics appear, the first step is to fully inform the parents of the facts and the controversies. Where the tic is major we usually suspend stimulants for several weeks to see if this lessens the problem. Usually it makes no difference and the parents ask for the drug to be reintroduced. But if the tic reduces with the suspension of medication, this necessitates a difficult decision.

If ADHD behaviors are major, most parents are terrified at the thought of stopping stimulants. For them we usually reintroduce the stimulant medication alone or reintroduce it with the addition of the tic-reducing drug clonidine. It is possible to stop the stimulants and treat the ADHD with one of the second-line ADHD drugs, for example Tofranil (imipramine) or Norpramin (desipramine), but in our experience they are less effective for ADHD and still have slight risks of promoting tics. Desipramine (similar to imipramine) is often recommended as superior to the stimulant-clonidine mix.

In summary

If a child has the brain-based condition ADHD, this puts him at much greater risk of developing the brain-based conditions of tics or even Tourette's syndrome. When tics are associated with ADHD, it is usually the ADHD which causes the child to underfunction behaviorally, academically, and socially, not the tic. When ADHD is causing significant problems, it is usual for parents, after giving their full, informed consent, to opt for continuation of stimulant medication. Occasionally tics appear to be made worse by stimulants, and when this happens a tricyclic preparation (imipramine, desipramine) or the combination of stimulant plus clonidine is used.

Ten years ago tics and Tourette's syndrome were seen as a contraindication to the prescription of stimulant medication—now this ruling has been lifted. Stimulants seem safe to prescribe in most cases, but we must exercise caution and watch as ongoing research makes the recommendation even clearer.

FIFTEEN

Practical Prescribing (Stimulants)

Before considering stimulants for the treatment of ADHD children, let's be quite clear who is in charge. *Parents,* not doctors, decide if they want a trial of medication and when it should be continued or stopped. These drugs will be given while the parent sees major benefits and no side effects. When there is doubt as to effectiveness, or the slightest concern over side effects, parents must stop the drug and talk to the prescribing doctor.

We make this point as antidrug activists frequently claim that children are put on stimulants unnecessarily while parents see absolutely no benefits, only side effects. This is ridiculous: if the asthma medication we prescribed didn't work or the penicillin caused a rash, you would stop it and call for help.

With stimulants the secret of successful prescribing is to start on a low dose, fine-tune to the individual, and if not happy with the response, try the alternative preparation.

To prescribe or not to prescribe

There is no black-and-white test that shows at what point stimulants should be prescribed. It all depends on the severity of the ADHD, the predominant behavior, the degree of learning difficulties, and how well both parents and school are managing. Where education, home relationships, happiness, and self-esteem are suffering, it's time to take a stand and start medication.

In the past we would only consider stimulants once behavioral, educational, and family programs had been tried and had failed. Now we commence medication early on as these other programs are so much more successful once the child is focused and in tune.

Starting stimulants

Ritalin comes as a 5 mg, 10 mg, or 20 mg tablet, while dextroamphetamine is available as a 5 mg tablet. As most of the troublesome side effects of stimulants occur at the time of introducing medication or increasing the dose, we urge you to start gently. In the young child (three years to five years) we start with a quarter of a 10 mg tablet, and with a half of a 10 mg tablet in the older (six years plus) child. Initially this is given in the morning with breakfast and if it causes no problems, it is then repeated at midday. The dose is then increased by quarter- or half-tablet increments. Many doctors don't recommend quarter tablets, but we find in the younger children a half tablet is often insufficient, one tablet is too much, and three-quarters is just right. After the trial, the most convenient strength of tablet will be prescribed and a long-acting preparation considered when necessary.

When trialing medication we are looking for evidence of response, not good behavior from dawn to dusk. Once we see benefits with this breakfast and midday dose we can then fine-tune to give the best result throughout the day.

A clinical trial

Academics who study ADHD would like to know if medication is going to work before it is prescribed, but they remain frustrated as there is no measure of potential drug response other than a carefully controlled clinical trial.

In our hospital-based practice we have been fortunate in having access to trial quantities of the two stimulants. This allows us to compare the effect of both preparations. Where possible, we start medication over a weekend so the parents are around to observe any benefits or possible side effects. We gradually introduce one drug over the first weekend and fine-tune it in the following week. The second drug is introduced over the next weekend. If both drugs are correctly adjusted and uncertainty remains, they are then alternated: two days of one drug, one day off medication, two days of the other drug, until both parents and school give a clear statement as to success or failure. After three weeks the parents are asked a simple question: "What do you want us to do now?" In these trials, we have found that of those who respond, 80 percent of parents will have a firm preference for one medication, while 20 percent see both as equal. Many of our colleagues dispute the difference between Ritalin and dextroamphetamine but many of them do not have the feedback of comparative trials.

Most doctors do not trial both medications. They prescribe 100 tablets of one drug (usually Ritalin), which is gradually introduced and instructions are given as to the limits within which parents can fine-tune and adjust. If this first medication is sufficiently successful, the other may not be tried. If there is doubt, the other is prescribed at review.

We rate the success of medication on a subjective, four-point scale. This is similar to the four or five stars used by film critics to rate new releases. A response of four out of four means a miracle. Three out of four is extremely good. Two out of four is good but indicates room for improvement. One out of four is a slight gain, but minimal. Zero means it's time to flush the remaining tablets down the toilet. The parents are asked to score each drug, and most of those we treat rate in the range of two and a half to four. Side effects of any significance are also noted beside each score.

There are more objective ways of recording response to medication. Some practitioners use the Paired Associate Learning Test or a Continuous Performance Test (e.g. Conners or TOVA), to measure memory and persistence before medication and later to measure its effects. These tests are of particular benefit in the "inattentive only" type of ADHD and when comorbid conditions cloud the picture. We may be out of step with the recommended practice protocols, but for us the best measure of response is to listen carefully to the parents and teachers.

Stimulants—short-acting drugs

When Ritalin and dextroamphetamine are effective the benefits are almost immediate but last for only a very short time. After the child takes a tablet his behavior will start to chain in 15 to 45 minutes, and the benefits will be lost between three and five hours later. There is an immense variation from child to child, some metabolizing the drug very quickly and others showing response for much longer periods.

It is extremely important for those monitoring the benefits of these treatments to be aware of this short span of action. If a tablet is given at 8:00 A.M. and behavior is disastrous in the early afternoon, this is not a failure of response—the child is not on active medication at the time of trouble. This is easily overcome by giving a second dose approximately half an hour before the time the first tablet started to lose effect, or by using a slow-release preparation.

The importance of this "drop-off" cannot be overemphasized. We frequently see children in whom medication is said to have lost effect, when in fact it works wonderfully but there are behavioral blowups in the gaps between doses. This is not failure; it is a problem of fine tuning.

Fine-tuning stimulants

As a rule of thumb, Ritalin is usually given up to a maximum dose of 1.5 mg per kilogram of body weight, per day. The maximum dose of dextroamphetamine is half this amount (0.75 mg per kilogram of body weight, per day). This is only a guide as the dose required varies greatly from child to child and is not directly related to body size.

Most in our care are maintained at approximately 50 percent to 60 percent of these maximum recommended doses, though occasionally we are forced to use levels up to 130 percent of the preferred maximum. Higher doses are prescribed only when we are sure there is not equal benefit at a lower level.

Studies show that stimulants start to lose their effect when approximately half the level remains in the body. For this reason the second dose can be smaller than the first as it rides on top of the residual half that remains. Most children in our care have bigger doses at the beginning of the day, which tail off toward the afternoon (e.g., two tablets 8:00 A.M., one and a half tablets 12 midday, one tablet 3:30 P.M.).

Choosing the right number of doses depends on what we are trying to treat, for example difficult behavior which is present all day, concentrating on schoolwork from 9:00 A.M. to 3:00 P.M., behavior at lunch break, or problems with homework. Though some children do well on two doses per day, most are maintained on three: given at breakfast, the middle of the day, and on returning from school. Some of our very young children require four to five smaller doses given two and a half to three hours apart.

Fine-tuning medication requires listening to parents and getting feedback from teachers. Many younger school children who used to get their second tablet at lunchtime are now performing much better when this is given at the mid-morning break. If the child's attention is lapsing in the half hour before lunch or they are getting into trouble at the start of the midday break, medication must be given earlier or a longer-acting combination prescribed.

Most parents know the moment medication is starting to lose its effect, which makes it easy to tune in a way which allows the best cover throughout the day. When stimulants cause problems of settling to sleep, the afternoon dose should be reduced or omitted. Where appetite and weight are a problem, doses are given with food and the afternoon tablet may possibly be withheld to allow a good appetite for the evening meal. (See end of this chapter, "Stimulant therapy—troubleshooting.")

Stimulants—what parents notice

- Better able to sit and stick at task (computer, drawing, playing).

- Less impulsive (they think before they act or speak).

- Less insatiable (they can let a matter drop, do not go on and on).

- Listens, will back down, more accepting of frustration.

- Less restless, fidgety, and "hyper."

- More reachable, closer, happier.

- Interrupts less, speech is more considered and on track.

- Home life becomes calmer.

- "You have given us the child we always wanted."

Stimulants—what teachers tell us

- Less distractible, disruptive, and fidgety.

- Less calling out in class.

- Able to get work finished without the need to be stood over.

- Less rush, will check for mistakes.

- Produces neater written work which is more consistent and better organized.

- Shows improvement in playground behavior.

- Relates better to other children, socially more in tune, has more friends.

- Grades improve. Confidence improves.

Start right—stay right

Stimulants are remarkably free of side effects and almost all the troubles come at the start of treatment or when doses are increased. Introducing medication gradually and taking time to fine-tune will always pay off. If you get it right at the start, it stays right.

Children rarely build up a tolerance to these drugs; if the dose is correct at the start, the same dose may often continue for some years. Though tolerance is extremely rare, occasionally a child stops responding for no apparent reason. When we suspect tolerance, we suspend the medication and observe what happens. Often the benefits are still there, but the parents have forgotten the way it used to be. If the dose has been retuned and the benefits have genuinely dropped off, then we trial the other preparation.

Beware drop-off and rebound

Most problems we meet are caused not by medication, but by the drop-off that can occur between doses. Some children slip smoothly off their medication, almost unnoticed. Most quickly revert to their old selves and a few rebound badly, behaving like a bear with a sore head.

If you think that the behavior is not property controlled on medication, check whether it is lack of drug effect or drop-off that is the problem. (See end of this chapter, "Stimulant therapy—troubleshooting.")

With or without food

Until recently it was believed that stimulants should be given a quarter of an hour before food. Now we are told it is more convenient and equally effective to give the drug with meals. As stimulants may suppress appetite it is best to avoid giving them in the hours before a meal. We make an exception when school problems are major—medication is then given at the most effective time for increased learning, which takes priority over a large lunch.

When school is uncooperative

In the past, many schools and senior educationalists were vigorously opposed to the use of stimulant medication. Though these unenlightened attitudes are rare nowadays, there are still a few antistimulant stalwarts. Such is the power of these people that parents are often fearful to admit their child has been treated for ADHD. When faced with this situation we first introduce the stimulants at home to ensure there is a strong response and no worrying side effects. If the teacher is approachable they are informed that a trial will take place over the next weeks and are asked to record behavior and work each morning. One dose of medication is given at breakfast time for three days, then stopped for two days; this on-off regime is continued, where the teacher does not know which morning the drug has been given and which it has not. This sort of trial usually turns the doubters into believers.

When the school is completely uncooperative, the same system is followed, without informing any school staff. If medication is really successful we see a pattern of good days with merit awards and bad days with detentions. Armed with this evidence an appointment is made to discuss the matter.

We must emphasize that these secretive suggestions are rarely required in these enlightened times. We urge all parents to work closely with their schools and keep them fully aware of what is happening.

Do you need holidays off medicine?

Some academics suggest children come off stimulant medication during holidays and weekends. There is no justification for this old-fashioned recommendation and if behavior causes big problems, we never stop stimulants at home. In the early 1980s it was believed that long-term medication could retard a child's physical growth—this is no longer of concern. There is no evidence that properly monitored, long-term medication will in any way harm children. It is, however, certain that untreated ADHD children can do immense long-term damage to family relationships and to their own happiness.

How long to treat?

Parents always ask us how long medication will be needed and the answer is simple—for as long as parents and teachers continue to see significant benefits. Children who have a major response to medication usually continue for many years; those whose response is less dramatic frequently fall away as the years go by. For many the benefits will last until the end of high school and even into college-level studies. As the use of these medications in adulthood becomes more accepted, it is likely that many of today's children will take stimulants right into their adult lives.

The parents we deal with are asked to continually monitor the benefits of stimulants. Most are aware of the drop-off after four hours and know when they forgot to give medication. If their child returns to the old ways this gives feedback as to the continuing need for stimulants.

When the ongoing benefit is in question we suggest the drug be suspended for one week, reintroduced for a week, suspended again, reintroduced. By this method both parents and teachers quickly know if it is necessary to continue. When stimulants are stopped this can be done immediately without any gradual tail-off.

Remember the first words of this chapter: *You, the parents, are in charge. You, with the advice of the school, tell us whether medication will or will not be continued. It is your decision.*

When stimulants don't work

Almost 90 percent of those with a major degree of ADHD will respond to one or the other stimulant medication. When a trial of medication has failed, first check that the drug was given in the correct dosage for that part of the day you were observing. If this has been given properly and there is no response, it's time to try the other preparation. If this also fails, move to the second line of medications (see Chapter 16). Some extremists suggest increasing the dose until you get either benefits or side effects. This is an unsound approach and it is our experience that if there is no response to a reasonable dose, trebling this level will never bring a miracle.

One of the commonest causes of failure is a misunderstanding of what we are trying to treat. Stimulants help the deficiencies in attention and behavior found in pure ADHD. Stimulants have no effect on the hostile attitudes of Oppositional Defiant Disorder or Conduct Disorder. Stimulants help the dyslexic child concentrate and work better, but they do not cure problems of reading. When there is no success with these comorbid conditions, this is a failure of expectation, not medication.

Are stimulants completely safe?

There is no such thing as a completely safe drug—people bleed with aspirin, have heart palpitations with tea or coffee, and even die from allergy to penicillin or natural treatments, e.g., Royal Jelly. As medicines go, the stimulants are exceptionally safe. They have been studied for over 40 years and found remarkably free of major problems. (See Appendix XVI, "Recent Review Papers," and Appendix XII, "The Stimulants—Small-Print Side Effects.") In medicine we must balance the benefits of treatment against the chance of any possible problem. The antistimulant activists forget that untreated ADHD is not without considerable risk. Every year impulsive, unthinking children are seriously injured and killed. Parents and children fall out of love, this wrecked relationship continuing for life. Clever children feel like failures, leaving school with a poor education, few friends, and low esteem. Nothing in this world is 100 percent safe but don't let yourself be so frightened by the small print that you miss the main message.

Stimulant therapy—troubleshooting

Your own doctor will advise how to fine-tune your child's medication and you must talk to him if you hit any problems. Meanwhile, here are the guidelines for troubleshooting we give to the parents in our practice.

- Behavior and learning are largely unchanged two hours after medication is given.
  Treatment is not working, increase dose or change medication.

- Behavior responds well for several hours, but drops off after three and a half to four hours.
  Bring forward the next dose, increase the previous dose or use Ritalin SR or Dexedrine spansules.

- The child has impossible early-morning behavior.
  Give medication on waking. A smaller dose may then be needed on leaving for school, for example at 8:45 A.M., or an additional small midmorning dose given, for example at 10:30 A.M., to hold him until lunchtime.

- Drugs cause difficulty getting to sleep.
  Did the child have equally severe sleep problems before starting medication? If not, suspend or reduce the 3:30 P.M. dose. If sleep is still a problem reduce or bring forward the midday dose. A few ADHD children sleep better when given a dose of stimulant an hour before bedtime. In this small group it helps them focus their circling brains and, like counting sheep, this focusing of attention calms them to sleep.

- There is a major rebound as level drops.
  Add an extra dose half an hour before the rebound. This usually means moving the lunchtime dose to mid-morning recess (11:00 A.M.) and introducing more in the afternoon (or use slow release).

- Emotionally upset, withdrawn, irritable, teary.
  Halve the dose. Suspend medication or change to the alternate medication.

■ Appetite reduction and weight loss.
Give drug with meals. Reduce or suspend afternoon dose to allow appetite for large evening meal. Encourage healthy, easy-to-eat snacks, for example flavored milk, yogurt. Introduce a major feed on return from school and supper before bed. Introduce a high-calorie booster, available over-the-counter from the pharmacist. If appetite and weight are still a major concern, the total dose of stimulant can be reduced or a different drug tried.

■ The effect does not last the full four hours.
Give four or even five more frequent small doses to maintain an even level throughout the day or a combination of short and long acting preparations.

■ Teachers report medication is now less effective.
Find out if there is a genuine lack of effect or if this is drop-off between doses. If it is drop-off, readjust medication to give a more even level. If uncertain of continuing benefits, have a trial off medication. If drug is genuinely losing effect, consider another medication.

■ School hostile to stimulant treatment.
Give a morning dose only and put the child on medication for two days, take them off for two days, and so on, without informing the school. If the difference is obvious, the case is proven, and you can take a stand. Give only a morning dose and a 3:30 P.M. dose.

■ Inattention causes problems in academic learning, not behavior.
Medication is given only for school and homework.

■ Behavior problems both at school and home.
Give medication every school day, weekend, and holiday for as long as the benefits continue.

■ School or parents feel medication no longer needed.
Stop medication for one week, then reintroduce for one week, then stop again. Observe what happens and make a decision, in association with the class teacher.

■ Behavior problems in the playground.
Take the midday tablet at the mid-morning recess or beginning of the lunch break, or use a long-acting–slow-release preparation.

■ Homework hassles.
Increase the 3:30 P.M. dose.

■ Bad behavior at after-school care.
Ensure 3:30 P.M. dose is given reliably.

■ Won't swallow the tablet.
Child should drink water to moisten the throat before putting the tablet in the mouth. Put with ice cream, with jam, dissolve in syrup. (Note: children find stimulants bitter.)

■ A teenager refuses to take medication.
Try to get the teenager to see what is in it for them. When on medication, they are in less trouble and more productive in schoolwork, especially math and written assignments. If they can't accept this, there is little more you can do.

■ In-laws criticize the use of medication.
The in-laws don't have to live with your child.

■ Father says ADHD is a lot of nonsense.
Maybe father needs his ADHD treated!

■ The child on stimulants develops tics.
If ADHD is minor, suspend all medication. If ADHD is major, stimulants will probably continue. Parents must be fully informed of the benefits and risks of treatment. (Read "Tics, Tourette's syndrome, and stimulant medication," at end of Chapter 14.)

■ An ADHD child has epilepsy or intellectual disability.
Stimulants can be given with care to the ADHD child with epilepsy. Stimulants are sometimes useful in a child with intellectual disability when the ADHD behaviors are significantly outside the norm for that child's developmental age.

■ Does the ADHD child have a say?
Listen to the child. Doctors must be sure that the child, as well as the parents, is happy with the effects (and side effects) of medication.

Prescribing stimulants—sample regimes

There are many possible ways to prescribe these medications. Here are the sorts of regimes we use in our practice. These are based on the standard 10 mg Ritalin and 5 mg dextroamphetamine tablets.

A four-year-old child

■ Start with a quarter tablet in the morning and, if there are no side effects, a quarter tablet at midday.

■ Maintain on:
A half tablet twice daily, or
A half tablet at breakfast and 11:00 A.M. One quarter at 2:00 P.M. (possibly one quarter at 4:00 P.M.), or
Three-quarters of a tablet at breakfast, a half tablet at midday, and a quarter tablet at 3:30 P.M.

A six-year-old child

■ Start with a half tablet in the morning and, if there are no side effects, a half tablet at midday.

■ Maintain on:
A half tablet twice daily, or
Three-quarters, one or one and a half tablets with breakfast.
Half, three-quarters, or one tablet at midday.
A half may or may not be needed at 3:30 P.M.

A 12-year-old child

■ Start with a half tablet in the morning and, if there are no side effects, a half tablet at midday. Next day the dose can be doubled.

■ Maintain on:
One, one and a half, or two tablets with breakfast.
One, one and a half, or two tablets at midday.
One tablet at 3:30 P.M.

SIXTEEN

Medication—The Nonstimulants

It seems unjust that the freely available drugs for ADHD are much more hazardous than the tightly regulated stimulants. Our main second-line drugs are the tricyclic antidepressants and clonidine, but these are only considered when stimulants have failed. The fact that we prescribe these drugs does not mean that we like them. The antidepressant drug moclobemide (Aurorix) is sometimes suggested in Europe and Australia but has not yet reached recognition in North America.

Clonidine (e.g., Catapres)

This is marketed as a drug to lower blood pressure but has been found effective in controlling impulsive, overactive behaviors and helping ADHD children to sleep. While stimulants work by enhancing normal brain function, clonidine has no effect on attention and, if anything, subdues rather than stimulates. For overactive/impulsive behavior, Clonidine is usually prescribed in combination with Ritalin or dextroamphetamine.

In the last couple of years clonidine has had some bad press. Four children treated with a combination of stimulants and clonidine suffered unexpected deaths, one of these occurring in Australia. There is also the report of one near death after clonidine had been suspended suddenly. Some of these deaths followed an unusual event, for example surgery, but some came out of the blue. This must raise questions about the safety of clonidine, but there is another side to the equation. Firstly, all children, whether on medication or not, have a small but measurable risk of unexpected cardiac death every year. In North America it is estimated at four in a million among children aged seven years to 15 years (see more on this under "Imipramine (Tofranil)," later in this chapter). When the total number of clonidine prescriptions is added up, the risks do seem to be increased, but not dramatically so. Secondly, those treated with stimulants and clonidine by definition are an extreme group of impulsive, accident-prone children. Their unthinking behavior places them at great risk of serious injury or death by misadventure. Also, families of this extreme group frequently fall apart, which has major long-term implications for the emotional health of parents and children.

In this country the risks and benefits have been investigated but opinion is still divided. The most influential authorities recommend the use of clonidine but advise caution. Others dislike the thought of an antihypertensive drug being used to control behavior or sleep.

From where we stand we recognize the risks and don't like the drug, but we still use the clonidine-stimulant combination. This is only in those extremely impulsive, overactive children who would destroy themselves and their families unless they receive this additional medication. We also use clonidine with major problems of settling to sleep when there is great disruption and other solutions have not worked. We believe the theoretical and at present unproven risks of clonidine are much less than the very real risk of injury, death, and destroyed families.

The preparation

Clonidine comes in 0.1 mg, 0.15 mg, and 0.3 mg tablets. To avoid confusion and the dangers of inadvertent overdose, we only prescribe one strength—the 0.1 mg tablet. Clonidine also comes in a convenient skin absorption patch in strengths that deliver 0.1 mg, 0.15 mg, and 0.3 mg Clonidine per day. This is the preferred preparation in the U.S.

To prescribe

In the eight-year-to-12-year-old child we would start with a half tablet (50 micrograms), given at bedtime. In the younger child the starting dose might be halved (a quarter tablet). This is given for seven days, after which a half tablet (for the older) and a quarter tablet (for the younger child) is now given with breakfast. After a further week another half or quarter tablet may be added.

For impulsive, extreme behavior, medication is usually given in two (occasionally three) doses per day. A child of eight to 12 years old would probably receive half or three-quarters of a tablet twice a day (breakfast and 3:30 P.M.). A four-year-old would receive a quarter tablet twice or three times a day. When used to treat severe sleep problems, a half or three quarters tablet for the younger child and a full tablet for the older child might be given an hour before bedtime. We are very conservative with our doses of Clonidine; some suggest significantly higher levels. (See R. D. Hunt et al., "Clonidine in Child and Adolescent Psychiatry," *Journal of Child and Adolescent Psychopharamacology* 1992; 1:87-102.)

The response

Most behavioral benefits are seen in the first four to six hours, though clinical improvement can last up to 12 hours. There may be initial benefits but it can take two weeks or longer for the effect to hit its peak. Our results with severe sleep problems are generally good, but the behavioral benefits are often less impressive than others describe. As clonidine is a drug which subdues impulsivity, rather than enhancing brain function, teachers see little improvement in distractibility and attention though parents report improved compliance.

Side effects

The most common problem we hit is sedation and sleepiness. Almost every child we treat for the impulsive daytime problems becomes unduly tired and many of our parents will stop the drug early on. The literature paints a much more favorable picture, stating that sedation usually eases over the first three weeks, with only a small minority refusing treatment for this reason.

Some children feel confused, while others have headaches. In theory blood pressure can drop slightly, but it does not seem a significant side effect when the child is healthy and we prescribe small doses. Low blood sugar is another theoretical side effect which is avoided if clonidine is taken with food. Currently the possible risk of unexplained cardiac deaths remains our greatest concern. Some colleagues suggest pre-treatment and follow-up regular electrocardiograph (EKG) tracings. This seems sensible but it may have little value in reliably preventing an extremely rare and not understood occurrence. As one death occurred after surgery, we gradually wean children off the drug in the weeks before a surgical procedure and reintroduce it several weeks later.

The drug Tenex (guanfacine) is another preparation similar to and possibly better than clonidine. Meanwhile we maintain our uneasy relationship with clonidine, prescribing only when the situation is extreme and then with the full, informed consent of the parents. Though some colleagues confidently use much higher doses, we choose to keep the levels low. Parents are warned of the dangers of exceeding the prescribed doses and instructed to gradually withdraw treatment, not stop abruptly. Clonidine must be stored securely as accidental poisoning is a hazard.

Clonidine is useful when tics accompany ADHD. When stimulant medication is perceived to aggravate the tic, the addition of clonidine often reduces or stops the problem and this combined treatment allows use of the stimulant to continue.

Desipramine (Norpramin) and Imipramine (Tofranil)

When stimulant medication is ineffective, the main second-line drug is either desipramine or imipramine. Imipramine and desipramine are tricyclic antidepressants, drugs which also have some effect on ADHD. For years they were used for depression, but they have now been superseded by the SSRI (selective serotonin reuptake inhibitor) drugs, for example Prozac and Zoloft. Though these new preparations have relatively few side effects, unfortunately they bring no benefits to the impulsive, inattentive behaviors of ADHD.

When tricyclics were the main treatment of adult depression, they were famed for the discomfort they caused in the early weeks before the antidepressant levels were achieved. Such were the side effects that many patients gave up, preferring depression to the drug. For ADHD we use relatively small doses compared with those needed for depression, and children seem to be much less troubled than the adults we used to treat.

Though the antidepressants help ADHD, they are less effective than stimulants. Hyperactivity, mood, and the emotional ups and downs are improved. Impulsivity is probably helped and there is a definite but limited effect on attention.

Though one U.S. research group (J. Biederman et al.) has found almost equal benefits can be gained from stimulants and tricyclics, this has not been our experience. We believe tricyclics are much less effective than stimulants and potentially much more dangerous.

The tricyclics are prescribed when stimulants have failed or cannot be used due to side effects. In theory a tricyclic should be the drug of first choice when tics or Tourette's syndrome complicate ADHD. In real life many doctors prefer the more effective stimulant medications and may or may not add clonidine.

The preparations

Tofranil comes in 10 mg, 25 mg, and 50 mg tablets. Norpramin comes in 10 mg, 25 mg, 50 mg and 75 mg tablets.

Action

These drugs stay in the body much longer than the short-acting stimulants and this brings the benefit of a once- or twice-daily dosage. After the start of treatment minor benefits may be reported in a matter of hours, with definite gains in one or two days, and the maximum benefits after several weeks.

Children can become tolerant to these, and if a previously good response lessens, the dose may be increased once—but after this it is best to move to another medication.

To prescribe

As a rule of thumb, children under eight years start with 10 mg at night and increase at two-weekly intervals by 10 mg increments, to reach a dose of 20 mg or 30 mg per day. Older children can be started with 10 mg or 25 mg and increased at either 10 mg or 25 mg increments, up to a maximum of 100 mg per day. This is usually given in two separate doses but occasionally three doses seem to suit the side-effect-sensitive child.

The review literature suggests a dose between 1 mg and 4 mg per kilogram of body weight, per day, but where possible the dose should be kept under 2.5 mg per kilogram, per day. We are probably overcautious in our use of these drugs, tending to treat a five-year-old with two 10 mg tablets a day and an eight-year-old with three 10 mg tablets a day. Our caution is not without reason; these drugs do have their problems.

Side effects

The most common side effect is sedation. Then to add further stress to parents there is a small-print concern over possible cardiac death. In the last 10 years there have been a handful of unexpected deaths in young people treated with desipramine. Though imipramine (Tofranil) is not desipramine, it is partly metabolized by the body to form desipramine. This means that in theory both preparations can have a potential risk.

Now stop for a minute before you overreact to this information. Remember that millions have been treated with desipramine and hundreds, if not thousands, of depressed and ADHD children are now alive and emotionally intact due to this successful intervention. Treatment is always a balance of the benefits against any possible problems.

When information about these deaths came to light, an expert panel analyzed the data. They discovered what we mentioned when discussing clonidine, that every child carries a small but definite risk of unexplained death (almost a Sudden Infant Death Syndrome of school age). The risk is minute, four in a million (possibly 250 children each year). With the addition of desipramine it was felt this risk was possibly eight in a million. After analyzing these figures in detail, the researchers found this was not a statistically significant risk (i.e., the risk was so small it probably happened by chance). (General risk, four in a million; tricyclic risk, eight in a million; suicide, eight in a million; car accident death, 70 in a million.)

In the panic that followed this finding—despite the assurances of researchers who demonstrated no significant risk—all psychiatrists and pediatricians were advised to arrange an electrocardiograph (EKG) before starting any tricyclic medication. If this shows a slight difference, for example a prolonged Q-T interval, the tricyclic should, if possible, be avoided. Recent studies show that this slight prolongation is extremely common in completely normal people, which lessens its value in predicting those at risk.

So what do we make of these theoretical risks? Though most trouble has been linked to desipramine, imipramine must also be treated with caution. There is a slight chance of unexplained cardiac death in any school-age child. This normal risk is marginally increased, but not to a statistically significant degree, in those treated with tricyclic antidepressants. An EKG is often performed before prescription, but its benefits may be more to protect the doctor than to help the child. Blood levels are of value in monitoring the high-dose treatments required for treating depression, but not the small doses of ADHD. The reported risks are minuscule, while the hazards of undertreated ADHD are immense. If stimulants fail and dysfunction continues to destroy children and families, tricyclic treatment is always the safest option.

Many children will feel tired and even "hungover" with the after-effects of the first evening dose. When medication starts to be given by day, tiredness, dry mouth, or a fuzzy head are often reported. All these problems cause most trouble in the early weeks or when the dose is increased. After a month the difficulties lessen or completely disappear.

The tricyclics are occasionally associated with blurred vision, constipation, confusion, and emotional upset. Some suggest that these drugs are more appropriate than stimulants for those with ADHD and tics, but they are not as effective as stimulants and tics may occasionally be worsened by these preparations.

Finally we urge you to stand back and look at the whole picture. Untreated ADHD is a high-risk condition, so if stimulants are unsuitable and tricyclics or clonidine help, be balanced in your decision.

The nonstimulants

Clonidine—Catapres

Action:

- Decreases impulsivity-hyperactivity.
- Decreases aggression-unthinking behavior.
- Improves sleep.
- Minimal or no effect on attention.
- May reduce tics.
- Usually given in conjunction with Ritalin or dextroamphetamine.

Problems:

■ Sedation almost universal.

■ Slight concern regarding cardiac deaths.

■ Medication should be withdrawn gradually.

■ Overdose is dangerous (keep drugs secure).

Dose:

■ A 0.1 mg tablet (or equivalent skinpatch).

■ For sleep a half tablet or one tablet at night depending on age.

■ For extreme impulsivity-hyperactivity, a quarter tablet twice or three times per day, up to one tablet twice or three times per day, depending on age.

■ Usually given twice a day with morning and afternoon stimulant.

Tricyclic antidepressants (imipramine—desipramine)

Action:

■ Imipramine or desipramine preferred tricyclics for ADHD—more effective than amitriptyline (Elavil).

■ Limited but definite effect on attention.

■ Decreases hyperactivity and probably impulsivity.

■ Improves mood, particularly when depressed or anxious.

■ More beneficial to sleep than stimulants.

■ Theoretically the preferred treatment for ADHD with tics.

Problems:

■ Sedation, dry mouth.

■ Hangover, fuzzy head.

■ Concerns regarding presumed cardiac death.

- Preferred gradual withdrawal of medication.

- Accidental poisoning may be fatal (keep drug secure).

Dose:

- Tofranil 10 mg, 25 mg, and 50 mg tablets.

- Norpramin 10 mg, 25 mg, 50 mg, and 75 mg tablets.

- A four-year-old child—10 mg twice a day.

- An eight-year-old child—10 mg morning, 20 mg night.

- In adolescents, 25 mg morning and 25 mg night.

- Note: We are extremely conservative—some clinics suggest doses which exceed 2.5 mg per kilogram body weight, per day.

- The size of the dose is influenced by the extent of the problem you are trying to help.

SEVENTEEN

Medication—All the Questions You Ever Wanted to Ask

When we attend large meetings of parents and professionals, it seems that 90 percent of questions concern medication. Here we have gathered up most of the common concerns. We apologize that in order to make this list stand alone we have repeated some information contained in the previous chapters. If the section on troubleshooting stimulants (at the end of Chapter 15) is combined with this list, almost every possible question on medication will be addressed. **In this chapter the word stimulant refers only**

to the drugs methylphenidate (Ritalin) and dextroamphetamine (Dexedrine).

■ Are we certain that long-term stimulant medication is completely safe?

There is no evidence of any major long-term problems. In the 40 years these drugs have been on the market there have been numerous claims and scares. All have been carefully investigated and the consensus opinion is one of long-term safety.

■ Are we certain that stimulant medication will not increase the risk of later substance abuse or addiction?

There is no evidence of any increase; in fact, stimulants probably decrease the risk. Research suggests that stimulants help children achieve at school, and maintain their relationships and self-esteem. Because of this, stimulant-treated ADHD children have a lower risk of later substance abuse and addiction than those who do not receive medication.

■ Why do children not become addicted to these potentially addictive drugs?

The untreated ADHD child has a brain that spins and spaces out. When a stimulant is effective it brings the child into harsh reality. No one ever got addicted to reality.

■ Does stimulant medication reduce physical growth?

Ten years ago there was concern that constant treatment with high-dose stimulants could result in lower-than-average final height. It should be noted that even when we worried about this, most parents felt that the risk of losing one or two inches was unimportant when compared with the major problems of ADHD. The most recent studies suggest no significant degree of growth suppression linked with stimulant medication. Some researchers believe that ADHD (and Anxiety Disorder) may be associated with a slightly smaller height—due to the condition, not to drug treatment.

■ When my child started stimulants, he just wouldn't stop talking.

Most children listen, think, and keep more on track when on medication. A few seem to talk nonstop, which if excessive is termed "overtalking" and is classed as a side effect.

■ Stimulants have removed the "spark" from my son. Friends ask "Is he on something?"

If medication has been fine-tuned correctly, no child should appear strange, different, or as though they are "on something." Medication should sharpen the focus but never remove the spark and brightness from a child. If concerned, talk to the prescribing doctor.

■ How do you get around problems of headache and abdominal pain?

These are relatively infrequent side effects. First check that the dose is not too high, and that it is being taken with meals and is balanced to give a steady level throughout the day. If headaches or abdominal pain persist, reduce the dose or trial the alternative stimulant. If these pains are a major problem, stop medication, but for mild headaches continue with the tablets, giving Tylenol for the pain. Remember, the stress of school is a common cause of headache and abdominal pain.

■ Do blood levels help us choose the most appropriate dose?

Stimulants are absorbed from the stomach and enter the blood, and from there some of the drug moves across to the brain. There is a great individual difference in the proportion that is transferred from the blood to the brain. For this reason blood levels are unhelpful in gauging effect.

■ What is the youngest age at which you would use stimulant medication?

Doctors think hard before prescribing stimulants in the under-five-year-olds. Having said this, there is no reason why medication cannot be used in younger children if the need is there. We have had amazing success treating extremely difficult three- and four-year-olds. Occasionally a two-and-a-half-year-old has been treated, but to think of medication for a child under the age of three years your back needs to be against the wall. When dealing with very young ages we usually ask for a second opinion from an experienced colleague before considering medication.

■ When our son was aged four years we trialed both Ritalin and dextroamphetamine without success. Is there any point retrying them now he is eight years?

Some children respond poorly under the age of six years and give a much better result at an older age. Some children have major side effects with one drug at a young age and when tried later this preparation suits them well. If a drug does not work early on, it is always worth retrialing it at a later age.

■ What is the maximum safe dose for stimulants?

The effective dose of stimulant varies greatly from child to child and is not closely related to size or body weight. Having said this, most can be maintained on Ritalin given in doses of less than 1 mg per kilogram for body weight, per day. Doses of over 1.5 mg per kilogram body weight, per day, are rarely necessary. Occasionally higher doses are needed, but only when lower levels have been clearly shown as insufficient. For dextroamphetamine the permitted dose is half that of Ritalin.

■ Some people now suggest stimulant medication be given in one heavy dose in the morning.
One dose is convenient as it avoids the need to take tablets at school. If large, this dose produces an initial overload which to us seems extreme and unscientific. We believe the best and safest results come with an even level throughout the day. If any morning-only regime is to be used, Ritalin SK or Dexedrine spansules provide a longer period of action.

■ What happens if we accidentally give double the correct dose of stimulants?
Probably no difficulties will be noticed though the child may be somewhat withdrawn, irritable, or unusual in his behavior. This only lasts for the next four to six hours. Stimulants are remarkably safe.

■ Our child showed no beneficial effects on the standard doses of stimulant medication—would higher levels work?
Some centers increase the dose until they either see benefits or hit side effects. In our experience, if you don't see some gain with a standard dose, a large dose will not produce an unexpected miracle.

■ How long should children be treated with stimulants?
These drugs will be continued for as long as parents, teachers, and the person with ADHD see definite benefits.

■ My doctor says we should stop medication every six months to ensure that it is still needed.
Some academics claim that ongoing benefits can only be demonstrated by regular periods off medication. To most parents of behaviorally difficult children this is a ridiculous, out-of-touch idea. When stimulants are effective, the insightful mother or father will know the moment the levels are starting to drop or when a dose has been forgotten. If the reason for treatment is a subtle problem of learning or there is any doubt about benefits, only then should the child be taken off medication and the situation reviewed.

■ What tests or questionnaires demonstrate the effect of medication?
Usually we use no formal tests, but rely on the observation of the parent

and teacher to report great gains. There are no completely reliable measures of the effect of treatment. The Continuous Performance Test and Paired Associate Learning Test are of benefit in monitoring the less obvious presentations (e.g. ADHD–predominantly inattentive, or ADHD clouded by comorbid conditions).

■ **My doctor says medication cannot be considered until ADHD is conclusively diagnosed with a computer or brainwave test.**
There is no electronic or other test which conclusively diagnoses ADHD. Questionnaires, computer programs, and brainwaves may point to the diagnosis, but they are not essential for either diagnosis or monitoring improvement. The main benefit of the computer programs (e.g. Continuous Performance Test) is in the underachieving "inattentive only" cases and those where comorbid conditions cloud the picture.

■ **Do you allow the parents you deal with to make changes in their child's medication?**
Doctors discourage patients from changing treatment without approval. With ADHD this is somewhat different as insightful parents quickly sense when drug levels are out of tune. In our practice parents are prescribed a certain regime, then given limits within which it might be adjusted to improve the fine tuning. It is our impression that good parents and teachers understand the individual effects better than we do.

■ **How regularly should the ADHD child be followed up?**
This is an impossible question to answer. In our experience, if medication is carefully introduced and fine-tuned to the individual, there is no need for frequent review. If you get it right at the start, it generally stays right. Obviously review must be closer when comorbid conditions, problem behavior, or poor response make management difficult. Many pediatricians aim at a three-month follow-up, but if things are going well a six-month review is fine. An urgent appointment should be available when things are falling apart.

■ **Should regular blood tests be performed in a child on stimulants?**
In Europe and Australia no routine blood tests are recommended. In the more lawyer-troubled practices in North America, a blood count and possibly liver-function tests may be suggested every six months or one year.

■ **A recent newspaper report said Ritalin causes liver cancer.**
In the mid 1990s a study was reported where excessively large doses of Ritalin were given to liver-cancer-prone rats. This increased the risk

of liver cancer. The antistimulant lobby used this to create "Stimulants Cause Liver Cancer" headlines. The current opinion is that stimulants remain safe in humans but care must be taken when prescribing excessive doses in cancer-prone rats.

■ **Much more stimulant is now being prescribed—are we overprescribing?**
Since the beginning of the 1990s, in North America (and most other countries) there has been a fivefold increase in stimulant prescription. Critics claim there is now overuse, but there is another explanation. Nowadays many more girls who underachieve at school are being recognized and treated. Adolescents no longer stop treatment at the age of 12 years. Many adults are being helped with medication, and drug holidays have been dropped. These reasons, plus a more acute awareness of the long-term dangers of undertreatment, have caused a marked increase in stimulant prescription.

■ How do we combat misinformation in the media?
Firstly, it's important to realize that much media misinformation is deliberately fed to the media by groups with an antistimulant agenda (e.g. the Citizens' Commission on Human Rights—Scientologists, discussed in more detail in Chapter 2). Secondly, we are all old enough to realize that what appears in the media is not necessarily true. Thirdly, it's important to understand the media tactic whereby two opposing views are presented as equally plausible: for example, if 999 parents had good experiences with stimulants and one had a bad experience, the media will represent a 1:1 argument suggesting both cases are equally common. The media is about ratings, entertainment, and creating controversy; it is not about accuracy. Having said this, newspaper editors and TV stations do not like to receive floods of letters criticizing their integrity. If you are angry you must voice your opinion.

■ Is one 10 mg Ritalin tablet equal in effect to one 5 mg dextroamphetamine tablet?
For convenience we state this is true but there seems to be an individual difference in the ideal dose of each from child to child.

■ How long do stimulants remain in the body?
Dextroamphetamine has a longer action than Ritalin but in our experience this is not always obvious. In both drugs the maximum effect starts to wane at three and a half to five hours, at which time only half the original dose remains in the blood. At approximately eight hours a quarter remains, and almost all will be gone by 12 hours. Most children seem

to get little effect once the levels have dropped to half (three and a half to five hours). A few seem sensitive and can have sleeplessness or other effects after 12 hours or occasionally longer. The long acting forms of these drugs stay in the body for a greater time, especially the Dexedrine spansules.

■ Do stimulants need to be given every day or can they be reserved for times of special stress?

As stimulants have an almost immediate effect, in theory they can be given only in times of crisis. A child who is in reasonable control in the normal routine of life may be medicated before a party or disrupting event. A university student may take medication to cover study or exams. Stimulants do not need to be taken regularly but in practice intermittent therapy is much less effective and is often disruptive to the child. Consistent treatment brings peace and stability to the whole living environment and this multiplies the gains of medication.

■ Do children develop a tolerance to Ritalin or dextroamphetamine?

In theory the effects of stimulants remain constant. Having said this, occasionally we see parents who are convinced that tolerance has developed. When this happens, if both drugs are equally effective, they are alternated (e.g. three months of one, three months of the other).

■ Can the stimulant medications be stored or do they lose potency?

Stimulants do degrade slightly with storage, and the side effects of the degradation products are uncertain. They can be stored for a reasonable length of time but should not be used after the "use by" date which is stamped on the container.

■ In what way is Ritalin different from dextroamphetamine?

Though both of these drugs are stimulant preparations, they have slightly different methods of increasing the neurotransmitter chemicals dopamine and noradrenaline. Ritalin is said to have a slightly shorter length of action than dextroamphetamine. Ritalin is thought to have a slightly greater effect on impulse control, while dextroamphetamine is believed to have a slightly greater effect on attention. In practice some children are better suited to one than the other. Finding the best drug is a case of trial and error.

■ Are there faulty batches of stimulants?

Occasionally parents claim that behavior has become worse since starting a new packet of stimulant. The quality controls are so high we believe this is a chance finding, nothing to do with the quality of the prescribed preparation. Occasionally we hear U.S. pediatricians claim that all brands of methylphenidate are not equal. The manufacturers strongly dispute this suggestion.

■ **My child has speech therapy in the late afternoon—should she be medicated at this time?**
If the child is still alert and attentive without medication, none need be given. If she is distractible, disorganized, and unable to concentrate during therapy, the session will be much more effective when combined with medication.

■ **My child needs therapy, but the therapist does not believe in stimulant medication and is refusing to provide treatment unless medication is stopped.**
If you are certain that the diagnosis of ADHD is correct and both you and your child's teacher are 100 percent happy with the medication, it is time to take a stand. Therapeutic dinosaurs still exist, but they should not let their out-of-date ideas disadvantage the children of the 1990s.

■ **If psychological or psychiatric interventions are commenced, does medication stop?**
Treatment is not an either/or question; both continue together. Modern psychiatrists know that their therapy is much more effective when they work with a receptive, organized, in-tune patient. Once more, if you are refused up-to-date treatment for your child, it is important for parents to take a stand.

■ **Do I stop medication on the day we come back for review?**
If the drugs are working, leave them in place. A good doctor will always listen to the description given by parents and teachers. We believe what you say without having our offices trashed.

■ **If they are sick, do they stop stimulants?**
As long as stimulants are seen to improve the situation they should be continued whether the child is sick or well. Obviously if they are off their food, vomiting, or extremely unwell, medication would be stopped.

■ **Should medication be stopped when a child is admitted for surgery?**
Stimulants would be stopped around the time of the operation, and reintroduced if behavior later became a problem. The situation is different with the drug clonidine, which should be gently tailed off in the weeks before admission for surgery and not reintroduced until full health is re-

stored. This latter drug has been associated with several unexplained deaths, at least one following a surgical procedure (see Chapter 16).

■ When other medical conditions exist, can stimulants be safely given?
Stimulants are in no way contraindicated when a child is being treated for any of the common medical conditions. Anticonvulsants and asthma medication can all be given in the usual doses without undue concern.

■ Are cold remedies and sedatives advised in children with ADHD?
Many ADHD children react to the sedative drugs and the sedating component of certain cold remedies by behaving like obnoxious drunks. Some cold remedies use pseudoephedrine, which has a slight stimulant effect. It is best to avoid ephedrine remedies rather than reduce the real stimulants. Cold remedies do not speed the resolution of the virus and are probably best avoided altogether.

■ Do stimulants block creativity?
This claim generally originates from the antipsychiatrist views of one high-profile American author. Many ADHD children and adults have immense creativity, but their disorganized brains prevent this from reaching realization. Stimulants may not increase creativity, but they increase creative output.

■ My child is an elite athlete—can stimulants be taken in top-level competition?
In the Olympics and all high-level competition the stimulants are illegal performance-enhancing drugs. At the time of writing, elite athletes who are subject to random drug testing cannot take any of the usual treatments for ADHD. If in any doubt check with the governing body of your sport.

■ My teenage son is planning a career in the army; will ADHD affect enrollment?
Current treatment with stimulant medication brands an applicant unfit to serve in any of the armed forces. If you plan to join the army make sure you are seen to be complying with their strict criteria before the interview. Check the current situation with the local recruiting office well in advance.

■ Is it safe to carry stimulant medication with us as we travel overseas?
With reasonable supplies of medication, travel within Europe should pose no problems. Travel within Asia is of greater concern. To be safe,

carry a limited amount of medication and ask the prescribing specialist for a formal letter stating its legitimate use.

■ **What are the main illegal substances taken by ADHD children?**
If the comorbid conditions of Conduct Disorder or Bipolar Disorder are not present, ADHD children seem at no greater risk of substance abuse. Alcohol, cigarettes, and marijuana are the main areas of concern. Hard drugs are a worry for all parents but misuse in properly treated ADHD is relatively rare.

■ **I have found that my ADHD child, who takes stimulant medication, is regularly smoking marijuana.**
This issue was brought up by several presenters at a recent U.S. parent support group scientific meeting. Their opinion was quite forceful: they felt it was foolish to give one drug to sharpen up concentration and another to blow it apart. You take one or the other; it is pointless using both. If marijuana is repeatedly taken, prescription of stimulants should stop.

■ **I am told that cocaine works on the same brain receptors as stimulants.**
This is true, but the effect of that highly addictive substance is quite different from that of the stimulants. Stimulants appear to affect the neurotransmitters in a smooth, gentle action, while cocaine seems to come and go in a flash. It is this tidal wave of reaction which gives the lift to addicts. The two drugs may have a similar site of action, but this does not mean they are in any way similar.

■ **Do addicts gain any pleasure from Ritalin or dextroamphetamine?**
Both these drugs do have a street value but they are usually taken in combination with other illegal drugs. When given alone either they are injected or the doses are many times those ever considered for ADHD. There have been some reports of Ritalin-sniffing and its dangers. It has been stated already that properly treated ADHD children or adults do not become dependent on or addicted to stimulants. The amphetamine favored by addicts is "speed," which is methylamphetamine, a very different preparation.

■ **If an ADHD adult is addicted to alcohol or other drugs, do stimulants have any part in therapy?**
If an adult wants to get on top of an alcohol addiction this will be much easier if their brain function is focused, organized, and in tune. Those experienced in this complex area find they are more successful at treating the addiction when the ADHD is first brought under control with

stimulant medication. Obviously this is highly controversial and great care must be taken not to introduce another drug of potential abuse. The drug Cylert (pemoline) is often used in these cases as it has no street value.

■ Does medication help adults with ADHD?
There are now a number of carefully controlled studies which show marked benefits of stimulants and the tricyclic antidepressants in adults with ADHD. If treatment is not effective it is possible the dosage is too low. One group of researchers suggests that Ritalin at 1 mg per kilogram of body weight, per day, has a 70 percent response rate. (See Appendix XV, "Adult ADHD.")

■ When stimulants help an adult, what behaviors change?
ADHD in childhood causes problems with school performance, relationships, and control of behavior. The same problems occur in adults who underfunction at work, have vulnerabilities in social relationships, and poor self-monitoring of behavior. These are the areas we improve with medication.

■ Do stimulants impair driving?
Untreated ADHD adults are said to have four times the risk of major motor accidents as those without ADHD. If stimulant medication helps organization, focus, and distractibility, driving should be improved, not impaired.

■ Can adults with ADHD take stimulants in pregnancy?
At present drug companies caution against the use of stimulants in pregnancy. This is not because of any known risk, but because of a complete lack of human and animal data to show safety or danger in pregnancy.

■ Do stimulants cause tics and Tourette's syndrome?
Any child who has ADHD is at a much greater risk of having a Tic Disorder and occasionally Tourette's syndrome. As tics and Tourette's are co-morbid conditions, this risk is present whether treated with stimulants or not. Tics occasionally become noticeable when stimulants are given, but it is felt by most that these would have eventually presented whether the drug was given or not. The presence of tics or Tourette's syndrome does not prevent the cautious use of stimulant medication. (See details at the end of Chapter 14.)

■ When tics are present do we treat the ADHD or the tic?
Recent studies show that tics, by themselves, cause remarkably little academic, behavioral, emotional, or social disadvantage. The same cannot

be said of ADHD. Where both occur together it is important not to under-treat the area that causes the most problems, the ADHD. (See "Tics, Tourette's syndrome, and stimulant medication," at the end of Chapter 14.)

■ **Why are stimulants used in preference to the tricyclic anti-depressants?**
Several studies have compared the action of the tricyclic desipramine, and found it to have an almost equal response to stimulants. (See Appendix XVI, "Recent Review Papers, 'Pharmacotherapy' ".) Though this appears in several academic papers, it is our view, and that of many of our U.S. and UK colleagues, that the tricyclics are considerably less successful than stimulants in ADHD. The tricyclics are usually recommended as the second-line preparations. Though tricyclics are not tightly regulated like amphetamine derivatives, they are potentially much more hazardous in both side effects and the risk of death from overdose.

■ **Should an electrocardiograph be taken before prescribing a tricyclic antidepressant?**
The tricyclic desipramine has been under suspicion as having a possible cardiac risk. In the last 10 years a small number of unexpected cardiac deaths have occurred in those treated with this tricyclic. This was investigated in great detail. (See details in Chapter 16.)

Pediatricians often recommend an EKG before prescribing one of these preparations, but this practice is not universal.

■ **Why do you use the blood-pressure-lowering agent clonidine for the treatment of ADHD?**
Clonidine was initially used as a drug for hypertension, but it also has a place in the treatment of those who are extremely impulsive, overactive, and aggressive, yet not fully controlled by stimulants. It also is used to help major sleep problems and to reduce tics in ADHD.

We find clonidine helpful in a few extremely difficult children but we treat it with great respect. Clonidine must not be stopped suddenly and accidental overdose can be serious.

Clonidine is a drug which is liked by some and hated by many. As with the tricyclic antidepressants there have been a small number of unexplained (presumed cardiac) deaths, these occurring in children taking the combination of stimulant and clonidine. (See "Clonidine," Chapter 16.)

■ **Are drug combinations safe in ADHD?**
Doctors are always encouraged to use one carefully aimed preparation rather than a combination of many. If we carefully fine-tune the main

preparations there is usually no need for polypharmacy. Sometimes two preparations are much more effective than one, particularly where co-morbid conditions make management difficult.

■ What are the common drug combinations used in ADHD?

* *Stimulants are sometimes given with clonidine to control major impulsive outbursts, to help settling to sleep, and where tics and ADHD coexist.*

* *A few psychiatrists now recommend the combination of stimulant medication and one of the SSRI drugs, for example Prozac or Zoloft, where ADHD is associated with coexisting depression, Obsessive Compulsive Disorder, or even anxiety.*

* *Stimulants can be combined with a phenothiazine, for example, haloperidol, for the treatment of major ADHD with coexisting tics or Tourette's syndrome.*

* *Occasionally stimulants can be given in association with a tricyclic anti-depressant, when either given alone is not fully effective.*

* *The stimulant Ritalin has, in extremely rare cases, been given in association with the stimulant dextroamphetamine. Most would see this as a crazy combination, but as both have slightly different actions, occasionally the mix has been reported to bring some benefit.*

■ Do the new SSRI antidepressants, for example Prozac and Zoloft, help ADHD?

Unfortunately this promising new class of drug has brought little benefit to the inattention and behavior problems of ADHD. Where depression coexists with ADHD some may prescribe them in combination with a stimulant preparation. Some prescribe Prozac or Zoloft in combination with an older tricyclic antidepressant, as this gives some ADHD effect in combination with the low-side-effect SSRI benefits for depression.

■ Does the new antipsychotic preparation risperidone (Risperdal) help ADHD?

Risperidone is a useful preparation, particularly for those with major psychiatric problems, but at present it is not recommended in pure ADHD. Though this is the official view, we are aware of a number of respected pychiatrists who claim great success with risperidone in complicated ADHD.

■ Does caffeine help those with ADHD?

Some adults with ADHD claim it was frequent cups of coffee that enabled them to study as mature age students. Caffeine is a stimulant which has been studied in ADHD. It brings marginal gains to concentration but the effect is crude and minimal compared with that of the true stimulants. Taking in large amounts of caffeine with stimulant medication can lead to feelings of tension, agitation, and irritability.

■ What is the effect of nicotine in ADHD?
There has been some interest in the benefits of nicotine gum or nicotine patches in those with ADHD. From the limited data available any effect is debatable and this is certainly not going to replace stimulant medication.

■ Are there new drugs on the horizon?
At the time of writing there is no exciting breakthrough in sight. Most of the improvements in treatment have come from a more effective usage of the original agents. In North America an old preparation, "Adderall," has recently been reintroduced, with some manufacturers claiming equal benefits and longer action than for Ritalin. This drug is made up of a combination of four salts of amphetamine. If Adderall continues to increase its profile, it seems this will only be an additional but not superior medication. The drug Tenex (guanfacine) has results that are similar to and possibly slightly better than clonidine, but neither preparation helps the concentration problems of ADHD.

■ What drug is most effective in Oppositional Defiant Disorder (ODD)?
No drug helps ODD, though if it is associated with ADHD, stimulants will make the child more reachable and less explosive (but sometimes more focused in their opposition).

■ An ADHD adolescent or adult is about to be sentenced for major criminal activity—should he be treated with stimulants rather than punished?
ADHD does not cause children to be deliberately hurtful or vindictive or to become involved in criminal activity. Poorly treated ADHD, associated with family dysfunction and hostile critical parenting, can increase the risk of major Oppositional Defiant Disorder and Conduct Disorder. In the early years this can sometimes be turned around with a change of parent attitude and medication. But by the time Conduct Disorder has become entrenched it is hard to alter.

Oppositional adolescents can be angry and blame the world for everything. Those with Conduct Disorder care little about how they abuse the rights of others. Oppositional Defiant Disorder and Conduct Disorder cannot be helped by medication, though the associated ADHD may become more manageable if treated with stimulants. Even intensive psychotherapy has limited benefits at this stage of these disorders.

The diagnosis of ADHD is not an excuse for major criminal behavior. Medication is unlikely to be of much help now, but if tackled 15 years before, things might have been different.

■ Do stimulants help children with specific learning disabilities?
The treatment of ADHD has no direct effect on specific learning disabilities. If, however, the distractibility, inattention, and active working memory problems of ADHD can be improved, the specific learning disability will become easier to treat. Stimulants do not change a child's basic abilities; they increase output and performance.

Though this is the official answer given at academic meetings, we see many ADHD children who become clearer in their language, write more neatly, and race ahead in their reading after the commencement of medication.

■ What is the most effective drug for aggressive behavior?
If aggression is due to the impulsivity and lack of self-monitoring of ADHD, the stimulants can bring a big improvement. If this fails, addition of the drugs clonidine or carbamazepine (Tegretol) may be considered.

Hostile behavior associated with Oppositional Defiant Disorder or Conduct Disorder is not believed to respond to medication, though several workers have claimed benefits from a combination of stimulant with the antipsychotic drug risperidone (P. Cosgrove 1996).

Children with totally unpredictable and almost bizarre outbursts may sometimes present with a childhood form of Bipolar Disorder. At this young age there is none of the adult manic activity, just major outbursts for some hours, followed by a short period of withdrawal. It is possible that as many as 10 percent of those with ADHD have a comorbid Bipolar Disorder. This is hot-off-the-press information which as yet is not universally accepted.

■ Are stimulants equally effective in the dreamy, "inattentive only" form of ADHD?
These children perform extremely poorly at school. Stimulant medication does work but is slightly less effective than when used in the full hyperactive-impulsive presentation of ADHD.

■ A number of plant preparations are currently being promoted as safer and more natural than the stimulants. Is there any evidence to back up these claims?

Over the last 20 years we have been bombarded by multiple quick-cure fads. These have included diet, vitamins, health drinks, minerals, skull realignment, swinging in a hammock, biofeedback, the use of various plant extracts, and administration of a mix of evening primrose and tunafish oil. While in favor, these products are heavily promoted by those who genuinely believe in their effects and those who are financially advantaged by their use. At the time of writing, a pine-bark extract is being promoted on the Internet, with claims that it is effective, natural, and safer than stimulants. Parents must be aware that what appears on the Internet may or may not be true. Natural health products are often introduced onto the open market without the detailed research and investigation into side effects that is compulsory before any medication can be licensed and sold. Just because a product is natural does not mean it is safe.

To this point there are 40 years of use and over 155 reputable research papers documenting the safety and benefits of stimulants. Those who claim that any new and almost-untried product is equally good and of greater safety seem to be stretching the truth. If two lottery tickets were available each costing $10, one giving a one-in-100 chance, the other giving one-in-100,000, few sane people would buy the ticket with the lower odds.

EIGHTEEN

ADHD in the Underfives

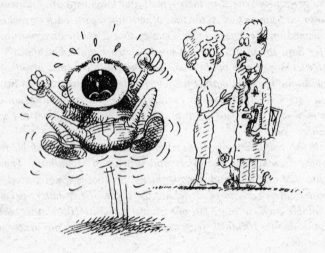

Everyone knows the "terrible twos" are an age of great "busy-ness" and no sense. The threes and fours are more predictable, but at all these ages the range of normal behavior is still extreme. The first features of ADHD usually show before the age of three years, but very few of these young children need anything more than minor guidance at this stage. This chapter is not about the majority of young ADHD children, who are more challenging than most other underfives but do well until the start of school. Our interest is in that small minority of explosive, impossible underfives, who destroy their parents.

The underfives—doubly difficult

The average child, under the age of three years, is a remarkably uncomplicated little person. Their behavior has no malice or aggression; they just don't think too deeply. At this age the brain's executive control, housed around the frontal lobes, is extremely immature. This accounts for the sparky behavior of the young, which rapidly improves as they come closer to school age.

The condition called ADHD is also the result of a relative lack of executive control. In this disorder the frontal areas fail to self-monitor and to inhibit unwise behavior. The average preschool child has plenty of active, unthinking behavior, but when ADHD is also present this produces a double dose of disinhibition.

Though the majority cause few problems until they hit the demands of school, there are a small number of exceptionally difficult young ADHD children. Their parents are overwhelmed, become increasingly punitive, and may begin to resent. Such are the destructive long-term implications of getting off to the wrong start; we can't afford to let this happen.

The presentation in the underfives

Surprisingly, the majority of young ADHD children in our care were unremarkable in their behavior as babies. A number were irritable, movement-loving criers in the early months, but as this behavior pattern in infants usually resolves itself, it is a poor predictor of ADHD. In the second six months a small number demand constant carrying, entertainment, and attention. We find that this pattern of constant demand is strongly related to an early presentation of ADHD in the preschool years.

Many of these difficult children were said to be busy and into everything as soon as they walked. A number were absconders who defied the usual separation anxiety of this age and bolted without fear. Most had an explosive passage through the "terrible twos." At age three years the complaints we hear from parents include low frustration tolerance; lack of sense; being demanding, generally dissatisfied, busy, noisy; and launching unthinking attacks on other children.

These behaviors are not the sole reserve of ADHD. They do occur in other children, but with less intensity and a much better response to the usual methods of discipline. Three problems cause most pain to our parents: **short fuse, immense demand,** and **unthinking attacks on other children**. This last behavior has resulted in many of our children being suspended or even expelled from day care.

The diagnosis

In the preschooler two problems make diagnosis difficult. Firstly, at this age there is such an extreme of behavior which is accepted as normal that it is hard to know where the "terrible twos" merge with ADHD. Secondly comes the problem of parental misperception.

Some of us enter parenthood with the expectation that our preschoolers will be obedient, self-entertaining, dress nicely, and behave like adults. Sometimes it is hard to determine whether a perceived problem of ADHD is real or due to the parents' misperception of a normal, high-spirited youngster. Though this concerns us as pediatricians, we must listen carefully to what parents tell us. Many children who in the past we believed were problems of parental misperception have recently returned as cases of ADHD that we missed.

There are lots of tests and questionnaires to help make the diagnosis of ADHD, but the most reliable measure comes from experienced eyes that see and ears that listen to what parents say. In simple terms, ADHD should be considered when a certain package of behaviors causes a child to be significantly "out of step" with others who are of the same developmental age and have an equal quality of parenting.

At this young age diagnosis involves excluding ADHD look-alikes. We frequently see young children thought to have ADHD when in fact their restlessness, low frustration tolerance, and lack of sense are due to intellectual disability. When in doubt about development, look at speech, understanding, interest, and the richness of play. If these are okay, the child's development is on track.

It is often said that autism, or Asperger syndrome, is indistinguishable from ADHD—but those with autism are distant, detached children, with a robotic quality to their language. This is totally different from the mischief-loving interest and energy of ADHD. The worst behaved children in our care are those with ADHD and a major degree of Language Delay. This combination seems to add extra frustration to an already explosive mix.

The parents

Parents of extremely difficult young children become "brain-dead" and bewildered. They can't understand why the behavior techniques that work so well for their friends are so ineffective with their children. They feel criticized by onlookers, friends, and family. They see no easy answers and they wonder what happened to the joy of parenting. With a difficult ADHD child of any age, parents seem to adopt one of three approaches.

- *They accept this temperamental difference, make allowances, relax, and parent from the heart.*
- *They become overwhelmed, feel like failures, and lose direction.*
- *They try to drive the bad behavior out of the child and force them to comply.*

Most parents, at some time, try the third, firm, confronting approach, but fortunately back off when it is seen to fail. Some get stuck in the middle ground, being overwhelmed and unable to move ahead. It seems that those who are successful in managing ADHD eventually discover the importance of the first approach, then accept, nurture, and parent from the heart.

Figures suggest that 40 percent to 60 percent of ADHD children will become oppositional and defiant, with 20 percent showing the more severe, almost amoral behaviors of Conduct Disorder. We believe the risk of these, particularly Oppositional Defiant Disorder, is greatly increased by this forceful, confronting approach. When parents decide they are going to "make" their child conform, a conflict of Bosnian proportions often results. At the end of the day the peacekeepers may be in place, but hateful relationships and lifelong distrust remain.

Turning around discipline

When the usual behavioral techniques don't seem to work it's time to reevaluate all available methods. Parents must not expect a miracle—instead they must seek out the techniques that bring them some success, then dump the rest.

Parents find it hard to let go of methods that work in every other child but are clearly not helping in theirs. *"Are you telling me we should stop punishing his bad table manners?"* "Is this working?" we respond. *"No, it makes things worse."* "Well, why do it?" *"Are you telling me to let him get away with everything?"* "No, but if it's not getting you anywhere why do it?" *"Are you telling me . . . ?"* "Read my lips!"

The best chance of success

This usually comes from anticipating problems before they hit; steering around the unimportant issues; clear, convincing communication;

diversion; time out, getting outside; putting on a favorite video; avoiding escalation; and keeping young children moving.

The best chance of failure

The methods that fail include nitpicking, escalating, addressing the unimportant issues, confronting, debating, shouting, smacking, withholding privileges, and overusing the word *no*.

Force and smacking are out

Parents who do not accept the ADHD child as different, and make no special allowances, are in for trouble. Those who are hell-bent on bringing up their children with the same rigid discipline of their parents' generation are also heading for failure.

In academic circles the thought of smacking is taboo, but in the real world it is an extremely common form of punishment. For children with an easy temperament, smacking may occasionally work, but there are much better forms of discipline. In the challenging child, smacking is ineffective; it escalates, creates resentment, and is dangerous. Parents smack to "make" their child conform. He defies, they smack harder—he resists, and things get out of control.

Medication can be a miracle

Pediatricians and parents are uncomfortable with the use of stimulants at this young age. Having said this, it is our experience, over the last 15 years, that stimulants can be surprisingly safe and successful in three- and four-year-olds. In theory, the drug clonidine and the tricyclic antidepressants might be considered ahead of stimulants, but in our clinics, stimulants—with their quick action, safety, and clearly documented effects—remain the first choice.

In these young children introduction and adjustment should be in quarter tablet (e.g. 2.5 mg Ritalin (methylphenidate)) increments. We trial both stimulants, Ritalin and dextroamphetamine, as these two preparations are definitely not equal in effect and side effects. After an initial three-week trial no drug will be prescribed unless the parents, with feedback from preschool/day care, are certain of the benefits and the freedom from unwanted side effects.

Medication response is quickly coded on a four-point scale. Four out of four is a miracle improvement. Three out of four is extremely good. Two out of four is good, but there is room for improvement, and one out of four is minimal. Most children who start on medication have a score of two and a half or above. The main effect is to lessen the explosive behavior and allow children to be reached. Once we can reach the child, our behavior plans start to succeed.

Some young children seem to metabolize medications quickly and rebound as their drug level drops. To combat this they are maintained on four, or occasionally five, small doses to give an even response throughout the day. A few who are extremely difficult will get their first dose the moment they wake.

During our trials of medication the most common parental complaint is of withdrawn, teary, upset behavior, occasionally with unexpected anger and irritability. This can be eliminated by changing the preparation or lowering the dose. Ten years ago we were reluctant to use medication in young children. Now we realize that with drug treatment children start to listen, parents start to communicate, and everyone becomes closer in their relationship.

Survival psychology

It's not fair, it shouldn't happen, but this young child is here and no one is going to miraculously change their temperament. Over the years we have moved from proposing clever behavioral programs that rarely worked, to regrouping and subsequently promoting the art of "survival psychology."

The first step is to accept the reality of the situation—the next steps are to introduce a few firm rules, then steer around the strife. If lengthy time in the supermarket is a nightmare, avoid it; use late-night shopping, or bundle the child into the shopping cart and use the "smash and grab" approach. If gatherings with friends and family cause embarrassment, drop in for a high-quality half hour and leave before the bomb blows. If travel is a torment, stay near home. If the child is an escape artist, fortify the compound. If ornaments get broken, lock them away. If the VCR is being reprogrammed, put it on a high shelf.

If parents feel trapped and need some space, put on a favorite video for a short period of peace—this is better than shouting, fighting, or having a nervous breakdown. Remember, it is emotionally better to spend time playing with a difficult child than squabbling and resenting the amount of time they demand. If they enjoy getting out, don't let two hours of fun in the park be destroyed by an argument on the way home. We are not looking for conflict; our aim is peaceful coexistence and a child who is still close to their parents at the age of 18.

The end result

Children who present with the extreme, explosive ADHD behaviors at preschool age will continue to be a challenge for many years. We can't wait until the age of six to take this seriously—if we don't get it right at the start, relationships may become permanently derailed.

Recently we worked with an extreme three-year-old and his defeated mom. We asked if his behavior was as difficult for everyone, to which she replied, *"Even our German shepherd is frightened of him!"* After redirecting the discipline, applying survival psychology, and undertaking a successful trial of medication she returned for review. When asked "What's different?" she smiled and said, *"Now I love him."*

NINETEEN

Encouraging Self-Esteem

ADHD is a real confidence crusher. If a child struggles at school, is socially inept, and in trouble all the time, it is no wonder that esteem sinks. Of course, some ADHD children are so thick-skinned that they bounce through with remarkable resilience. Then there are those who excel at sports, which helps shore up their confidence. Unfortunately, for most it is a hard road they tread, but one that can be made more comfortable if we boost, not crush, confidence.

The negative spiral

Parents need to be almost superhuman to remain positive and encouraging as they live with an ADHD child. Certainly, at the time the diagnosis is made, many parents are already at a pretty low ebb. They blame themselves and feel like failures. Others find fault in everything their child does and are now engaged in a no-win war. Some start to wonder if their child is deranged, brain-damaged, or moving toward prison.

It is sad to see parents, who were so full of hope and enthusiasm when their children were little, become so negative and disillusioned. Even worse is the effect of these unhealthy attitudes on the child.

Children can't see themselves; they judge their self-worth from the reactions of those around them. We are the mirror that shows them how they are appreciated, and through this they shape their self-image. If esteem is to remain high we must encourage, value, help, and watch what we say to our children so that they will savor success.

Confidence crushers

Parents and teachers can undermine esteem, not just by the words we use, but also by the way we use them. Intonation, lack of interest, put-downs, and implied incompetence all take their toll. After a while this erosion of esteem becomes so easy, we hardly know we are doing it.

Don't listen

When you live with a child who nags, complains, and babbles on, you switch off to survive. But if children are to feel valuable, what they say should be valued. When they rush in from school wanting to tell of some great adventure they need an audience, not: "Wait until the news is over," or "Oh yes." Yawn!

It is not easy, but if we don't encourage communication, soon they will stop trying to tell us anything.

Put-downs

ADHD children may appear to be insensitive and irritating, but it doesn't mean they are not upset by hurtful remarks. Be particularly careful of the "You" statements. "You know it all, don't you?" "You never think of anyone else." "You annoy me all the time." "You make a mess of everything."

"You" statements are never so hurtful if turned into "I" statements. "I get upset when we don't get along together." "I find it hard work tidying up all this mess." Remember, it is the behavior and not the child you dislike.

Overprotect, undertrust

When you have seen the ADHD child stumble into so many dangerous and stupid situations, it is natural to become overprotective. But it is hard to feel you are a competent person when parents constantly say: "Don't climb, you know you always fall," "Don't slice the bread, you'll cut your finger," "Don't run, you will trip," "Don't go in the surf, you'll do something stupid," "Don't ride your bike, you ride too dangerously."

There is a difficult dividing line between keeping our children safe and stifling them with overprotection. Children need to feel trusted if they are ever going to achieve independence and good self-esteem.

Comparisons

Children are unique; they don't need to be compared with their cousins and classmates. The ADHD child will not be as tidy as his brother or study like his sister, but so what? Children need to be respected for their individuality and not have their noses wiped in it. When human beings of any age try to live up to other people's inappropriate ideals, they crack and lose confidence.

Fault Finding

Every one of us knows how much it hurts when we produce our best work, yet receive nothing but criticism. Children are just as sensitive: *"Look what I made."*—"Oh, what is it?" *"I got dressed all by myself today."*—"It would look better if your shirt wasn't inside out." *"I've just washed the dishes for you."*—"There's grease on that one, let me do it. I'll wash them properly." When children do their best, they need to be encouraged, not undermined.

Words that wound

When we are utterly exasperated it is easy to say things we know we should never say. "You're such a pest." "Can you do nothing right?" "You know how to make everyone's life unhappy." "I can't trust you to do anything." We need to get rid of words like "dumb," "stupid," "ruin," and "pest." If we don't drop destructive language, it is esteem that will drop instead.

The focus on failure

There is one great difference between adults and children. Both have their individual strengths and weaknesses, but only adults are allowed to promote what they are good at and hide their problems.

Clumsy children have to front up with 30 others and be embarrassed as they exercise. Poor readers have to expose this weakness as they read in front of the class. Children who cannot spell can't hide it with illegible writing or a good secretary.

Parents often lose sight of their children's need to savor success. All the focus seems to be on failure. "He runs like he's impaired." "He can remember nothing." "His reading is awful." "He has no style to his swimming."

It is hard enough living with parents who can only see your weaknesses, but when you struggle through school and arrive home to find an army of tutors and therapists ready to focus further on your bad points, life becomes pretty negative.

Converting to confidence

For children to feel good about themselves, they must see that their words are valued, that their talents are appreciated, and that they themselves are respected and trusted. At the same time those who care for them need to encourage esteem, and in everything the focus must move from failure toward savoring success at something.

Wonderful words

Take time to listen as the ADHD child talks. Acknowledge what the child says, keep eye contact throughout the conversation, and let them finish without interrupting them. Show you're interested and let them know you care. Use plenty of encouragement. "You're great." "I like it." "Give it a go." "I believe in you." Sometimes they won't accept your praise and respond, "No, it sucks," "I hate it!" The secret is to be more specific in your encouragement. "The spelling is so much better." "This is the neatest paragraph." "I liked the goal you saved near the end of the game."

Well done

Take time to watch what they are doing, appreciate their effort, and give help when it is needed. When things are not right, guide, *don't* criticize: "Gosh, if you tidy this a tiny bit, it will be perfect!" Look past the bad bits to see the good. For example, their writing may be messy and their spelling poor, but the story is full of talent. Let them know you are pleased. "That's good." "You're right." "You bust yourself, but you did it." "That's so much better." "You're really improving."

Respect and trust

Things may get spilt or broken and the work may be substandard, but at least the child is trying. Encourage them to do as much as they can without putting anyone at too much risk. Without responsibility and our trust, children feel inadequate and lack independence.

A wonderfully wise mother recently gave us her views of esteem: "If you treat your children the way you would like to be treated yourself, you will never go far wrong."

Confidence in the classroom

Teachers tread a tightrope. They know the ADHD child needs a lot of extra attention, but they realize that esteem suffers if they are seen to stand out as different. It is quite a balancing act, particularly when the child is often unpredictable, disruptive, and difficult.

School is stressful for children with ADHD. It takes twice the effort for them to achieve the same results as anyone else. Equal effort gets them nowhere. If teachers are to maintain esteem and interest, they need to continually encourage the child. When attention is hard to hold, use material that is of interest. If the child is into fishing, let him read, write, talk about, and count fish. If it is sport, dinosaurs, or whatever, encourage his interest.

Teachers should follow the same suggestions already mentioned for home. They need to watch their choice of words, to encourage the children, and let them feel important. The ADHD child may be intensely irritating, but his behavior and self-image will be stronger if he is noticed, can share special tasks, and is allowed the same privileges as would be granted to the potential Rhodes scholar or the number-one nerd in the class.

Savoring success

A life which is all failure and no fun gets pretty depressing. As parents, we need to look past the problems of school to find hobbies, interests, and outside activities our children enjoy. We must move the focus from what our children cannot do to what they can do. Confident children are those who savor success at something and it is up to us to find out what that something is (see also Chapter 20 for suggestions on sports, interests, and hobbies).

TWENTY

Choosing the Right Sports, Hobbies, and Other Activities

At the end of the school day, the active ADHD child hits the outside world like an escaped prisoner. He wants space, freedom, exercise, and enjoyment. It is imperative that these school-stressed children have outside interests. It is up to parents to find what suits the child best.

Avoiding social stress

Many ADHD children are uncomfortable in social situations. They look awkward, don't know what to say, and feel out of place. As we plan outside interests it is important to find ones that bring maximum enjoyment and minimal social stress.

The secret is to look for activities that give space and leave the child firmly in charge of his or her own communication. Those we have found most successful are hiking, bike riding, and swimming.

On a hike, you can walk, talk, run ahead, look around, then talk some more. On a bike, you can speak to a friend, do a few wheelies, and speak again. At the pool or beach, you can meet new friends, splash around, then come back and talk some more. With activities like these, the child is in charge of his own communication and can avoid uncomfortable social pressure.

Another way to keep things comfortable is to ensure that they have friends with similar interests. The bikers, horse riders, and football fans don't need small talk; they can chatter on all day. As they talk about bikes, horses, and their sports heroes, it may bore us out of our brains, but in this company they are stars.

The best sports and activities

Swimming

In Australia this is our number-one recommendation for ADHD children. Not only is it an outlet for energy, it also provides a socially useful interest which they will still have in adulthood. These children can learn to swim safely at an early age, but it often takes quite a few years to get their arms, legs, and breathing synchronized in style. Many parents tell us that their children hate swimming. It is not swimming they dislike; it is the long, boring lessons and waiting their turn which puts them off.

Swimming is not only about style; it is about being safe and enjoying yourself in the pool or the surf. ADHD children need fewer lessons and far more fun, and preferably splashing around with a parent beside them in the water.

Soccer and other team sports

Some of our ADHD children are sensational at sports and this success brings a great boost to their esteem. Others don't have the coordination or concentration to do well, but they still enjoy the outing.

Soccer is one of the best sports for young ADHD children, but inattention means that many go wandering off, lose interest, run in the wrong direction, or drift off to pat a passing dog. Little League works well when the team is winning, but most are particularly poor losers.

If they show any interest in team sports, they should be encouraged. They don't need to pass like Pele or bat like Jeter, but if they enjoy what they are doing it does not matter how good they are.

Bicycles

ADHD children are not the safest riders on the road, but for many, bikes give space, freedom, and an escape from the frustrations of life. If they are old enough and the roads are relatively quiet, get them up on two wheels. After a hard day at school it is great to burn off some energy and this allows them to mix in a socially comfortable way. Many of the world's most talented mechanics were once ADHD children who started by stripping and tuning their bikes.

Fishing

There is something about fishing that seems to soothe. Many of our ADHD children fish from piers and rocks. Some of the most active can even sit relatively still in a small boat. Fishing gives space and is free from social stress. If you live near water, why not give it a go?

Judo and tae kwan do

Parents are reluctant to direct an impulsive, immature child into anything that might encourage violence. Certainly no one would recommend pistol shooting, knife throwing, or pyrotechnics, but judo and tae kwan do are different.

These martial arts have been greatly enjoyed by many of our children. They teach organization and anticipation, and have the right amount of interest and discipline to keep the attention of the usually inattentive.

Cubs, Scouts, and other groups

About two-thirds of our ADHD children seem suited to Scouts. They enjoy the activity, the practical parts, and the interest in the outdoors. Some children do not fit comfortably into this structure and should be withdrawn when it starts to seem like school to them.

Athletics, gymnastics, and dancing

Ten years ago it was fashionable to encourage clumsy children to do Saturday-morning athletics. This helped coordination, enhanced socialization skills, and strengthened their muscles. But running last was never good for self-esteem.

If your child enjoys sprinting, jumping, and cross-country running, that's great, but when it seems all pain and no pleasure let them give it a miss.

Gymnastics and dancing are two other options. These give a great outlet for all that ADHD energy. The aim is fun and enjoyment, not an obsessive interest in style.

Cooking

Some of the world's great chefs have ADHD—maybe it's the late nights that suit them! It is surprising how children enjoy cooking when encouraged by their parents. Some of our ADHD boys are immensely creative in the kitchen. Unfortunately, they are less creative when it comes to cleaning up. Cooking is an interest we often overlook. If they enjoy it, encourage it.

Hobbies, crafts, and interests

The children in our care have all sorts of pastimes. We have potters, painters, football fanatics, collectors, actors, singers, music lovers, gardeners, hikers, horseback riders, water skiers, woodworkers, mechanics (and thousands of television addicts).

Every ADHD child has some talent just waiting to be tapped. Parents need to be on the lookout for new activities and interests all the time. We must be patient, as ADHD children swing from immense enthusiasm to total turnoff in what seems like a millisecond. But don't give up; keep looking for new talents to encourage, which will bring enjoyment and boost the child's esteem.

Computer games

ADHD children may be unable to concentrate in class, but put some in front of a computer game and they will outplay anyone. Parents must realize that it is the game, not the computer, they like. If you slip in some boring remedial program their interest may evaporate. It is important for ADHD children to be competent with computers, and computer games are a good way to start them off (see Appendix XIV, "Computer Programs to Help Learning.")

Conclusion

The school-stressed child needs to develop a protective shield of outside activities. These can be sports, hobbies, clubs, or anything that brings enjoyment and a sense of success.

Parents must encourage these activities but not include too many lessons. It is wonderful when an ADHD child stars and has perfect style, but it is more important to enjoy than to excel.

TWENTY-ONE
Adults with ADHD

Adult ADHD first came to be noticed when pediatricians began to recognize that some of the parents in their care had the same symptoms as their children. The idea of this adult condition took time to gain acceptance but it received the seal of approval when, in 1993, the main U.S. parent support group changed its name to become Children and Adults with Attention Deficit Disorders.

It is believed that at least half of our ADHD children will bring some of the features of their condition into adulthood. Adult psychiatrists now accept this as a real condition and are prepared to consider medication for its treatment.

We are told that some of the most creative, driven, and famous people in today's society are adults with ADHD. Unfortunately, not everyone who grows up with ADHD has such a success story—many of the adults we see have one thing in common: a secret feeling of failure. These are clever people who have had to struggle twice as hard for everything. This has left them with an inner feeling of inferiority, underachievement, immense frustration, and even guilt. Hopefully with the new understanding of ADHD in childhood, and its acceptance as an appropriate adult diagnosis, this situation is about to change.

The picture

Adults have very much the same difficulties as children with ADHD. The school problems now become work problems. The hyperactive-impulsive behaviors usually mellow but there remains a restlessness and a tendency to impulsive actions.

Many ADHD adults wonder what is wrong—they work hard, but still feel unachieving and unfulfilled. Those who study find it difficult to organize and finish assignments; information is not easily remembered, and they may forget as they read. Many students become immensely frustrated, then overwhelmed, and drop out. Relationships and mixing can be a problem where the adult misreads the expectations of a situation or seems insensitive to the needs of those who are emotionally close.

The greatest attribute and the greatest disability of adult ADHD is the restless, circling brain. As this spins, a cascade of thoughts intrudes into the mind. Occasionally this brings immense creativity and invention, but more often it distracts the mind from the important issues of the moment. This inner restlessness is at its worst when there is boredom and lack of structure. It is at its most focused in times of crisis, imminent deadlines, and the heat of battle.

The need for novelty and high drama makes some adults exceptionally hard to live with. They run their lives at top speed and expect everyone to follow their lead. Some fear the quiet times when things are going smoothly, and feel compelled to stir things up just for the buzz.

It is no wonder that relationships at work and home can suffer in ADHD. This need for pace and challenge leaves some adults dreading the end of a high-pressure project or the quiet of family time together. Winston Churchill was a classic example of adult ADHD. He thrived on the stress, excitement, and ever-changing challenges of war, but when peace came he dreaded the quiet, which he feared would lead him to pathological depression.

This adult picture varies greatly in its presentation and severity. Most who read this chapter will have learned to live with their weaknesses of attention, memory, and organization. But some will be in major strife, largely due to their inability to self-monitor behavior and the repercussions of their impulsive actions.

Adult ADHD—The Most Frequent Presenting Complaints

- Inability to concentrate.
- Lack of organization.
- Forgetfulness and poor memory.
- Poor self-discipline.
- Inability to establish and maintain a routine.
- Confusion, trouble thinking clearly.
- Inability to perform up to intellectual level in study.
- Performance on job below level of competence.
- Difficulty in finding and keeping jobs.
- Depression, low self-esteem.

ADHD in day-to-day life

The adult with ADHD may have a restless mind, a restless body, an impulsive temperament, poor short-term memory, attention deficit, "circular speech," overfocused interests, and difficulties with organization. Let's look at these and other behaviors in more detail.

A restless mind

Adults tell us they have "a busy brain." As they sit in a lecture their mind is bouncing around all sorts of ideas, most of which have nothing to do with the topic. "Did I lock the car properly?" "Should I have a hamburger on the way home?" "I wonder who is winning the football game?" Adults with ADHD can't stop distracting themselves, particularly when things are boring.

In outside life their heads are alive with ideas, but these thoughts are rarely captured and turned into action. When this creative potential can be harnessed, there is true brilliance, but for most of the time it is an immense annoyance to those with ADHD and the people they live with.

A restless body

Though the activity of ADHD is at its worst in the early years, many people remain busy in adulthood. A few continue with an almost childlike hyperactivity, while the majority are restless, with occasional bursts of busyness. This restlessness is shown as jiggling feet, clenching of the jaw, flitting eyes, tapping, clicking pens, or just appearing "overcharged." If the adult can harness this immense drive and energy they can be amazingly productive. Unfortunately, it's hard to live with so much busyness.

Impulsive, "sparky" behavior

The worst excesses of impulsivity have usually mellowed by the later years, but some adults are still remarkably hotheaded. They get into trouble with unwise spending, poor business decisions, unthinking outbursts, and unpredictability. Adults with ADHD are more accident-prone than others and at greater risk of injury on the roads.

This impulsivity and lack of self-monitoring make the ADHD adult an inconsistent parent. They alter the rules, explode inappropriately, and can't let the irrelevant behaviors pass unnoticed. This results in the ADHD child being more difficult to manage. Sometimes we wonder if we should be treating the parent before the child.

Poor short-term memory

Though long-term memory is generally good, the short term is a particular problem in adults with ADHD. Ideas come quickly and evaporate unless recorded immediately. Instructions and information are forgotten unless backed up by a written note. Poor memory is an immense irritation to those with ADHD, who hold their lives together with notes, lists, memory jogs, and the tightest of structure.

Inattentive—distractible

While the circling brain of ADHD distracts from within, annoyances in the external environment steal attention from the outside. Those with ADHD become rapidly bored and lose their focus. They miss the steps of instructions. They can read a page with little thought for the print that has passed their eyes. Minor irritations can become immensely distracting: the drip of a tap, the flicker of a fluorescent light, the coworker's sniff, or the hum of a water cooler.

Attention usually sharpens in times of high energy and crisis, but working with a drama-driven adult is a stressful and aging experience.

Poor time management

Adults with ADHD find it difficult to get organized and do what needs to be done. For them, procrastination is the greatest curse, and once they have started on a task it is hard to sustain energy, then finish on time. Work is unevenly divided, with most effort allocated to the least important activity. There is often an inability to estimate time, which results in missed appointments and taking on more than can be managed.

"All or nothing" response

It seems that some ADHD adults have no middle ground; they are either in fast forward, stop, or full reverse mode. There is a great tendency to jump in, boots and all, and when interest drops, rush off in another direction. All this impulsive coming and going is immensely stressful.

Hyperfocus—preoccupation

Those with ADHD are inattentive but they can also get stuck, preoccupied, and overfocused. An idea hits the mind, and is pursued to the death. This determination and single-mindedness has made many famous ADHD adults great, but it can also be quite destructive. When the preoccupation is negative or self-critical some adults become almost paranoid. In a relationship, the overfocus on other agendas can make the adult unavailable and distant to their partner.

Disorganization

Forgetfulness, distractibility, impulsive actions, and poor time management are a sure recipe for chaos. Disorganization is one of the commonest concerns of the adult with ADHD, and here strict structure averts total turmoil. Those who succeed are almost obsessive in their pursuit of order; they know that once they drop their guard, all falls apart. Some of the most successful ADHD businessmen are held together by a good wife or secretary, who acts as their frontal lobe.

Circular speech

Most ADHD adults have good speech skills but some wander all over the place. Good communication starts by introducing a topic and taking the listener along a predictable course. These circular talkers start appropriately, but keep adding, correcting, and sidetracking. This characteristic is painfully evident when I listen to the teaching tapes made by some of the high-profile psychiatrists who have ADHD themselves. After all the verbal coming and going I wonder if an hour of interrogation by the KGB would have been easier on my brain.

Social clumsiness

Adults with ADHD have a genuine wish to get along well with their coworkers and be successful in their relationships. Unfortunately there are parts of this disorder which lead to social stress. Many fail in their relationships as they don't sense the usual cues that guide socialization. It is easy to become so engrossed in our own agenda that we forget the needs of those who depend on us. The impulsive behavior can cause adults to be erratic, short-tempered, and unpredictable. Though it is the ADHD adult who is the cause of these social problems, they can become paranoid that the other ratbags are at fault and don't want to be friendly. It's no wonder that emotional and work relationships can hit such lows.

Specific learning disabilities

Many children with ADHD also have some specific weakness in learning, and this is the same for adults. The most common problem is one of weak reading and spelling. Many ADHD adults do not read for pleasure and are poor spellers, but they cope. A few have major ongoing reading and writing problems, which cause immense frustration and demoralization for these intelligent adults.

Protecting relationships

The risk of marriage stress, broken relationships, and sole parenthood is greatly increased in adult ADHD. There are no miraculous ways in which we can help, but if we are alert to the danger areas, much of this trouble can be avoided. It's important to start with sensible expectations. Life is no fairy tale—we can make things less rocky for those with ADHD, but we can't provide the golden coach and say that everyone will ride off and live happily ever after.

Stay in tune

Wives of ADHD partners often feel there is little appreciation of their emotional needs. When home life is stressful they want someone to encourage and listen, but their need is not acknowledged. They have busted themselves on some project and would like a sign of appreciation, but it doesn't come. The children have been impossible all day, the mother is exhausted and requires relief, but the problem is not picked up.

People can live together without being sensitive to each other's needs, but this will only be half a relationship. We can't expect the impossible, but if partners can try to stop for a minute and think how others feel, things do go better.

Think before you act

It is a sad fact that in most adult relationships a partner is treated with less politeness and respect than a boss at work. When our adult lives are tough, it's important not to dump on those we love. Adults with ADHD speak and act before they think, but they must try to be aware how this explosion or insult feels for others. Learn to step back for some minutes, walk around the block, take deep breaths, or practice a relaxation technique. It is easy to act impulsively; it is hard to repair the damage after the event. When disciplining children, think before you open your mouth. Is this important? Is it worth fighting over? Am I interfering in my partner's discipline?

Impulsivity leads to overspending and poor money management. Watch how you use credit cards and beware of debt. Don't rush into business decisions without careful thought. Ask advice of an impartial friend, sleep on it, reconsider before you sign. Before spending your savings think of your partner's needs—with two small children still in diapers, is the priority a washing machine or a new VCR?

Slow down

In ADHD there is often an oversupply of energy. This is a great asset in physical work but it causes stress in the home. Be aware that pacing, jiggling, and flitting does generate tension. Try to unwind outside the home with walking, going to the gym, or other exercise. If you want to be busy, work on some project in the house. If you want to be quiet, relax, meditate, or listen to music. Have healthy addictions such as exercise or following football, not alcohol.

Why did we marry?

When things are going badly it's important to remember why you got together in the first place. There are boring people in this world, but none of them has ADHD. Excitement brought you together and excitement is still there. But now, with two children and a large mortgage, your partner could do with less excitement and more support. Sometimes it is our needs, not the person we married, that have changed.

When work gets busy and home responsibilities seem immense, it is easy to give up on the fun things you used to do together. Adults with ADHD plan poorly, then hit the weekend with no tickets for the show and no activities arranged. Try to organize your leisure and together time just as carefully as your work.

Sex and ADHD

With such a growing interest in adults, sex is a frequent topic at seminars on ADHD. Some adults keep such strange hours it is quite a feat to get both partners in bed and awake at the same time. Successful sex requires concentration, and this is a weakness in ADHD. Several psychiatrists have claimed that prescribing stimulant medication to some females with ADHD had a marked effect on the women's sex life. It is presumed that this keeps the inattentive mind on the task. But this may not be the same for the male. At a recent meeting, I mentioned the reported action of stimulants on wives with ADHD, which led to a strange disclosure at question time. There were about 500 parents in the audience and one mom was bursting to have her say. "Dr. Green, this is not true," she said. "Since my husband started Ritalin, it has turned around his work but not his sex life. When he's on medication he gets all philosophical and won't stop talking. When he's off—there's more of the animal about him!" In lectures there are some memorable moments; this was one.

Helping ADHD in the workplace

At school, those with ADHD were unable to cope with an unaccepting, nitpicking principal. As adults, those with attention deficit don't cope with a boss at work who suffers from "attention surplus disorder"! They need someone who sees the big picture, who appreciates their qualities and does not highlight their weaknesses.

It's important to choose the right sort of job. Adults with immense pace and activity need space and an outlet for their energy. The disorganized slow readers and writers should avoid a high-intensity, pen-pushing job. Structure, organization, time management, sustaining energy, and maintaining relationships are vital to success at work.

Structure—organization

With adult ADHD there is often lack of output for the effort expended. This is due to poor planning, inconsistent pace, and disorganization. Success needs structure and an obsessive interest in order.

Start the day on time and try hard to keep to time. Don't leave things until the last minute; deadlines are only stressful when they are about to be missed. Have a "do list" and tick it off as you go. Take a step back and see the priorities, then deal with them first. Be on guard against the ADHD "Achilles' heel"—procrastination. Take big projects and break them into small chunks which are much easier to manage.

Adults with ADHD are usually better at doing their own jobs then coordinating a group of others. Beware a promotion which moves you from your area of brilliance to a managerial role which highlights your weakness.

Improving memory and attention

In ADHD attention and memory are usually weak. Don't allow yourself to be rushed through an important sequence of instructions. Write notes or slow down and visualize the logic of each step. When important instructions are given on the run, record them in a pocket notebook, on a memo tape, or ask that a hard copy be sent to you. Use the same memory jogs which helped in high school: a watch alarm, a knot in the handkerchief, a watch temporarily worn on the wrong wrist, and notes stuck to prominent places. Use the visual clue of color to code important information. Help memory with all the rhymes and mnemonics that were discussed in Chapter 12 (e.g., "i before e, except after c"). If you can't remember names at the time of introduction, use word association, where "Arnold" is Schwarzenegger, "Bill" is the president, and so on.

Without regular breaks, attention fades, which leads to poor output and inaccuracy. Have periods of full-on work, a short gap, then start again. Distractions in the workplace can be just as troublesome as distractions in the classroom—try to move away from heavy office traffic or a talkative coworker. With flexible work hours, starting early and working late allows times of undisturbed attention.

Coping with overactivity

Busy bodies need to release pent-up energy. Get into the habit of exercise before work, after work, or during the lunch break. When the computer or papers on the desk are driving you to distraction, make an excuse for an errand which involves a few runs up and down the stairs. Remember that pacing, jiggling, and tapping are infuriating to those who do not have ADHD.

Social relationships

Where possible we must try to associate with people who appreciate us and spend the minimum of time with those who don't. As adults with ADHD often have problems of impulse control, be on your guard against outbursts, bad language, and impulsive remarks you may later regret. Be particularly careful when tired or overwhelmed as these leave you vulnerable. When upset, don't escalate the situation; move away, get some space, take deep breaths, or use one of the "breathing-counting" relaxation techniques. Don't threaten to resign in the heat of the moment; thousands of ADHD adults have learned this lesson the hard way.

Watch the ADHD habits of fidgeting, overpowering, and acting smart, as these may unnerve the thin-skinned coworker. Don't get paranoid that you are being unfairly treated; take a step back and work out the reason for the problem. Sometimes "the truth is out there"—those who behave like idiots are treated like idiots.

Problems of reading, writing, and study

Weak readers struggle with manuals, academic articles, and heavy literature. This is not all the fault of the reader; much of the blame must go to authors who present their work so poorly. Always look for the literature which is well set out, interesting, and cleverly written, then dump the rest.

Technical information is easier to understand if books have plenty of diagrams and illustrations. When studying, use a highlighter pen to register the main points. Write notes as a series of headings that act as memory jogs and give structure to what is important. Weak spellers must have a dictionary at hand or move to a computer with a spell-check facility. Typing brings legibility to illegible writing and word processing allows an edit before presentation.

Adults who find reading difficult can improve with practice, but they will rarely become comfortable with heavy literature. When reading is extremely difficult, books can still be enjoyed through libraries which provide talking books for those with special needs.

Do we disclose?

It is rarely advisable to tell your coworkers that you have "a disorder." There is, however, great advantage in being quite frank about your individual weak spots. "I have such a hopeless memory—I need to write things down." "Let's cool down—I'm a bit of a hothead." "I'm pretty busy—I need to burn off some energy." "I've never been able to spell." Approached in this way you are like everyone else, just with a greater scattering of strengths and weaknesses.

Professional help and the use of medication

To get diagnosis and treatment for adult ADHD, referral is made to an adult psychiatrist. There must be a current history of ADHD behavior which has been present from childhood. There is no simple diagnostic test for adult ADHD. The diagnosis is made when a number of ADHD behaviors cause problems in relationships, learning, and work. The ADHD symptoms must predominate and not be overshadowed by associated conditions such as major depression, alcoholism, addiction, antisocial behavior, violence, or personality disorders.

If the behaviors described in this chapter strike a chord, first try the self-help ideas we have suggested. If you want to take it further you must find a practical-minded psychologist or psychiatrist who understands ADHD.

Medication is now known to have an important place in the treatment of adult ADHD. The stimulants are the preferred drugs, and studies now show response in approximately 70 percent of treated adults. (See Appendix XV, "Adult ADHD".) Others claim lesser response rates but the lack of success is often blamed on the use of inadequate dosage. The Biederman group (see Appendix XV) states that "There is a robust response with a robust dose," which to them means 1 mg per kilogram body weight, per day, of Ritalin. The drug desipramine (Norpramin), which is very much the same as imipramine (Tofranil), is said to bring significant benefits when the stimulants don't suit. Medication is often used in association with cognitive behavior therapy where it helps adults to draw back from their negative areas of preoccupation and allows refocus on a more positive and constructive mind-set.

Some professionals provide a service to coach the ADHD adult in the skills of organizing their lives, for example efficient study, managing the stresses of work, and improving social interactions.

The current services for adult ADHD are somewhat limited. If statistics are correct and 50 percent of our ADHD children will suffer symptoms in adulthood, we must now prepare adult psychiatrists for the needs of these children in the future.

Adult ADHD and its danger to parent support groups

Parents with ADHD are outstanding in their ability to lobby, promote, and get things done. These driving adults can also become overfocused on the unimportant issues, get sidetracked, and become quite destructive. Over the last decade I have been saddened to watch the demise of many excellent support groups. All parents were united in the same goal, but often irrelevant issues or unthinking actions destroyed the organization they set out to promote.

Parent support groups have dramatically changed the acceptance, understanding, and treatment of ADHD. With so much drive and energy found in the members of these groups, we must not lose sight of the target. Successful parents shoot at the target, not at their foot.

Final thoughts

ADHD is a very real condition which troubles a large number of children and adults. With understanding and help, we can bring great improvement to lives, relationships, education, employment, learning, and self-esteem.

Despite the current interest in ADHD we see many parents who are unaware that this condition was the cause of their troubles in childhood. One of the saddest parts of our work is to meet intelligent, talented adults who still believe they are inferior, inadequate, and dumb. It is criminal that this unnecessary assault on their esteem was ever allowed to take place. We can't change the past, but we can be doubly determined that the same will never happen to the ADHD children of this present generation.

TWENTY-TWO

The Associated Problems of Learning and Language

Children with ADHD frequently have associated weaknesses in reading, spelling, writing, mathematics, and language. The incidence of these specific learning problems is usually quoted as between 35 percent and 50 percent, meaning that about half of the ADHD children also have these related problems. Some say it is as low as 10 percent and others as high as 90 percent. (See "Cormorbidity," M. Semrud-Clikeman, in Appendix XV.)

ADHD by itself causes children to underfunction academically for their intellect through inattention, poor memory, and lack of impulse control. When these problems are combined with specific learning disabilities, the child is faced with double trouble.

Attention, memory, and executive control

Inattention (lack of attention) is probably the most common reason for a child not achieving full potential at school. Attention is quite a complicated concept. One of the many possible ways to understand this was given in Chapter 5. Here another way is suggested, where attention is divided into a number of overlapping parts such as *selectivity*, *monitoring*, and *maintaining effort*. These parts are in turn closely associated with memory. Collectively they are called the "executive functions."

Executive function

Animals do not usually think before they respond, but humans do usually reflect before they react. This difference is due to executive function, which is a function of areas around the frontal lobes of the human brain. These areas are the conductor that keeps the orchestra of learning and behavior playing in harmony. Children with ADHD have a weakness in this area that results in problems of prioritizing, planning, using time wisely, anticipating consequences, learning from the past, and staying in tune socially. This not only affects behavior, it also causes the ADHD child to underfunction at school.

ADHD is now thought to be best characterized as a disorder of executive function. Executive function is self-regulation. Executive functions are the control processes which lead to inhibition and delay in responding, at least long enough to allow the child to read feedback and integrate information from past experience in order to modulate present behavior and predict future consequence. So the child can stop himself from moving to those activities that are more attractive, persist with tasks that have less interest value, and be motivated in this because of an orientation towards a future event—e.g., project due or exams next week.

The implications of executive dysfunction become greater and greater the higher a child gets in school. The presence of executive dysfunction causes even a child with no other risk factors for learning disability to present with poor school output.

Weaker executive functions mean that the ADHD child is unable to be his own tutor through the incidental learning of good study techniques. He will continue to require tutoring through his school years. There is a tendency to lapse into passive learning—lack of self-regulation in keeping himself on task, in rehearsing and efficient encoding in memory. This leads to rapid erosion of learned material.

Attention

Inappropriate selectivity

Children with ADHD find it hard to see the forest for the trees. When information comes in they pick up on one small part of it but don't identify the main message. In answering a question they go off on a tangent and get sidetracked. When attempting projects or exam questions they spend all their time coloring in their diagram and don't get on with the answer. If we can't wisely select what to give our attention to, we can't succeed at school.

Inadequate self-monitoring

Children need to attend and to review their work if they are to spot their errors before the teacher who is marking their schoolwork. When they write, ADHD children make silly mistakes which are not noted in their inattentive rush. When reading aloud to the class, they blurt out a word without checking if it matches the meaning of the sentence. Inattention is partly to blame for this but there are also the problems of poor self-monitoring and impulsivity. This lack of quality control leaves many ADHD children underfunctioning for their true academic ability.

Inability to maintain effort

Inattentive pupils find it impossible to stick with uninteresting tasks. They become bored and don't pay attention to schoolwork, while a fast-moving video game will hold their attention for hours. This lack of persistence and switching off from difficult schoolwork is a particular problem in the primary-school years.

Mental fatigue is a big problem in ADHD children. Complicated work requires so much concentration that they soon suffer "terminal brain fade." These children can maintain such effort, but it is at great personal cost. It is no wonder they don't want to start their homework or to see the tutor waiting for them when they arrive home after school.

Memory

It is hard to distinguish between problems of attention and memory. If we can't attend to the work in front of us, it cannot be photographed by our minds, integrated, and stored away. Children with ADHD usually have a good long-term memory but a poor recall for the present. They remember what happened a year ago, but not the information that has just been given.

Short-term memory

Most ADHD children are no good at remembering instructions. They forget large chunks of what is being taught and have particular problems when information is given in a sequence. This shows up as a poor memory for lists and confusion with the steps required to solve a problem.

Active working memory

This part of short-term memory refers to a child's ability to hold a number of bits of information in the mind so they may be processed. If you can't keep several groups of figures in your head at one time, mental arithmetic is impossible. If we are to understand what we read, the words at the beginning of the paragraph must still be remembered by the time we reach the end of the paragraph. With language, active working memory helps us to juggle words in our minds so that we can craft them to make the maximum impact upon use in our speech and written language.

Specific learning difficulties

Children with ADHD are already disadvantaged by their problems of attention, memory, and executive control. To make life even more difficult, many also have a specific learning disability. The most common of these are weaknesses in the areas of reading, spelling, writing, mathematics, and language. Children who have ADHD without the impulsive-overactive package of behaviors (ADHD–predominantly inattentive) have a higher incidence of these learning difficulties than those with the more recognizable presentation of ADHD with hyperactive-impulsive behaviors.

Reading and spelling

How we learn to read

The first step in reading is to learn some "sight words." This recognition starts at preschool age as children see street signs, advertisements, and everyday labels. Soon they recognize their own name and words such as "stop," "walk," "McDonald's," "Coca-Cola," and "Toyota."

Children entering school vary greatly in the number of words they can recognize and this skill increases rapidly throughout the kindergarten year. The ability to recognize words by their shape is an important part of adult speed reading, but before we get to this level we must move through some very complicated steps.

To be a proficient reader the next skill required is the ability to decode new, unfamiliar words by breaking them down into their component parts. The first step is to learn each letter of the alphabet. The next step is to associate the correct sound with each of these letters (sound symbol association). The letter "b" in the alphabet is called "bee," but sounds out as "buh." The first stage in reading phonetically is to associate a sound with every letter of the alphabet.

Next a child learns to look at a word and break it up into its individual sounds (segmentation). Speech pathologists tell us that the smallest unit of sound is called a phoneme; therefore this ability to segment a word and be aware of the phonemes is called phonemic segmentation and phonemic awareness. As a child looks at the word *cat* they must now learn that it is made up of three sounds— "ku," "aa," "tuh." They then start to blend a consonant and a vowel together, for example "ca," "at" ("ku-aa," "aa-tuh"), and also two consonants (consonant blends), such as "pl" and "tr."

Once they have mastered breaking down words the child moves on to learn those that don't fit the simple sound rules. Diphthongs are where two vowels come together to make one sound, for example, "oi" in "oil" and "ou" in "out." Consonant diagraphs are where two letters join to make a different sound, for example, "th," "sh," "ch," "ph," and "gh."

Finally, children have to learn anomalies, where groups of letters sound different from word to word, for example, "**gh**ost," "tou**gh**," "**c**at," "**c**all."

The child uses these newfound rules to sort out the sounds they see, then blends them to make a meaningful word: "c-a-t" means "cat." After this it is just a matter of time, practice, and inherent ability that turns one into a strong reader.

Good adult readers skim through the text using an advanced form of shape recognition helped by cues from the context, the grammar, and pictures. Adults who are fast, natural readers can't understand why dyslexic children switch off the moment they see the print. When you realize how complicated the process is, it is no wonder!

Reading difficulties

The majority of children with reading problems have difficulties with phonemic awareness and segmentation (the ability to recognize and break words into the component sounds). A smaller number of weak readers have trouble with shape recognition, which is the skill needed for effective sight reading. A third group is doubly disadvantaged with problems in both areas (the mixed type).

Children whose weakness is phonemic awareness will do well in the early stages of learning to read when shape recognition is all that is needed. They quickly come unstuck when they have to sound out what they see. Children with this sort of reading problem look at the word *cat* and see only one sound rather than three. When they proceed beyond this simple sounding out, the rules and variations make reading difficult. These children, who have the problem of sounding out, are taught to read by building on their shape recognition skills, then using grammar, context, and pictures to tune into the meaning.

Weak readers who have difficulty with shape recognition are said to have visual perceptual dyslexia. They are slow to develop a sight-word vocabulary and, as they have to sound out each word, their reading is slow. They start out confusing "b's" with "d's," and clever teachers give prompts, for example, the letter "b" has a bat before a ball. The letter "d" has a drum before a stick.

When children have a mixed type of reading difficulty, teachers have to use anything that works.

If it is not already enough to have a specific weakness in reading, in addition there are the problems of ADHD. Even if the words are correctly decoded, poor active working memory lets the meaning get lost by the end of the sentence. With poor self-monitoring the appropriateness of a word in a sentence is not checked. Finally, they spend so much time decoding, unraveling, looking at individual words, and trying to understand the meaning, that the effort is not maintained and they lose interest. With so much mental energy required for so little success, it is no wonder weak readers will make any excuse to avoid heavy literature. (See Chapter 23, "Hints to Help with Reading," and also Appendix XIV, "Computer Programs to Help Learning.")

Mathematics

Problems with mental arithmetic are almost universal in ADHD children and on top of this quite a number have a specific learning weakness in the area of the mechanics of mathematics (dyscalculia). With this problem the child has difficulty sorting out relative size and understanding the processes needed to add, subtract, multiply, and divide, as well as the concepts needed for algebra and other subjects. Dyscalculia is like dyslexia. It is part of the child's makeup and no amount of tutoring will turn the weak student into an advanced mathematician. For some reason specific learning difficulties in math are frequently associated with problems of handwriting.

Learning mathematics

The first step in becoming a mathematician takes place around the age of two and a half years, when little children start to repeat numbers in a meaningless, parrotlike fashion, called rote counting. By the time they arrive in preschool, children have learned to attach meaning to the numbers. With this skill they can look at a picture and count the three fish or look at their fingers and count to 10. This is called correspondence counting. Now they know the relative sizes of numbers, realizing that four is more than three.

Once school starts children learn the basics of addition and subtraction (math operations). Then figures are written in columns, to be added and subtracted. The times tables are memorized, followed by learning multiplication and division. Now they move to fractions, decimals, algebra, geometry, and then on to all the more complicated concepts (abstract numerical reasoning).

Children with ADHD usually have little difficulty in repeating numbers parrot-fashion by rote and can correspondence-count using their fingers to count to 10, but when fingers and objects can no longer be used as a calculator, they are in trouble.

To manage math we need to be organized and to have a good

active working memory. Without this we lose track of what we are adding, borrowing, subtracting, and multiplying, and mental arithmetic is a nonevent.

Many ADHD children have dyscalculia. They are slow to grasp the relative size of figures, to learn tables, to remember the correct sequence of digits, to understand the meaning of mathematical signs, to master fractions, and to comprehend the concepts of higher mathematics. It is sometimes unclear whether there is a pure specific disability in the area of mathematics or whether the problem is mostly inattention and memory. Whatever the cause, the result is the same. Many ADHD children find mathematics is far from fun.

Language problems

At the end of the 1990s there is great interest in the way language is associated with ADHD and reading. Children with ADHD often have a particular pattern of speech and many of the associated problems of reading come from a difficulty in the decoding of language in the brain.

Learning language

In the months before their first birthday a baby's tuneful babble turns to speechlike sounds. Between the ages of one and two they attach meaning to each sound and have a large, single-word vocabulary.

Around the second birthday they learn the relationships between words, and how to put them together in phrases and then sentences. Over the next year they start to add grammar and then to plan and organize their ideas into a simple narrative.

As they leave the toddler years children learn the rules of two-way conversation. They listen, wait, and respond in a socially appropriate way. By school they start to tune in to unspoken cues and know what is and is not acceptable. By the end of primary school, language has become much more complex, such as talking around the subject using innuendo, riddles, and jokes.

The understanding part of speech starts just before the first birthday when they find the word *no* means no. By 14 months they may respond to simple commands such as "point to your nose" or "close the door." After age two, ideas such as "bigger," "smaller," "up," and "down" are taken on board and they start to cope with more than one item of information at a time. From here the child moves on to more abstract concepts, for example, "If you had a dog, a hen, and a fish, which one would have hair?" Finally, they start to understand all the subtleties which are hidden in double meanings, our intonation, and in what we don't quite say.

There is a great difference between the simple question/answer language of the young child, for example, "Show me the fire station," and the language that is used by those who express and comprehend really well, for example, "Why can't you park the car in front of the fire-station door?" Children may be familiar with quite a lot of words and have learned many answers but they may still be quite disabled by their lack of high-level language.

The difficulties with attention, active working memory, and executive control cause most of the concerns with language.

ADHD children don't listen before they respond. They impatiently break into others' conversations. They are disorganized, so their speech frequently slips off track and they skip from one topic to another. With their problems of selectivity they get caught up in unimportant detail, become sidetracked, and miss the big picture. Stories are punctuated by long pauses, "umms," and "ahhs" which often hide a problem of finding the right word. When you ask questions they answer, "Good," "I don't know," or "I can't remember," rather than struggling to organize their substandard speech. When it comes to comprehension ADHD children have problems with sequencing, for example, "before," "after," "yesterday," and "tomorrow."

With these language problems, many ADHD children are unable to maintain a proper two-way conversation. They can't regulate the content to the needs of the listener, so people switch off. This difficulty with the social use of language is referred to as a problem of pragmatic skills (see Chapter 24, "Hints to Help with Language Problems.")

Conclusion

About half of all children with ADHD also have some specific learning weakness in an area such as reading, writing, spelling, or language. On top of this almost all have problems with attention and short-term memory. These problems of specific learning weakness become so intertwined with difficulties of ADHD that we find it hard to see them separately. The exact proportion of the blend may be uncertain, but there is no dispute about the end result. If we don't help children with ADHD they will underfunction for their intellect.

Summary: the learning problems of ADHD

Lack of executive control

■ Poor self-motivation, planning, and use of time (difficulty anticipating, prioritizing, and staying in tune socially).

Poor attention span

■ Inappropriate selection (off tangent, can't see forest for trees).

■ Inadequate self-monitoring (poor checking and quality control).

■ Inability to maintain effort (loses interest, quickly bored, mentally fatigued).

Poor memory

■ Short-term memory (instructions forgotten, half-heard messages).

■ Active working memory (trouble holding several pieces of information in mind, mental arithmetic, speech and reading problems).

The specific learning problems

Reading delay

■ Problems of phonetics (difficulty sounding out words).

■ Problems of sight word reading (difficulty recognizing words by shape).

- A mixed reading problem (both phonetics and sight word reading).

- Problem of comprehension (understanding what is read).

- ADHD reading problems (impulsive, poor self-monitoring, loses meaning due to weak active working memory).

Mathematics weak

- Dyscalculia (poor concept of size, slow to learn tables and master concepts of math).

- ADHD problems with math (loses track, disorganized, poor self-monitoring, sequence difficulty; poor active working memory affects mental arithmetic).

Language problems and ADHD

- Expressive speech (slips off track, loses sequence, use of blocking words, for example "Don't know").

- Social language (interrupts, misanswers, poor eye contact, misses social cues).

- Comprehension (information lost with inattention, poor selectivity, and weak active working memory).

TWENTY-THREE
Hints to Help with Reading

FISH

Many ADHD children also have a developmental reading disorder (dyslexia), which in our experience is usually of hereditary origin. This inheritance follows an interesting pattern in families. If a person has either pure ADHD or pure dyslexia, it usually passes to the next generation in this same form. If ADHD is associated with dyslexia, those that inherit the dyslexia will often have this double trouble.

Reading problems

The way we learn to read was discussed in detail in Chapter 22. There we noted how dyslexia could present in four possible ways:

- ■ A weakness with phonetics (sounding out words).

- ■ A weakness with sight words (recognizing words by shape).

- ■ A mixed reading problem (phonetics and sight words).

■ A weakness with reading comprehension (understanding what is read).

  With these problem areas in mind parents should promote reading by first strengthening the child's strong points, and from this firm foundation then work on the weak points. Here are some of our suggestions.

Ways to encourage sound recognition

■ First teach the child the letters of the alphabet.

■ Next link each letter with its sounds (sound symbol association), for example, the letter "u" sounds "uh."

■ Strengthen this sound symbol skill by associating this letter with pictures that start with the sound, for example, the letter "u" sounds out as "uh," as in "umbrella."

■ The next stage is to memorize the sounds of certain word clusters. These word clusters are the diphthongs ("ae," "ou," "ei," "oo," "ee") and the consonant diagraphs ("ch," "ph," "gh," "th"). These cannot be deciphered by sounding out and can only be mastered by constant practice.

■ Now you must go back to the basic sounds, and teach the child how to blend two together, for example, "tu," "wi," "ca," "wu" and "ft," "lt," "gr," "pl." These give the basic building blocks for creating words.

■ Combinations of letters can now be blended, for example, "tu" → "tuf" → "tuft"; "wi" → "wil" → "wilt."

■ Blending can be helped by using a box framework, which puts each letter of a word in a box, like one sees in a crossword puzzle. This focuses attention on one letter at a time and keeps the sequence in order.

■ Teach the child to see each word as a number of component sounds which come in a set order. To help this they can count out the syllables or tap out the parts they can hear in a word, for example, the word *envelope* (en-vel-ope) has three parts.

■ Teach the child to divide big words into little words, for example, skate-board, post-box, fish-tank, out-side, sun-light, butter-fly.

■ The focus continues on the individual sounds in words. Ask them to isolate the sounds at the beginning, end, and any named position within a word, for example, what is the beginning sound in the word *leg*? "L"-eg. What sound is in the fourth position of *strip*? str-"I"-p. Children can again be helped by presenting words in a box framework. This enables them to focus on each sound, one at a time.

■ As parents we can read, talk, and work with our children to help sort out the sounds of words, but often it takes more than this. Remedial reading tutors can be recommended through a school or a parent support group.

■ Some parents engage a speech pathologist to help improve their child's ability to discriminate sounds. One of many programs used for assessment is the Lindamood Auditory Conceptualization Test. This uses colored blocks to represent units of sound, and through its companion method, the Auditory Discrimination In-depth Remedial Program, the child is trained to segment words in readiness for reading. This strengthens one step in the reading process.

■ The enthusiasm of parents and teachers is important in keeping the child interested in an area that causes such pain.

Ways to encourage word recognition

■ Make up some index cards, each representing one important word (flashcards). Ask the child to view them regularly and introduce more words when the first ones are learnt.

■ Expand their sight vocabulary by teaching lists of phonetic and nonphonetic words in their word families, for example:

| bat | hat | cat | fat | sat | pat | rat | mat |
| sight | light | | might | | tight | | bight |

■ Play word-recognition games with flashcards along the lines of the card game Snap.

■ Certain spelling rules need to be learned, for example the silent "k" ("**k**nock," "**k**nee") and the silent "e" ("chees**e**," "goos**e**").

■ Spelling can be helped using games such as Junior Scrabble.

■ When you are reading to the child, cover the print in mid-story and ask him or her to use the grammar, context, and pictures to guess the next word.

■ The above steps are helpful, but most sight word recognition comes as we read simple stories with our children.

Ways to encourage sound and word recognition

When both phonetic and sight word parts of reading are weak (mixed reading problem), we have to take elements from all the above techniques to help the child's reading. There is usually one part of reading which is stronger, so start by building on this so they can fall back on it. With these children the secret is to go with whatever seems to work. Stress the positives and don't dwell on the negatives.

Ways to help reading comprehension

Children who find reading difficult can spend so much mental energy decoding the words that they miss the meaning. This defeats the purpose as there is no point reading the sentence if we don't understand what it means. Comprehension can be improved by doing the following:

■ Select high-interest books written at the right level for the child.

■ Present reading material in manageable-sized chunks. Don't give them more than they are able to digest.

■ With the correctly sized portions, encourage children to actively think about what they have read and then talk about it before they move on.

■ In the early stages of reading it is often best for the parent to read and ask questions about comprehension as you go along. Stop every now and then so that the child may read a word. As time goes on give him or her longer chunks to read.

■ When the child gets stuck with a word he can't understand, ask him to identify it, based on the grammar and context. Also point out any illustrations to see if they act as a word prompt.

- Choose books carefully—the child will be more motivated if the topic is of interest to him. Start with few words and lots of pictures.

- Don't be afraid to read the same storybook several times. It all helps.

- Don't be in a hurry as you read with your child. Children with reading difficulties need time to work out the words and understand the message.

- As reading becomes stronger children should be encouraged to give you a summary of what they have read.

- Try to have a regular reading time every day, preferably just before bedtime when the house is quiet.

- Keep the reading material well within the child's abilities. When he is succeeding, he feels encouraged and is spurred on to greater things.

- There are now some good computer programs which can be used to develop reading, spelling, writing, and mathematics skills. Some parents swear by these, but we must not forget that even the most expensive program will give more pain than pleasure to children with these learning difficulties (see Appendix XIV for suitable software packages).

- As well as parents helping comprehension, teachers and remedial tutors can work wonders. There are also some speech pathologists who promote, among other techniques, the Lindamood Visualizing and Verbalizing Program. This trains the children to build up a mental picture of what they are reading, then talk about the image in their mind.

- As in all parts of learning, parents are important teachers. Teaching the weak reader can be slow and extremely frustrating, but go gently. Pushing can become a great turnoff for the struggling reader.

A common problem

A weakness in reading is extremely common in the child with ADHD. It is not caused by ADHD, but the presence of ADHD makes it a bigger problem. It is not that these children are lazy, stupid, or poorly taught; they just find the effort of reading gives little pleasure. Where the difficulty is in decoding the sounds, the word-recognition skills must be boosted while the sounds are slowly sorted out. Where word recognition is a problem the phonetic skills of reading should be boosted while flashcards and constant practice improve the recognition skills.

Even when reading appears to be quite good there is often so much effort put into the reading that much of the meaning is missed.

Please be patient. Children with major reading problems frequently continue to have some reading weakness no matter what technique is used. Read, talk, question, and never push too hard. A patient parent is the top teacher.

TWENTY-FOUR

Hints to Help with Language Problems

Language problems are more common with ADHD than most people realize and there seems to be very little published information on practical ways to help. When it came to writing this chapter, we sat down with our speech-pathologist colleagues and pinpointed the main difficulties we saw in our ADHD children. In simple terms there seem to be six problem areas we are trying to help:

■ Speech which slips off on a tangent.

■ Problems with sequencing information.

■ Communication which is socially out of tune.

■ Difficulty comprehending long instructions.

■ Picking up on the wrong part of the message.

■ Difficulty with vague, open-ended questions.

This may look a very learned list, but don't be fooled: it is much easier to describe the problems we see than to make them disappear. Here are our top tips to help.

Ways to keep language on track

Children with ADHD are impulsive, inattentive, and disorganized. When talking they may ramble on, become sidetracked from the topic, or get stuck on some unimportant detail.

■ When their conversation drifts off on a tangent, gently steer them back to the main topic.

■ Use verbal prompts to give conversation structure. "You were telling me about whales. What was it they ate?"

■ Rehearse their language by playing games. "Now you are on the latest TV game show. We each get a topic and you must talk about it for 20 seconds."

■ Take time to listen and appear interested.

■ Encourage clear communication, but never become a nitpicking parent.

Ways to strengthen the presentation of information in sequence

Presenting information in sequence is a particular problem. As the ADHD child tells us about some exciting event, the end may be at the beginning, the middle at the end, and the start is nowhere. It is hard to be an interested listener when language is so jumbled and out of order.

■ First, work out what they meant to say and then gently encourage the child to go back and have another go.

■ Organize the child by asking specific questions. "So what were you doing when it started?" "Who was first to see it?" "What happened next?"

■ Sequence is something we teach our children in our everyday lives. It starts in infancy and continues as we talk our way through changing diapers, starting the car, and making a slice of toast. Keep talking; this allows children to learn about "first," "next," "and then." This brings order to language.

■ As you read a story check that the child is keeping up with all that is happening by asking simple questions. Recap and point out the sequence of the story.

Ways to keep communication socially in tune

Children may be familiar with language but still communicate poorly. For conversation to be in tune we need to listen and then respond appropriately at the right time. We must be sensitive to gesture and tone of voice, then answer in the right way. This use of effective communication in day-to-day life is referred to as the pragmatics of language, which are often weak in ADHD children.

These children tend to interrupt, talk over others, or answer without listening. They go off in their own direction without tuning in to the other party. They misread the social cues and barge in, soon wedging their foot well and truly in their mouths. The pragmatics are further upset as they interrogate, come on too strong, and can't keep eye contact.

- When the two-way conversation is breaking down, gently put the brakes on it. "Wait a minute, you've lost me." "Can we just check that again?"

- Encourage eye contact and tell the child when it is not happening. "Who are you talking to now?"

- Let the child know when they are being annoying or rude, but don't make a big deal of it.

- Role-play polite ways of handling situations, but take it gently and keep it light.

- Playing board and card games helps to develop turn-taking skills.

- Teach the child to wait and not interrupt using a hand signal or timer. Set the timer for the amount of time you want him to wait. When it rings, answer him. Don't keep him waiting too long or he will forget what he wanted to say. Praise him for waiting.

- When you are on the phone, involve the child in a short segment of the conversation. Then firmly ask him to leave.

- Practice greeting each other at home. Coach him to use greetings before visitors arrive. Don't take it personally when he is rude.

- Help him realize the connection between emotion and behavior. Identify the feeling (e.g., anger) and the reason for it (i.e., cause and effect). Let him have a say in what to do next time he is angry. Guide him in his ideas.

- Praise and encourage when communication is clear, appropriate, and on target.

- Never become a negative nagger, who turns a happy, inappropriate speaker into an angry, obstinate mute.

■ These ideas are sound in theory but in most ADHD children the pragmatics are painfully slow to improve.

Ways to encourage comprehension of long instructions

ADHD children are often easily distracted, quickly bored, and have a poor active working memory. This severely limits the amount of information they can cope with at any one time.

■ Before you start speaking gain their attention and make good eye contact.

■ Structure what you say with the first things presented first.

■ Keep it simple; remove unnecessary words.

■ Communicate away from competing noise.

■ Be specific about the messages you wish to get across. This helps the child to be specific about what we demand of him.

■ Complicated information must be broken into short, easily understood chunks.

■ With little children, get down to their eye level and physically hold their hands still when an important message must be transmitted.

■ Use cue words to catch attention. "Ready to listen." "Wait for it."

■ Teach the child to seek clarification if he does not understand. Give constructive feedback when he does so.

■ Be enthusiastic. Say what you mean and mean what you say.

Ways to help the child see the whole picture

When impulse control is poor many ADHD children will respond rapidly to the least important, "wrong" part of a message. This is like a quiz-show contestant who hits the buzzer when only the first quarter of the question has been given. Responding without listening makes the ADHD child particularly irritating to live with.

- Gain eye contact, keep the environment quiet, and sort out what you want to say before you say it.

- Emphasize the key words. "**Point to all** the animals in the picture that **do not** eat the grass."

- As you read at bedtime, talk about the story, perhaps discussing other relevant topics.

- Discuss what you have just been watching on television during the commercial breaks. Make it simple and lighthearted, not an interrogation session.

- Emphasize by action and gesture.

- Take it slowly and check that they have understood what is important before encouraging their response.

Ways to help with vague, open-ended questions

When you are somewhat inattentive, impulsive, and have a poor short-term memory it is easier to work with concrete black-and-white information. Children with ADHD often find it difficult to respond to questions that require reasoning, thinking, planning, and drawing on past experience.

- As you go about your daily activities sometimes try to move away from questions about the here and now and approach events in a more abstract way, for example, "When we fill the car with gasoline, why does it say no smoking on the gas pump?"

- As you read a story, stop before you move to the next page and ask, "What do you think is going to happen next?"

- If the child cannot come up with his own ideas, give him some alternatives, for example, "Do you think it says no smoking on the gas pump because it's bad for your health?"

- Use information from films, videos, current affairs, or children's shows to talk "around" a topic, that is, to use the topic as a basis for other discussions.

- Talk in an interested, casual manner and keep it fun.

■ With all these ideas, there is a fine dividing line between encouraging good communication and annoying the stubborn child so that he won't talk at all.

Acknowledgment: The ideas in this chapter come mostly from Jeanette Cowell and her Speech Pathology colleagues at Royal Alexandra Hospital for Children, Sydney.

TWENTY-FIVE

Hints to Help Handwriting and Coordination

Proficient handwriting is not a skill that comes easily to the ADHD child, so be patient. Aim for legibility and content, not calligraphy. Spend short periods practicing these ideas with the child, and keep it positive and fun.

Helping handwriting

Check posture

Make sure the child is sitting in a chair that supports his back. The table must not be too high or too low as this results in tense shoulders and slouched posture. Elbows should rest comfortably on the table and feet should be placed flat on the floor. It helps if the child leans slightly onto the nonwriting arm, as this stabilizes the paper and allows the writing arm to move freely across the page. Sometimes writing on a surface with a slope, like the old-style school desk, can help sitting position.

Check pencil grip

Some children develop a tense, awkward pencil hold which slows down written work and tires the fingers. A thicker pencil or special plastic grip can help to reduce this tension.

Circular and stick movements

Ask the child to practice counterclockwise and clockwise circular patterns across the page, or while standing at a whiteboard. When seated at the table, use a large sheet of unlined paper working from left to right, then repeat the drawings using paper with widely spaced lines. Eventually introduce the lined paper that is used at school. Also practice drawing straight and oblique lines. Dot-to-dot games are a good activity for pencil control.

Individual letters

Start the child drawing letters which are formed in a counterclockwise movement—a, o, c, e, s, d, g, q—and then move on to the clockwise letters—r, n, m, h, k, b, p. Now string together a continuous row of "n's" and "u's." Stick lines involving vertical, horizontal, and the oblique should also be practiced to make the letters l, t, f, i, x, z. Now the child should move on to letters drawn with a "curvy" movement—v, w, y.

Check the child's sitting posture at the table and his pencil grip as you go. Try not to correct everything at once as this leads to overload and will add to the child's frustration.

Encourage

Handwriting is a complex and skilled task which does not come easily to many ADHD children. Praise and keep them practicing. If teachers are still concerned with the quality of handwriting, ask an occupational therapist for help. Stimulant medication often brings a marked improvement to the quality of written work, particularly in the primary-school age group.

Helping coordination

Children with coordination difficulty will often have problems swinging a bat, throwing and catching balls, tying shoelaces, riding a bike, running with style, and assembling things with their hands. When children see themselves as clumsy they can lose confidence in themselves, and when playing with other children they can be made to feel as if they don't belong.

Parents can help to some extent, but no amount of practice will turn the poorly coordinated child into a top tennis player, football legend, or star of the ballet. To help, take the pressure off them and avoid competitive sports, unless they enjoy them. Here are a few simple suggestions which should be followed in a fun way.

Throwing and catching

Throwing can be practiced by aiming at a large target, such as a rubbish bin, gradually decreasing the size to an empty milk carton. With catching, arms can't coordinate quickly enough to trap the ball. Practice with a large ball, such as an inflatable beach ball, gradually working down until the child can bounce, throw, and catch a tennis ball with reasonable reliability.

Hand movements

Manipulation can be improved through simple activities, such as paper weaving, threading paper clips, and clay work. Construction sets should be encouraged, starting with large pieces and working toward those that are smaller. Simple craft suggestions help coordination, for example putting nails in a piece of wood and weaving string designs. Have a desk area set up with color markers, crayons, and reams of paper permanently on hand.

Bicycle riding

Some children find it hard to master a two-wheeled bike. They go quite well until the move from training wheels and after this it is hard work. Find an open space where steering will be unimportant, and the surface not too tricky. After this there are no shortcuts; it takes hours of running behind with parents holding lightly to the seat. If this gets too hard put the bike away for a few months and then try again.

Swimming

ADHD children find it easy to kick and easy to move their arms but extremely difficult to kick, move arms, and breathe all at the same time. Be reassured—all these children will become proficient swimmers, as long as we don't turn them off water while they are learning.

Swimming lessons that involve a lot of sitting around waiting to participate generally fail. A teacher who insists on perfect style rather than safe swimming may also be unsuccessful. Most ADHD children do best splashing around the pool having fun with a parent. This is better than a whole academy of swimming instructors.

* * *

Note: These ideas come from Neralie Cocks, occupational therapist, the Child Development Unit, Royal Alexandra Hospital for Children, Sydney, and author of the book *Watch Me, I Can Do It! Helping Children Overcome Clumsy and Uncoordinated Motor Skills*. Australia: Simon & Schuster, 1996.

TWENTY-SIX
Debunking the Myths

Parents are bombarded with all sorts of conflicting and often incorrect information. Some misinformation comes from well-meaning friends; however, much is put out by the media and professionals who hold strong opinions but don't understand ADHD. Here is a list of the most commonly promoted myths. We apologize that some of this information has been repeated in other parts of this book, but our aim is for this list to stand alone and be as complete as possible.

■ ADHD is the latest in a long line of trendy fads. It won't be around for long.

This condition was first described almost 100 years ago. In North America the modern view of ADHD has been widely accepted and appropriately treated for well over 20 years. The research-based knowledge of this complex condition increases every year. ADHD is not going to go away; in fact, we will hear more about it, particularly with the growing interest in adult ADHD.

- **The behaviors attributed to ADHD are indistinguishable from those seen in completely normal children.**
  ADHD behaviors occur to some extent in all of us. The difference between ADHD and normal behavior is the degree of the problem and the difficulties it causes. For a diagnosis of ADHD to be made the child must be significantly out of step with the expected behavior for his developmental age and environment. If we compare ADHD with the common condition of depression: all adults feel sad from time to time, but there is a great difference between having a down day and being immobilized by deep depression.

- **These children need nothing more than a bit of firm discipline.**
  ADHD is not a problem of poor discipline. You can be as punitive as you like, but the problem will continue. The danger of heavy discipline is the creation of a resentful, oppositional child.

- **ADHD is a lame excuse for poor parenting.**
  Those with no knowledge of ADHD are quick to blame parents. Most parents have tried all the usual techniques and met nothing but failure. The child with ADHD has a biological condition which is influenced by the actions of parents but not caused by poor parenting.

- **ADHD is predominantly a condition of the children of affluent North American parents.**
  This is often quoted, but is untrue. ADHD is a strongly hereditary condition which can drag clever parents and children down the social and financial scale. More of the affluent population will attend expensive clinics, but this is due to their ability to pay, not the lack of need in all classes. The incidence of ADHD appears to be approximately the same in most countries and races. Unfortunately the professionals in some regions do not choose to open their eyes and recognize the condition.

- **Where family dysfunction exists, this condition needs treatment, not ADHD.**
  Many of our parents also suffer ADHD. This affects their impulse control, social skills, and the ability to be receptive to the needs of their partners. As a result the presence of ADHD in adults increases the risk of stress, dysfunction, and breakup in their relationships. ADHD fathers or mothers may then pass the gene to one or more of their children.

  Family dysfunction does not cause the ADHD in an affected child, but inconsistent, stressed, dysfunctional parents can greatly increase the problem. Dysfunction and ADHD often coexist. Both problems require help but it is often more successful to treat the ADHD than the entrenched difficulties of a dysfunctional adult relationship.

■ Mothers of ADHD children often have a history of postnatal depression, problems of bonding, and failure of attachment. These mothers need psychological help to repair their emotional wounds—their child does not need the diagnosis of ADHD.

This is frequently quoted by the old-fashioned breed of "talking-cure" psychiatrists. Postnatal depression is extremely common, affecting about 15 percent of all mothers, and seems to lead to no increase in the incidence of ADHD. Most of the parents we see bond with and form a close attachment to their ADHD child even though it is difficult to be close to an infant who may be irritable, demanding, and sleepless. Relationship and emotional difficulties do not cause ADHD, but the problems of ADHD are often more troublesome when upset parents have only a low charge left in their emotional batteries.

■ The increased risk of ADHD in adopted and fostered children comes from problems of attachment to an infant who is not the natural child of the parents.

Adopting and fostering in the 1990s is a high-risk occupation. This has nothing to do with bonding or attachment; it results from the origin of those children who currently present for adoption. In these days of better education, contraception, termination, and support for sole parenthood, few children come up for adoption. A high proportion of those available come from disorganized, impulsive, learning-disabled, or drug-abusing backgrounds. Genetic risk factors in this group bring a higher incidence of many problems, one of the most common being ADHD.

■ A child who is not excessively overactive cannot have ADHD.

This is an idea which went out of date 20 years ago. Though a number of ADHD children are restless and fidgety, many show no obvious signs of overactivity. The condition described in this book involves inadequate self-monitoring of behavior and attention-based problems of learning and memory. These cause difficulties in education, home behavior, and maintaining relationships. The focus on overactivity is out-of-date and unhelpful.

■ ADHD is a short-term condition which will pass if untreated.

In the 1970s we used the term "Hyperactivity" to describe the behavior of the busy child who usually calmed down around the age of seven years.

Most of these "hyperactive" children in fact had ADHD and though the hyperactive behavior seemed to settle at seven years, the problems of learning and behavior continued. In the 1980s it was believed that children outgrew ADHD in their early teens and at this point medication should be suspended. Certainly most ADHD adolescents become better at self-monitoring their behavior, but the problems of academic underachievement usually continue.

In the days when medication was thought unnecessary in high school, many children underfunctioned academically or became dropouts. It is now recognized that ADHD needs to be taken seriously right through the school years, in college-level studies, and for many, right through life.

■ The behaviors of ADHD must be obvious in all areas of the child's life. If he can behave in the doctor's office or concentrate on their favorite computer game, the diagnosis is not valid.
Many academic papers on ADHD, especially those from Europe, state that the behavior and attentional problems must show in home, school, and all other situations. Though this is usually true, there is a certain amount of selectivity in the presentation of ADHD. The most distractible of all children may be fully focused when guarding the goal at football and may appear attentive in the one-on-one situation of the psychologist's office.

■ A child cannot have ADHD if he sleeps well.
Most ADHD children sleep well, though two specific sleep problems are more common in these children. A significant proportion of ADHD children have difficulty settling to sleep in the evening, and a small number are amazingly early risers. In between settling and rising, they may be restless, but most sleep well.

■ If a child is diagnosed as having dyslexia, intellectual disability, Oppositional Defiant Disorder, Conduct Disorder, or depression, they do not have ADHD.
In the early 1980s this was one of the most damaging mistakes made by professionals. If a child had one of these "comorbid" or associated conditions, those of us who recognized and treated the ADHD were said to have made an incorrect diagnosis. At that time in Australia the organizations interested in specific learning difficulties (e.g. dyslexia) only addressed the reading problem—and misunderstood the behavior, attention, and memory difficulties. Psychiatrists would diagnose Oppositional Defiant Disorder, which was often treated with little success, while the major

and treatable problems of ADHD were missed. Over half of all children with ADHD will have associated comorbid conditions, and all these problems need help.

■ Preservatives and colorings in the diet cause ADHD.
In the mid 1970s it was believed that diet and "Hyperactivity" were closely related. The modern literature states that diet does not cause ADHD: this is a biological, brain-based, highly hereditary condition. A small number of children with ADHD may have worse behavior when exposed to certain artificial or natural food chemicals. Most researchers and the parent support group, CHADD, do not promote diet as a major part of treatment.

■ Sugar makes many ADHD children hyperactive.
Carefully controlled trials have shown no relationship between high sugar levels and the behaviors of children with or without ADHD.

■ The standard disciplinary techniques used for all our children work equally well on those with ADHD.
This is often stated by experts who have no real understanding of ADHD. The ADHD child tends to act before he thinks, and is rarely satisfied with usual rewards. It is not that the normal techniques are entirely ineffective; they need to be modified and our expectations lowered.

■ Multimodal treatment is a must. Help is needed in education, remediation, behavior management, occupational therapy, and parent support before medication is considered.
"Multimodal" was the buzzword of the late 1980s. Treating many areas sounds good but in reality this sort of help is expensive and hard to find. As you work with ADHD it is obvious that some interventions are much more important than others.

As this book is being written, a large U.S. multicenter study is looking at the effect of single and multiple treatments for ADHD. This impressive study will not report for some time, but provisional impressions suggest that without first introducing medication, nothing works very well. You will hear us say many times in this book, "You have to reach before you can teach."

■ Stimulant medication is new, controversial, and largely unproven.
These drugs are not new; they have been on the market for over 40 years. At the last count there were 155 quality research papers which documented their safety and effect. Most studies have looked at the action of stimulant medication in school-age children (147). There are a few pa-

*pers on the benefits of these drugs in preschoolers (five) and the action
of stimulants in adults (currently three—but the number is increasing
rapidly).*

■ **Ritalin and dextroamphetamine are sedative drugs which make
children quiet and compliant.**
*Drugs such as Valium, alcohol, and barbiturates sedate and numb. Stim-
ulants enhance brain action, sharpen focus, and normalize. Stimulant
medication has a minimal effect on those whose brains are functioning
normally. In ADHD these drugs allow the brain to self-monitor and self-
regulate behavior. Sedatives rob children of their natural abilities; stimulants allow children to use their talents to the fullest.*

■ **ADHD children are being given "speed," which is increasing the
problems of addiction in society.**
*"Speed" is the street name for methylamphetamine, also known as "ice."
This drug, favored by addicts, is related to, but not the same as, Ritalin
or dextroamphetamine. A codeine headache pill comes from the same
family as heroin, and the painkillers used by dentists are related to cocaine. Ritalin is related to "speed" but they are different.*

*Stimulants have been studied for 40 years and do not cause addiction
in those treated for ADHD. There is evidence that children correctly
treated with stimulants improve in education, relationships, and self-
esteem, all factors which lessen the risk of drug abuse in later life.*

■ **Every child and adult, with or without ADHD, could learn and
behave better if given stimulants.**
*This is a half-truth put about by those keen to confuse and to discredit
stimulants. If an ADHD child responds, the change is dramatic and affects every aspect of his life. If non-ADHD children or adults are trialed
on stimulants, it is likely that neither they nor anyone around them
would notice any difference. But if these same non-ADHD people were
trialed in the test laboratory, slight gains may be measured on some research instruments.*

*It is misleading to claim that stimulants work equally well whether
there is ADHD or not. There is a great difference between an unnotice-
able but statistically significant laboratory measurement and the complete
turnaround of a troubled life.*

*The Olympic Committee views the bronchodilator inhalers we puff
for asthma as performance-enhancing drugs. In carefully controlled
laboratory tests nonasthmatics will marginally improve their lung
function. Though this has caused these preparations to be banned from*

high-level competition, I doubt if you or I would notice the slightest difference if we took a puff of Ventolin. With stimulants, it is also a question of the degree of response.

■ **Stimulants have a high placebo effect; many of the reported benefits are only in the parents' minds.**
This view is often put forward by antimedication psychiatrists who quote a single study which is now 17 years out-of-date. The most recent research shows a remarkably low placebo response when compared with the high levels of reported benefit. Even if parents are incorrect in the belief that medication is helping, this will not continue for long. Most parents and teachers who see gains report these benefits for many years.

■ **Stimulants are frequently used by pushy parents as a "clever pill" to make a slow child perform better than they are naturally able.**
We worry when a previously undiagnosed child presents for treatment in the weeks prior to final exams. Our policy is to prescribe on-going medication only when both parents and teachers report significant gains. Some parents do request stimulants for children who we don't believe have major ADHD. Often the degree of response that follows our treatment shows that the parents, not the doctor, were right.

■ **Stimulants are "mother's little helper" given for the benefit of the parent, not the child.**
This claim causes immense anger in the parents we deal with. It implies that they choose to dope their normally exuberant child due to their lack of tolerance. Stimulants do not sedate; they enhance and normalize the child with ADHD. They bring an underfunctioning child up to potential and improve the communication, happiness, and quality of relationships.

■ **Stimulants remove the "spark" from ADHD children and rob them of creativity.**
This frequently stated claim comes from a controversial author, not from any research-based work on ADHD. Many of the most creative people in history were probably adults with ADHD. But many more might have been equally famous if the disorganization of ADHD had not blocked the expression of their genius. Children with ADHD often run in unproductive circles, like a dog chasing its tail. Once we introduce organization, attention, and the ability to communicate, this allows the expression of creativity.

■ **Stimulants make ADHD children depressed.**
The problems of academic and social failure that follow ADHD increase

the risk of depression. Proper treatment hopefully reduces this risk. If medication is introduced in too large a dose or the wrong preparation prescribed, some children become withdrawn, teary, and emotional. This is a transient reaction to the introduction of a medication, which passes within four hours. This is not depression.

■ To be sure medication is genuinely effective, all ADHD children should be trialed blindly with similar-looking tablets, some with active medication, and others with an inactive placebo substance. This would prevent parents claiming to see benefits that don't exist.

In our experience, when medication works well, everyone is in no doubt. Parents not only know that a drug is helping their child, they quickly become aware as the levels drop off at four hours.

Those who push this placebo approach insult the intelligence of the average parent. If it were depression we were treating you would not alternate between periods on Prozac and others on a sugar tablet. In the case of depressed adults, if, following treatment, they state their lives have turned around, it would be unethical to challenge this belief with sugar tablets.

■ Medication should be given only during school hours, not in the afternoon, on weekends, or during school holidays.

If ADHD predominantly affects attention and learning there is no need for out-of-school treatment (except to cover homework). If treatment brings big benefits to behavior, relationships, and self-esteem, it must be given throughout the full day, weekends, and holidays. Home and family relationships are of immense importance and must never be disadvantaged by underusing a safe and effective form of treatment.

■ Stimulants build up in the body and for the sake of safety all children should have regular periods off medication.

The effect of a dose of Ritalin or dextroamphetamine is already at half its power by four hours and mostly out of the body by 12 hours. These are extremely short-acting drugs which do not have cumulative side effects. Ten years ago we worried about the possibility of treatment slowing physical growth. This no longer is an issue.

■ If the medical treatment of ADHD is working there will be no further crises or difficult days at school.

Some schools complain that our treatment is unsuccessful because the child has a blowup or bad day. The nature of ADHD is to have good and bad patches. Even the best-managed child will stumble into some crises, but hopefully these are far fewer than before treatment. Our job is to help parents and children as best we can; we don't perform miracles.

■ ADHD children frequently sell these amphetamines on the street.

Antistimulant lobby groups come to the media with many such stories. The claims sound impressive but when investigated are usually based on hearsay and are without evidence. Whether genuine or not, these claims and the resultant uproar by U.S. columnists and talk-show hosts have made this a big issue. Those of us who work with ADHD adolescents recognize that street sale is possible, but believe it is exceptionally rare. Ritalin and dextroamphetamine do have a street value, but the main amphetamine of interest to addicts is methylamphetamine ("speed" or "ice").

■ Children become dependent on their stimulant medication and use it as a prop.

Most adolescents with ADHD recognize that when they take their medication they function better at school and get into less trouble. Despite this they see medication as an imposition and need a nudge if it is going to be taken regularly. They do not become dependent—these tablets are seen as an annoying necessity which they usually resent.

■ If the diagnosis of ADHD is incorrect, stimulants will still be effective.

When stimulants work well, they bring an immense change to both learning and life. These major benefits are only seen in ADHD and could not occur if a diagnosis was incorrect.

■ The drugs Ritalin and dextroamphetamine are identical and only one needs to be trialed.

These two drugs are not identical in either their pharmacological action or their clinical effect. Our view is out of step with mainstream U.S. opinion, but we believe, where possible, both should be tried, followed by prescription of the one that best suits the individual. When we look at the data from our comparative trials with younger children, approximately 20 percent of parents believe both drugs to be identical, while 80 percent see one as superior.

■ There is current controversy surrounding the condition ADHD and its treatment.

There is no doubt that ADHD exists and that the modern treatments are both safe and effective. The research findings are so conclusive now that there is no controversy, just residual pockets of ignorance.

■ There is uncertainty regarding the long-term safety of stimulant
drugs.
*The question of long-term safety was recently put to an expert panel at
the last Annual Scientific Meeting of CHADD (the U.S. parent support
group). The consensus opinion from the main researchers was entirely
favorable. After 40 years of use there is absolutely no evidence of any
long-term problems. There is, however, no research that has conclusively
shown long-term benefits. These are presumed but as yet have not been
scientifically established.*

■ As ADHD is not a life-threatening condition, medication should
be greatly restricted in its use.
*ADHD is not as obvious as leukemia or kidney failure, but it is still a se-
rious, debilitating condition. It robs children of their education, wrecks
relationships, and often produces school dropouts with little esteem and
chips on their shoulders. The results of underestimating the seriousness
of ADHD lead to major problems in the present and possibly in the next
generation.*

Appendices

APPENDIX I

The Criteria for Diagnosing Attention Deficit Hyperactivity Disorder (DSM-IV 1994)

A. Either (1) or (2)

1. Six (or more) of the following symptoms of **inattention** have persisted for at least 6 months to a degree that is maladaptive and inconsistent with developmental level:

Inattention
   (a) often fails to give close attention to details or makes careless mistakes in schoolwork, work, or other activities
   (b) often has difficulty sustaining attention in tasks or play activities
   (c) often does not seem to listen when spoken to directly
   (d) often does not follow through on instructions and fails to finish schoolwork, chores, or duties in the workplace (not due to oppositional behavior or failure to understand instructions)
   (e) often has difficulty organizing tasks and activities
   (f) often avoids, dislikes, or is reluctant to engage in tasks that require sustained mental effort (such as schoolwork or homework)
   (g) often loses things necessary for tasks or activities (e.g. toys, school assignments, pencils, books, or tools)
   (h) is often easily distracted by extraneous stimuli
   (i) is often forgetful in daily activities

2. Six (or more) of the following symptoms of **hyperactivity-impulsivity** have persisted for at least 6 months to a degree that is maladaptive and inconsistent with developmental level:

Hyperactivity
   (a) often fidgets with hands or feet or squirms in seat
   (b) often leaves seat in classroom or in other situations in which remaining seated is expected
   (c) often runs about or climbs excessively in situations in which it is inappropriate (in adolescents or adults, may be limited to subjective feelings of restlessness)
   (d) often has difficulty playing or engaging in leisure activities quietly
   (e) is often "on the go" or often acts as if "driven by a motor"
   (f) often talks excessively

Impulsivity
   (g) often blurts out answers before questions have been completed
   (h) often has difficulty awaiting turn
   (i) often interrupts or intrudes on others (e.g. butts into conversations or games)

B. Some hyperactive-impulsive or inattentive symptoms that caused impairment were present before age 7 years.

C. Some impairment from the symptoms is present in two or more settings (e.g. at school [or work] and at home).

D. There must be clear evidence of clinically significant impairment in social, academic, or occupational functioning.

E. The symptoms do not occur exclusively during the course of a Pervasive Developmental Disorder, Schizophrenia, or other Psychotic Disorder and are not better accounted for by another mental disorder (e.g. Mood Disorder, Anxiety Disorder, Dissociative Disorder, or a Personality Disorder).

Code based on type:

314.01 Attention Deficit Hyperactivity Disorder, Combined Type: if both Criteria A1 and A2 are met for the past 6 months

314.00 Attention Deficit Hyperactivity Disorder, Predominantly Inattentive Type: if Criterion A1 is met but Criterion A2 is not met for the past 6 months

314.01 Attention Deficit Hyperactivity Disorder, Predominantly Hyperactive-Impulsive Type: if Criterion A2 is met but Criterion A1 is not met for the past 6 months

Coding note: For individuals (especially adolescents and adults) who currently have symptoms that no longer meet full criteria, "In Partial Remission" should be specified.

314.9 Attention Deficit Hyperactivity Disorder not otherwise specified

This category is for disorders with prominent symptoms of inattention or hyperactivity-impulsivity that do not meet criteria for Attention Deficit Hyperactivity Disorder.

APPENDIX II

The Criteria for Diagnosing Oppositional Defiant Disorder
(DSM-IV 1994)

A. A pattern of negativistic, hostile, and defiant behavior lasting at least 6 months, during which four (or more) of the following are present:

    (1) often loses temper
    (2) often argues with adults
    (3) often actively defies or refuses to comply with adults' requests or rules
    (4) often deliberately annoys people
    (5) often blames others for his or her mistakes or misbehavior
    (6) is often touchy or easily annoyed by others
    (7) is often angry and resentful
    (8) is often spiteful or vindictive

Note: Consider a criterion met only if the behavior occurs more frequently than is typically observed in individuals of comparable age and developmental level.

B. The disturbance in behavior causes clinically significant impairment in social, academic, or occupational functioning.

C. The behaviors do not occur exclusively during the course of a Psychotic or Mood Disorder.

D. Criteria are not met for Conduct Disorder, and, if the individual is age 18 years or older, criteria are not met for Antisocial Personality Disorder.

Reprinted with permission from the *Diagnostic and Statistical Manual of Mental Disorders*, Fourth Edition. American Psychiatric Association, Washington, DC, 1994.

APPENDIX III

The Criteria for Diagnosing Conduct Disorder (DSM-IV 1994)

A. A repetitive and persistent pattern of behavior in which the basic rights of others or major age-appropriate societal norms or rules are violated, as manifested by the presence of three (or more) of the following criteria in the past 12 months, with at least one criterion present in the past 6 months:

Aggression to people and animals
(1) often bullies, threatens, or intimidates others
(2) often initiates physical fights
(3) has used a weapon that can cause serious physical harm to others (e.g. a bat, brick, broken bottle, knife, gun)
(4) has been physically cruel to people
(5) has been physically cruel to animals
(6) has stolen while confronting a victim (e.g. mugging, purse snatching, extortion, armed robbery)
(7) has forced someone into sexual activity

Destruction of property
(8) has deliberately engaged in fire setting with the intention of causing serious damage
(9) has deliberately destroyed others' property (other than by fire setting)

Deceitfulness or theft
(10) has broken into someone else's house, building, or car
(11) often lies to obtain goods or favors or to avoid obligations (i.e. "cons" others)
(12) has stolen items of nontrivial value without confronting a victim (e.g. shoplifting, but without breaking and entering; forgery)

Serious violations of rules
(13) often stays out at night despite parental prohibitions, beginning before age 13 years
(14) has run away from home overnight at least twice while living in parental or parental surrogate home (or once without returning for a lengthy period)
(15) often truant from school, beginning before age 13 years

B. The disturbance in behavior causes clinically significant impairment in social, academic, or occupational functioning.

C. If the individual is age 18 years or older, criteria are not met for Antisocial Personality Disorder.

Specify type based on age at onset:
Childhood-Onset Type: onset of at least one criterion characteristic of Conduct Disorder prior to age 10 years

Adolescent-Onset Type: absence of any criteria characteristic of Conduct Disorder prior to age 10 years

Specify severity:

Mild: few if any conduct problems in excess of those required to make the diagnosis and conduct problems cause only minor harm to others (e.g. lying, truancy, staying out after dark without permission)

Moderate: number of conduct problems and effect on others intermediate between "mild" and "severe" (e.g. stealing without confronting a victim, vandalism)

Severe: many conduct problems in excess of those required to make the diagnosis **or** conduct problems cause considerable harm to others (e.g. forced sex, physical cruelty, use of a weapon, stealing while confronting a victim, breaking and entering)

Reprinted with permission from the *Diagnostic and Statistical Manual of Mental Disorders*, Fourth Edition. American Psychiatric Association, Washington, DC, 1994.

APPENDIX IV

The Criteria for Diagnosing Tic and Tourette's Disorder (DSM-IV 1994)

Diagnostic criteria for 307.21 Transient Tic Disorder

A. Single or multiple motor and/or vocal tics (i.e. sudden, rapid, recurrent, non-rhythmic, stereotyped motor movements or vocalizations).

B. The tics occur many times a day, nearly every day for at least 4 weeks, but for no longer than 12 consecutive months.

C. The disturbance causes marked distress or significant impairment in social, occupational, or other important areas of functioning.

D. The onset is before age 18 years.

E. The disturbance is not due to the direct physiological effects of a substance (e.g. stimulants) or a general medical condition (e.g. Huntington's disease or postviral encephalitis).

F. Criteria have never been met for Tourette's Disorder or Chronic Motor or Vocal Tic Disorder.

Specify if:
Single Episode or **Recurrent**

Diagnostic criteria for 307.22 Chronic Motor or Vocal Tic Disorder

A. Single or multiple motor or vocal tics (i.e. sudden, rapid, recurrent, nonrhythmic, stereotyped motor movements or vocalizations), but not both, have been present at some time during the illness.

B. The tics occur many times a day nearly every day or intermittently throughout a period of more than 1 year, and during this period there was never a tic-free period of more than 3 consecutive months.

C. The disturbance causes marked distress or significant impairment in social, occupational, or other important areas of functioning.

D. The onset is before age 18 years.

E. The disturbance is not due to the direct physiological effects of a substance (e.g. stimulants) or a general medical condition (e.g. Huntington's disease or postviral encephalitis).

F. Criteria have never been met for Tourette's Disorder.

Diagnostic criteria for 307.23 Tourette's Disorder

A. Both multiple motor and one or more vocal tics have been present at some time during the illness, although not necessarily concurrently. (A *tic* is a sudden, rapid, recurrent, nonrhythmic, stereotyped motor movement or vocalization.)

B. The tics occur many times a day (usually in bouts) nearly every day or intermittently throughout a period of more than 1 year, and during this period there was never a tic-free period of more than 3 consecutive months.

C. The disturbance causes marked distress or significant impairment in social, occupational, or other important areas of functioning.

D. The onset is before age 18 years.

E. The disturbance is not due to the direct physiological effects of a substance (e.g. stimulants) or a general medical condition (e.g. Huntington's disease or postviral encephalitis).

Reprinted with permission from the *Diagnostic and Statistical Manual of Mental Disorders*, Fourth Edition. American Psychiatric Association, Washington, DC, 1994.

APPENDIX V

The Criteria for Diagnosing Major Depressive and Manic Episodes, (Adult Criteria) (DSM-IV 1994)

Criteria for Major Depressive Episode

A. Five (or more) of the following symptoms have been present during the same 2-week period and represent a change from previous functioning; at least one of the symptoms is either (1) depressed mood or (2) loss of interest or pleasure.

Note: Do not include symptoms that are clearly due to a general medical condition, or mood-incongruent delusions or hallucinations.

  (1) depressed mood most of the day, nearly every day, as indicated by either subjective report (e.g. feels sad or empty) or observation made by others (e.g. appears tearful). **Note:** In children and adolescents, can be irritable mood.

  (2) markedly diminished interest or pleasure in all, or almost all, activities most of the day, nearly every day (as indicated by either subjective account or observation made by others)

  (3) significant weight loss when not dieting or weight gain (e.g. a change of more than 5% of body weight in a month), or decrease or increase in appetite nearly every day. **Note:** In children, consider failure to make expected weight gains

  (4) insomnia or hypersomnia nearly every day

  (5) psychomotor agitation or retardation nearly every day (observable by others, not merely subjective feelings of restlessness or being slowed down)

  (6) fatigue or loss of energy nearly every day

  (7) feelings of worthlessness or excessive or inappropriate guilt (which may be delusional) nearly every day (not merely self-reproach or guilt about being sick)

  (8) diminished ability to think or concentrate, or indecisiveness, nearly every day (either by subjective account or as observed by others)

  (9) recurrent thoughts of death (not just fear of dying), recurrent suicidal ideation without a specific plan, or a suicide attempt or a specific plan for committing suicide

B. The symptoms do not meet criteria for a Mixed Episode.

C. The symptoms cause clinically significant distress or impairment in social, occupational, or other important areas of functioning.

D. The symptoms are not due to the direct physiological effects of a substance (e.g. a drug of abuse, a medication) or a general medical condition (e.g. hypothyroidism).

E. The symptoms are not better accounted for by Bereavement, i.e., after the loss of a loved one, the symptoms persist for longer than 2 months or are characterized by marked functional impairment, morbid preoccupation with worthlessness, suicidal ideation, psychotic symptoms, or psychomotor retardation.

Criteria for Manic Episode

A. A distinct period of abnormally and persistently elevated, expansive, or irritable mood, lasting at least 1 week (or any duration if hospitalization is necessary).

B. During the period of mood disturbance, three (or more) of the following symptoms have persisted (four if the mood is only irritable) and have been present to a significant degree:
   (1) inflated self-esteem or grandiosity
   (2) decreased need for sleep (e.g. feels rested after only 3 hours of sleep)
   (3) more talkative than usual or pressure to keep talking
   (4) flight of ideas or subjective experience that thoughts are racing
   (5) distractibility (i.e. attention too easily drawn to unimportant or irrelevant external stimuli)
   (6) increase in goal-directed activity (either socially, at work or school, or sexually) or psychomotor agitation
   (7) excessive involvement in pleasurable activities that have a high potential for painful consequences (e.g. engaging in unrestrained buying sprees, sexual indiscretions, or foolish business investments)

C. The symptoms do not meet criteria for a Mixed Episode.

D. The mood disturbance is sufficiently severe to cause marked impairment in occupational functioning or in usual social activities or relationships with others, or to necessitate hospitalization to prevent harm to self or others, or there are psychotic features.

E. The symptoms are not due to the direct physiological effects of a substance (e.g. a drug of abuse, a medication, or other treatment) or a general medical condition (e.g. hyperthyroidism).

Note: Maniclike episodes that are clearly caused by somatic antidepressant treatment (e.g. medication, electroconvulsive therapy, light therapy) should not count toward a diagnosis of Bipolar I Disorder.

Criteria for Mixed Episode

A. The criteria are met both for a Manic Episode and for a Major Depressive Episode (except for duration) nearly every day during at least a 1-week period.

B. The mood disturbance is sufficiently severe to cause marked impairment in occupational functioning or in usual social activities or relationships with others, or to necessitate hospitalization to prevent harm to self or others, or there are psychotic features.

C. The symptoms are not due to the direct physiological effects of a substance (e.g. a drug of abuse, a medication, or other treatment) or a general medical condition (e.g. hyperthyroidism).

Note: Mixed-like episodes that are clearly caused by somatic antidepressant treatment (e.g. medication, electroconvulsive therapy, light therapy) should not count toward a diagnosis of Bipolar I Disorder.

Reprinted with permission from the *Diagnostic and Statistical Manual of Mental Disorders*, Fourth Edition. American Psychiatric Association, Washington, DC, 1994.

APPENDIX VI
ADHD Rating Scales

Barkley and DuPaul

Child's name: _____

Age _____ Grade _____ Completed by: _____

Circle the number in the one column which best describes the child.

	Not at all	Just a little	Pretty much	Very much
1. Often fidgets or squirms in seat	0	1	2	3
2. Has difficulty remaining seated	0	1	2	3
3. Is easily distracted	0	1	2	3
4. Has difficulty awaiting turn in groups	0	1	2	3
5. Often blurts out answers to questions	0	1	2	3
6. Has difficulty following instructions	0	1	2	3
7. Has difficulty sustaining attention to tasks	0	1	2	3
8. Often shifts from one uncompleted activity to another	0	1	2	3
9. Has difficulty playing quietly	0	1	2	3
10. Often talks excessively	0	1	2	3
11. Often interrupts or intrudes on others	0	1	2	3
12. Often does not seem to listen	0	1	2	3
13. Often loses things necessary for tasks	0	1	2	3
14. Often engages in physically dangerous activities without considering consequences	0	1	2	3

Reproduced by permission from R. A. Barkley, *Attention-Deficit Hyperactivity Disorder: A Handbook for Diagnosis and Treatment,* New York: Guilford Press, 1990.

Edelbrock Child Attention Problems

We have found this form useful in screening for the child who has major inattention but who does not have hyperactivity. Such a child is often missed by the other questionnaires, which, in our experience, mainly pick up the hyperactive-impulsive ADHD child.

Child's name _____

Child's age _____   Filled out by: _____   Child's sex M [ ]   F [ ]

Directions: Below is a list of items that describe pupils. For each item that describes the pupil now or within the past week, check whether the item is Not True, Somewhat or sometimes true, or Very or often true. Please check all items as well as you can, even if some do not seem to apply to this pupil.

	Not true	Somewhat or sometimes true	Very or often true
1. Fails to finish things he/she starts			
2. Can't concentrate, can't pay attention for long			
3. Can't sit still, restless or hyperactive			
4. Fidgets			
5. Daydreams or gets lost in his/her thoughts			
6. Impulsive or acts without thinking			
7. Difficulty following directions			
8. Talks out of turn			
9. Messy work			
10. Inattentive, easily distracted			
11. Talks too much			
12. Fails to carry out assigned task			

Please feel free to write any comments about the pupil's work or behavior in the last week.

_____

_____

_____

_____

Reproduced by permission from C. S. Edelbrock. The Pennsylvania State University. For more information see R. A. Barkley in Appendix XVI.

APPENDIX VII

Tests of Persistence, Memory, and Attention

The Paired Associate Learning Test

Here the examiner helps the child to learn some items of paired information. An example might be, "In London Zoo there is an elephant, in Sydney there is a camel, and in New York there is a lion." As this information is taught, a visual stimulus is shown, for example a picture of a lion, and the child responds, "New York."

This is a test of attention, short-term memory, and visual auditory learning. As it goes on, incorrect responses are put right, so that the child keeps learning all the time. The test is continued until the child achieves a perfect run or until a predetermined number of attempts has been made.

Paired association is a demanding task which is particularly useful when studying the effects of medication. When drugs are being trialed, this test helps document the best preparation and correct dose.

The Continuous Performance Test

This is a computer task. The child sits at the keyboard watching the screen. He is instructed to press the space bar as soon as a special sequence of letters is seen on the screen. Alternatively the child is asked to stop himself from pressing the space bar when a specified target appears. The child is scored on the number of successful targets he spots, those he misses, and his reaction time.

The Continuous Performance Test has been standardized on thousands of children both with and without ADHD. This gives a reasonably objective measure of impulsivity and, to a lesser extent, distractibility. It is of particular value when diagnosis is obscure or in documenting the effect of medications. There are a number of commercially marketed versions of this test, each differing in its convenience, expense, and ease of scoring.

APPENDIX VIII
Quantitative EEG (QEEG)—Brain Mapping

The standard electroencephalograph (EEG) measures brain electrical activity. Tracings are made from electrodes placed around the skull. The resulting paper record is read by a neurologist who will note major abnormalities which suggest conditions such as epilepsy. This technique is too crude to pick up the subtle electrical differences present in ADHD.

QEEG brings computer technology to this old EEG method. Quantitative diagnostic features are extracted from the standard EEG, cortical-evoked potentials and brainstem-evoked potentials to give an objective statistical evaluation of brain electrical activity. The results of this evaluation are represented by colorful maps and tables of data which highlight areas of activity that stand out as different from what would be expected for the average child of the same age.

This technique is available for children aged six years and older. It is noninvasive, painless, and unlike other scans, can cope with some movement in the restless child.

The technique

Brainwaves are recorded from electrodes placed at standardized sites on the head. The electrodes are attached to a special cap which is fitted on the child. Data are collected in two main ways. Firstly, data are recorded from EEG tracings as the child sits quietly with eyes closed. Next, brainwave activity is collected while the child is presented with various stimuli. Flashes of light, checkerboard-pattern reversals, and tones or beeps are presented while measuring cortical-evoked potentials. Loud clicks at 80 decibels are used while recording brainstem auditory-evoked responses.

One expects to see certain patterns of response in the "average" child or adult. The areas where the dysfunctions occur give an indication of the anatomical and functional integrity of the brain. It must be remembered that QEEG picks up those electrical messages that reach the outside of the skull. This may not accurately measure subtle activity deep in the brain.

In the child with ADHD, there is a slowing of the brainwaves which appears most prominently in the frontal regions. In children with specific reading disability certain patterns of functioning are observed which deviate from normal. Children with primarily auditory difficulties show different patterns to those with poor visual processing.

By providing a quantitative estimate of the maturational level of the brain and adequacy of information processing, one can document changes that come with medication and maturity.

QEEG is relatively new to the fields of pediatrics and neurology. There are a number of clinics worldwide utilizing this in the assessment of ADHD, reading disability, and various psychiatric disorders.

Current research is focusing on the use of QEEG in cognitive disorders, both in children and in adults. We have no doubt that this has a place in the diagnosis and monitoring of ADHD. Whether this is just another pointer toward the diagnosis or something far more specific, time will tell.

APPENDIX IX
Brain Imaging in ADHD

Positron Emission Tomography (PET) and Single Photon Emission Computed Tomography (SPECT)

For a long time researchers have tried to pinpoint the seat of ADHD in the brain. Initially they used the brain-wave test, electroencephalogram (EEG), but this mainly detected abnormalities in the superficial layers called the cortex and did not tap into the deeper parts. Methods such as CT and basic MRI scans showed up the anatomy of the brain, but in ADHD there were no significant lesions. In the late '80s new types of scans became available which could reflect brain function. The SPECT (Single Photon Emission Computed Tomography) and PET (Positron Emission Tomography) scans look at blood flow and metabolism in different parts of the brain. This is able to indicate the areas that are being relatively over- or underused.

With SPECT and PET scans, it was found that regions located centrally and deep within the brain (called the caudate nuclei/striatum) were the most consistent areas of underfunction in ADHD, as were the frontal lobes and the posterior periventricular region. In the SPECT and PET scans, blood flow and glucose metabolism to these areas were low, which reflected reduced activity.

The striatum, frontal lobes, and posterior periventricular region are thought to be important for controlling and directing what we attend to. As well as having complex connections with each other, these three regions are richly interconnected with the sensory cortices—the regions of the brain that receive sensations. They act as a gate, allowing important information to register but filtering out the noise of interfering information which may prevent us from focusing on relevant messages. Because these "gates" are underfunctioning in ADHD they are unable to filter out the hundreds of unimportant stimuli that arrive every minute. This constant, unchecked bombardment shows up in the sensory cortices. They become flooded with incoming messages and can be seen on the SPECT scan as high blood flow to the areas that receive vision and sound, the occipital and temporal lobes.

When methylphenidate (Ritalin) was administered to ADHD children, its effect showed up on Xenon-133 SPECT as a redistribution of blood flow in the brain. Methylphenidate appeared to increase the level of function of the underperfused regions at the striatum, posterior periventricular region, and, to a lesser extent, the frontal lobes. This normalization allowed the clutter of irrelevant messages to be screened out and was seen as a reduction in blood flow to the vision and hearing areas. This filtering of irrelevant distraction suppresses reflex responses and helps concentration.

More recent PET and SPECT scans have mostly (but not all) backed up these differences in regional metabolism. The changes in function described after the administration of Ritalin have not been conclusively replicated. (See Appendix XV, "PET and SPECT scans.")

Magnetic Resonance Imaging (MRI)

Functional scans such as the SPECT and PET scans involve a high level of ionizing radiation. This has limited studies in children using these imaging techniques. Now there is a new modality for this purpose, the functional MRI. In an MRI scan, a picture is constructed from the radio signal that is emitted from atoms in the brain when a magnetic field is applied to it. There is no ionizing radiation involved. Previously MRIs were used only to study the anatomy of the brain. Now, by superimposing the change in the composition of the radio signal caused by changes in metabolic activity, it is possible to map the regions of the brain involved in executing a particular clinical activity. Currently, studies using functional MRI are investigating the areas of the brain that are involved when children are engaged in a continuous performance task (CPT). Early evidence indicated that this task, which requires inhibition of responses, is localized to the prefrontal lobes. A preliminary study using blood oxygen level-dependent functional MRI (called B.O.L.D.), reports hypoperfusion (lack of activity) in the right caudate area, which was reversed by Ritalin treatment.

Another new use for the MRI is for detailed volumetric measurements of specific regions of the brain. Extensive and time-consuming measurements of the head and body of the caudate nucleus and the frontal lobes have supported their role in ADHD. The volumetric measurements of the caudate nucleus indicate a smaller right caudate nucleus in ADHD boys in comparison to normal boys. The usual "right-greater-than-left" caudate asymmetry was reversed in ADHD. The greater the reversal, the greater the difficulty experienced by the subject in inhibiting responses on clinical testing. The frontal region of the brain and the cerebellum were smaller and the normal age-related changes in the volumes of the caudate and lateral ventricals were absent in this condition. Abnormalities of the corpus callosum, which houses nerve fibers running between the frontal lobes and striatum, have also been reported on volumetric MRI. The side of greatest difference in the caudate volumes has not always been consistent, nor has the specific region involved in the corpus callosum.

That there is still conflict in the results obtained by different research studies may be accounted for by differences in the subtypes of ADHD, the presence of comorbid disorders and methodological differences inherent in the use of these PET, SPECT and MRI scans.

In summary
The findings from structural and functional studies are in agreement with each other and with earlier neurocognitive studies in the localization of ADHD to the fronto-striatal circuit. There are rich dopaminergic connections between the frontal/prefrontal regions and the caudate/striatal regions. Advances in the field of neuroscience suggest that executive functions—inhibition, intention, and active working memory—are the cognitive deficits underlying ADHD. The frontal and striatal circuits have been demonstrated to subserve such executive functions, this being shown by a wide body of researchers (see Appendix XVI, Goldman-Rakic).

APPENDIX X
Interpreting the *WISC-III*

This is a test of overall intelligence for children aged six to 16 years. The child's level of intelligence is represented by a number, called the intelligence quotient or IQ. On the Wechsler Intelligence Scale for Children-III (WISC-III), mean IQ is 100 with a standard deviation of 15. If a child is of normal intelligence, his IQ would therefore be anywhere from 85 (low-average IQ) to 115 (high-average IQ).

The WISC-III comprises 13 subtests, which, broadly speaking, can be divided into those which reflect verbal ability (information, comprehension, arithmetic, similarities, and vocabulary subtests) and those which measure nonverbal intelligence by assessing intelligence without placing great demands on the child's language skills (picture completion, picture arrangement, block design, object assembly, and coding subtests). These two clusters give rise to the verbal IQ and performance IQ respectively. The remaining three subtests—digit span, mazes, and symbol search—are supplementary.

Factor analysis of the WISC-III resulted in the formation of four Kaufman factors: *verbal comprehension*, *perceptual organization*, *processing speed*, and *freedom from distractibility*. The verbal comprehension factor is computed from the information, comprehension, similarities, and vocabulary subtests. The perceptual organization factor is calculated using the picture completion, picture arrangement, object assembly, and block design subtests. These derived quotients from the Kaufman factors are a "purer" reflection of a child's verbal and nonverbal intelligence.

The speed with which a child can process information is reflected by the processing speed factor, which is derived from the coding and symbol search subtests.

The subtests arithmetic and digit span are used to form the Kaufman factor called freedom from distractibility. The freedom from distractibility factor is low in some children with ADHD, but this is by no means diagnostic, as performance on these three subtests is affected by reasons other than inattention.

Wechsler Intelligence Scale for Children-III

VERBAL SCORES

+ • Information

+ • Similarities

• × Arithmetic

+ • Vocabulary

+ • Comprehension

× Digit span

PERFORMANCE SCORES

° Picture completion

° Picture arrangement

° • Block design

° Object assembly

* Coding
  Mazes

* Symbol search

× Places greatest demands on ability to concentrate
• Most related to general intellectual ability
+ Best reflects the understanding and application of verbal knowledge
° Measures the interpretation and organization of visually presented material
* Requires ability to attend and to coordinate eye and hand function at speed

APPENDIX XI

Neuropsychology Tests

These are tests of frontal lobe function used in assessing children with ADHD.

The Stroop Color-Word Test

This is an interference test requiring the child to filter out and inhibit competing information before responding correctly. The speed with which the child completes the test is recorded.

There are three different tasks:

1. Reading a list of color names (red, blue, and green) which are printed in black ink.

2. Naming the color of different-colored patches.

3. Naming the color of ink which is used to print a list of words. The words are themselves color names which may be the same as or different to the color of ink in which they are printed.

The Trail Making Test

A test of speed and of mental flexibility.

Part A: A dot-to-dot task where the child is asked to connect a series of numbered circles (1-2-3 . . .)

Part B: The child is asked to connect circled numbers alternating with circled letters of the alphabet (1-A-2-B-3 . . .)

The Wisconsin Card Sorting Test

A test of problem-solving ability and of mental flexibility.

The child is required to sort a deck of cards. The cards contain geometric designs which can be sorted into different sets according to their common features, such as shape, color, and number of squares.

A computerized version is available where groups of cards to be sorted appear on the screen and the child clicks the mouse at the cards he thinks belong together.

APPENDIX XII

The Stimulants—Small-Print Side Effects

Every drug has the potential to cause side effects in some people. The common problems associated with stimulants are covered in Chapter 14. Some of the less common side effects are:

Dizziness

Strange feelings and fears

Drowsiness

Nail biting

Talking less

Talking more

Tingling of fingers

"Edgy"—ill at ease

Obsessional

Minor increases in heart rate and blood pressure

Lowered convulsive threshold

Psychosis (at the high dose—reversible)

If you are ever concerned about a significant side effect, the stimulants must be stopped immediately and the prescribing doctor contacted. Almost every action we take in life has some minute degree of risk. We are justified in prescribing medication as long as the benefits greatly outweigh any possible dangers.

APPENDIX XIII

Food Intolerance—Treatment Through Diet

The foods we now eat have been selected using trial and error over thousands of years. As we all are different in our sensitivities, it is no surprise that many people are intolerant to some foods.

Food allergy vs. food intolerance

When the body reacts to a protein in food, this is called a food allergy. When the body is sensitive to some of the chemical constituents, this is a food intolerance. *Food allergies* are more frequent in infants and young children, particularly those who suffer from eczema. The most common problems come from proteins in eggs, cow's milk, and peanuts, though others may also cause difficulties.

Allergy typically presents with an immediate local reaction around the mouth, sometimes followed by vomiting, hives, swelling, breathing difficulties, and even shock. With allergic reactions, antibodies are found in the blood and the offending protein can be isolated by a skin-prick test (a series of possible products are placed on the forearm, the skin surface is broken, and a local reaction is noted when there is allergy).

Food intolerance is a much less clear-cut condition. Many foods may be involved, and the response is dose-related and frequently cumulative. A little of the offending product may be taken from one food, more from another, and finally the body is tipped over the edge by eating some from a totally different source. This makes intolerance hard to diagnose as the food that tips the balance may not be the main culprit. The reaction may be to one or a number of chemicals, either natural or added.

The timing of reactions can be anywhere from 30 minutes up to 24 hours or more after eating a problem food. Where behavior is affected by diet, this is generally due to food chemical intolerance, not allergy.

The symptoms of intolerance can include irritability, tenseness, out-of-control or out-of-character behavior, overactivity, headaches, abdominal discomfort, mouth ulcers, irritable bowel symptoms, rhinitis, leg cramps, and recurrent hives. Symptoms can occur in isolation or in any combination. The possibility of intolerance is much higher when there is a significant family history of similar symptoms. Diagnosis of intolerance can only be made by a carefully monitored elimination diet followed by selective challenges to isolate the problem foods. Food sensitivity is highly individual and no one diet is suitable for every child.

Food intolerance—four problem areas

Salicylates These are a family of plant chemicals found naturally in many fruits, vegetables, nuts, herbs and spices, jams, honey, yeast extracts, tea and coffee, juices, beer, and wines. They are also present in flavorings (such as peppermint), perfumes, scented toiletries, eucalyptus oils, and some medications, such as aspirin, which is a member of the salicylate family.

Amines These come from protein breakdown or fermentation. Large amounts are present in cheese, chocolate, wines, beer, yeast extracts, and fish products. They are also found in certain fruits and vegetables, for example bananas, avocados, tomatoes, and broad beans.

MSG (monosodium glutamate) Glutamate is a building block of all proteins and is found naturally in most foods. In its free form (not linked to protein) it enhances the flavor of foods. This is why foods rich in natural MSG are used in many meals, for example tomatoes, cheeses, mushrooms, stock cubes, sauces, meat extracts, and yeast extracts. Pure MSG can also be used as an additive to increase the flavor of soups, sauces, Asian cooking, and snack foods.

Food additives People who are sensitive to natural food chemicals are usually also sensitive to one or more of the common food additives. These are either preservatives which are used to keep foods fresh or colorings which are added to make foods look more attractive. The ones most likely to cause reactions are:

Colors

Artificial	102, 107, 110, 122 to 129, 133, 142, 151, 155
Natural (annatto)	160b

Preservatives

Sorbates	200 to 203
Benzoates	210 to 213
Sulfites	220 to 228
Nitrates, nitrites	249 to 252
Propionates	280 to 283
Antioxidants	310 to 321

Flavor Enhancer

Monosodium glutamate (MSG)	621

Most other additives are unlikely to cause reactions, for example anticaking agents, bleaches, emulsifiers, mineral salts, propellants, food acids, sweeteners, thickening agents, vegetable gums, and vitamins.

A simplified guide to diet
Doctors and dietitians who specialize in the area of diet and behavior claim much greater success than is accepted by the general medical population. They believe that others fail through a misunderstanding of the correct way to create an individual elimination diet and challenges which are inappropriate.

The list that follows is given as a guide. It should be supervised by a specialist in diet. In the initial weeks it is often suggested that milk and wheat be eliminated also. They will be the first to be reintroduced after the elimination phase.

The diet should be followed strictly for two to six weeks. Challenges may commence after five symptom-free days. If there is no improvement in four weeks, contact your dietitian. If six weeks have passed without change, diet is unlikely to be the answer.

Food chemicals in vegetables
Low: White potatoes (peeled), green beans, iceberg lettuce, brussels sprouts, cabbage, celery, chives, dried beans, dried peas, leeks, lentils, parsley, shallots.

Very high: Tomatoes, broccoli, broad beans, cauliflower, eggplant, gherkins, olives, mushrooms, spinach.

Food chemicals in fruit

Low: Pears (ripe, peeled), pears (canned in sugar syrup).

Very high: Citrus fruits (oranges, mandarins, lemons), raisins, pineapple, kiwifruit, berry fruits, prunes, tomatoes, stone fruits, avocadoes, dates.

Note: Salicylates are highest in unripe fruit and this decreases with ripening. Amines increase with ripening in fruits that go mushy, for example bananas and avocados. Much of the natural chemical is close to the skin, which is why we suggest pears be peeled.

Food chemicals in meat, chicken, fish, and eggs

Low: Beef, chicken (fresh, no skin), fish (fresh white), eggs, lamb, rabbit, veal.

Very high amines: Anchovies, fish roe, dried, pickled, salted, smoked fish, smoked meat and chicken, canned tuna.

Very high salicylates, amines, and MSG: Meat pies, salami, sausages, seasoned meats, chicken.

Note: Browning, grilling, or charring meat will increase natural amine levels.

Food chemicals in dairy foods and soy products

Low: Butter, cream, fresh cheeses, milk, plain whole milk yogurt, soy milk.

Very high: All tasty cheeses, soy sauce.

Food chemicals in drinks

Low: Water, milk, soy milk, decaffeinated coffee, carob powder, unpreserved lemonade (not more than a glass per week).

Very high salicylates only: Cordials and soft fruit-flavored drinks, tea, peppermint tea.

High amines only: Cocoa powder, chocolate-flavored drinks.

High salicylates and amines: Cola drinks, orange juice, tomato juice, vegetable juice.

Food chemicals in herbs, spices, and condiments

Low: Chives, garlic, parsley, poppy seeds, saffron, sea salt, shallots, vanilla.

Very high: Meat extracts, soy paste, soy sauce, vinegar, tandoori, gravies, pastes (fish, meat, tomato), all sauces, stock cubes, tomato sauce, yeast extracts.

Food chemicals in cereals, grains, and flours

Low: Rice, wheat flour, rolled oats, arrowroot, barley, buckwheat, cornstarch, malt, rice flour, rice cereals (plain), sago, soy flour, rye flour, wheat, wheat cereals (plain).

High salicylates only: Cornflakes, cornmeal, breakfast cereals with honey.

High amines only: Breakfast cereals with cocoa.

High salicylates and amines: Cereals with fruit, nuts, and coconut.

Food chemicals in jams, spreads, sugars, and sweets
Low: Golden Syrup, sugar, toffee, caramel, carob, malt extract.

Very high salicylates: Honey, jams, licorice, mint-flavored sweets, peppermints, chewing gum, fruit-flavored sweets and ices.

Very high amines only: Chocolate (all), cocoa.

Food chemicals in fats and oils
Low: Butter, ghee, margarine (unpreserved, no antioxidant), safflower oil (no antioxidant), sunflower oil (no antioxidant).

High: Coconut oil, olive oil, sesame oil, walnut oil.

Food chemicals in nuts, snacks, and crisps
Low: Cashews (raw, up to 10 per day), plain potato chips.

Very high salicylates only: Fruit flavors, honey flavors, granola bars.

Note: Cheese flavors have high levels of amines and MSG; spicy flavors have high levels of salicylates, amines, and MSG.

Toiletries
Allowed: Unflavored toothpaste, plain, lightly perfumed soaps, shampoos, and moisturizers; sunscreen without PABA; unscented roll-on deodorants; unscented laundry detergents and soap powders.

Avoid: Flavored, colored toothpaste; mouthwashes; strongly perfumed products; perfumes; aftershave lotions; aerosol deodorants and hair sprays; sunscreen with PABA; fabric conditioners; washing and ironing sprays. (*Note:* Some ADHD children eat toothpaste.)

Challenges
Once behavior has improved with diet, that is just the first step. Challenges are needed before the offending food or foods can be isolated.

After five consecutive symptom-free days, milk and wheat are reintroduced, if they have been removed from the elimination diet. Following this, the dietitian advises on the order of the challenges. Usually salicylates are top of the list followed by amines, MSG, Propionates (Code 280, 283), Sorbates (200, 203), and so on.

It can take up to 48 hours before there is any reaction, so it is important to be patient; otherwise all the effort can be lost. Three symptom-free days must be allowed before moving to the next challenge. The eventual aim is to provide an individual diet tailored for the particular child, which gives the maximum benefit for the least restrictions.

Acknowledgment: The information in this section comes from the work of Dr. Anne Swain, Dr. Velencia Soutter, and Dr. Robert Loblay of the Allergy Unit, Royal Prince Alfred Hospital, Sydney. This group and their publications act as a resource to dietitians around Australia.

The Food Lists are an extract from their comprehensive book, *Friendly Food: the Complete Guide to Avoiding Allergies, Additives and Problem Chemicals,* Sydney: Murdoch Books, 1991. (Distributed by Gordon and Gotch, 68 Kingsgrove Road, Belmore NSW 2192.)

Computer Programs to Help Learning

There was a time when ADHD children refused to load anything educational into their computers. But modern software has changed all that. Now those once boring programs have hi-tech sound, arcade-style gimmicks, and enough hype to hold the attention.

With the help of a group of computer-interested teachers and parents, we have come up with the following list of software which is both fun and educational.

Title	Grade Range	Age Range
Reading/Language		
1. Reader Rabbit 2 Deluxe	Preschool to Grade 2	4 to 7 years
2. Reader Rabbit 3 Deluxe	Grade 1 to Grade 4	5 to 9 years
3. JumpStart Kindergarten	Kindergarten to Grade 3	5 to 8 years
4. Interactive Reading Journey	Preschool to Grade 2	5 to 7 years
5. Living Books Framework (Just Grandma and Me, Just Me and My Dad)	Preschool to Grade 2	5 to 7 years
6. JumpStart Adventures	Grade 2 to Grade 4	7 to 9 years
7. Reading Blaster	Grade 2 to Grade 4	7 to 9 years
8. Reading Blaster	Grade 4 to Grade 7	9 to 12 years
9. Super Solvers Treasure Mountain!	Grade 2 to Grade 4	7 to 9 years
10. Super Solvers Midnight Rescue!	Grade 3 to Grade 8	7 to 10 years
Spelling		
1. My First Incredible, Amazing Dictionary	Preschool to Grade 2	3 to 7 years
2. Ready to Read and Write 2	Grade 1 to Grade 4	6 to 9 years
3. Word Quest for Windows	Kindergarten to Grade 6	5 to 11 years
4. Children's Dictionary	Grade 2 to Grade 7	7 to 12 years
5. Superspell	Grade 2 to Adult	7 to Adult
6. Carmen Sandiego Word Detective	Grade 3 to Grade 9	8 to 14 years
Mathematics		
1. Millie's Math House	Preschool to Grade 2	3 to 7 years
2. Math Blaster Junior	Preschool to Grade 2	3 to 7 years
3. James Discovers Maths	Preschool to Grade 2	3 to 7 years
4. Math Rabbit	Preschool to Year 4	3 to 9 years
5. Math Blaster: In Search of Spot	Grade 1 to Grade 6	6 to 11 years
6. Math Workshop	Grade 2 to Grade 6	7 to 11 years
7. Super Solvers Outnumbered	Grade 2 to Grade 8	7 to 13 years
8. Math Blaster: Secret of the Lost City	Grade 3 to Grade 8	8 to 13 years

Title	Grade Range	Age Range
Keyboard Skills		
1. JumpStart Typing	Preschool to Grade 2	4 to 8 years
2. Type Quick	Grade 3 to Adult	8 to Adult
3. Ultra Key	Grade 4 to Grade 10	9 to 15 years
Story Writing		
1. Mavis Beacon Teaches Typing for Kids	Preschool to Grade 3	4 to 8 years
2. Storybook Theatre Bundle	Grade 1 to Grade 4	6 to 9 years
3. Storybook Weaver	Grade 1 to Grade 6	6 to 11 years
4. Creative Writer 2	Grade 3 to Grade 10	8 to 15 years
Oral Language/Spoken English		
1. Triple Play Plus!	Grade 4 to Grade 12	9 to 17 years

Early Childhood Activities

These games help the young child to develop prereading and premathematics skills in readiness for school.

1. Cat in the Hat	Preschool to Grade 2	3 to 6 years
2. Candy Land	Preschool to Grade 1	3 to 6 years
3. The Backyard	Preschool to Grade 1	3 to 6 years
4. The Tree House	Preschool to Grade 2	5 to 8 years
5. Thinkin' Things	Preschool to Grade 2	5 to 8 years

APPENDIX XV
Abstracts From the Latest Research Literature

The diagnosis of ADHD

Blondis, T.A., Accardo P.J. & Snow, J.H. "Measures of attention deficit. Part 1: Questionnaires," *Clinical Pediatrics*, 28:222-228, 1989.
Looks at questionnaires which may be used to supplement office evaluation of hyperactivity, noting that most have deficiencies.

Blondis, T.A., Accardo, P.J. & Snow, J.H. "Measures of attention deficit. Part 2: Clinical Perspectives and test interpretation," *Clinical Pediatrics*, 28:268-276, 1989.
Discusses difficulties in the interpretation of psychological testing arising from the significant overlap between ADHD and associated learning disabilities.

Sleator, E.K. & Ullmann, R.K. "Can the physician diagnose hyperactivity in the office?" *Pediatrics*, 67:13-17, 1981.
Emphasizes the importance of historical information gathered from parents together with teacher reports as reliable aids in the diagnostic process. Eighty percent of children subsequently diagnosed to be hyperactive showed exemplary behavior in the office.

Adolescent ADHD/ follow-up studies

Biederman, J., Faraone, S., Milberger, S., Curtis, S. et al. "Predictors of persistence and remission of ADHD into adolescence: Results from a four-year prospective follow-up study." *Journal of the American Academy of Child & Adolescent Psychiatry*, 35(3): 343-51, March 1996.
Remission can equally occur in childhood as in adolescence. A positive family history, a presence of comorbidity, and environmental adversity are related to persistence of ADHD.

Biederman, J., Faraone, S., Milberger, S., et al. "A prospective four-year follow-up study of attention-deficit hyperactivity and related disorder," *Archives of General Psychiatry*, 53 (5):437-46, May 1996.
ADHD children are at risk of developing impairments in cognitive, interpersonal, school, and family functioning with increasing age.

Mantzicopoulos, P.Y. & Morrison, D. "A comparison of boys and girls with attention problems: Kindergarten through second grade," *American Journal of Orthopsychiatry*, 64(4):522-33, October 1994.
Children with predominantly attentional problems in kindergarten were rated as having an increasing degree of behavior problems as they progressed to the higher grades, presumably due to the greater demands put on them.

Lie, N. "Follow-ups of children with Attention Deficit Hyperactivity Disorder," *Acta Psychiatrica Scandinavica*, 85:Suppl 4-40, 1991.
Comprehensive review of follow-up findings in adolescents and adults who were previously diagnosed with childhood ADHD. It finds that pure ADHD without conduct disorder has a good prognosis in relation to psychopathology, antisocial behavior, alcohol and illicit drug abuse, education, and occupation.

ADHD with hyperactivity versus ADHD without hyperactivity

Wolraich, M.L., Hannah, J.N., Pinnock, T.Y., Baumgaertel, A., et al. "Comparison of diagnostic criteria for attention-deficit hyperactivity disorder in a county-wide

sample," *Journal of the American Academy of Child & Adolescent Psychiatry*, 35(3): 319-24, March 1996.
DSM-IV criteria are better at characterizing the heterogeneity that is within ADHD.

Hynd, G.W., Lorys, A.R., Semrud-Clikeman, M., et al. "Attention deficit disorder without hyperactivity: A distinct behavioral and neurocognitive syndrome," *Journal of Child Neurology*, 6:S35-S41, 1991.
Describes the entity of ADHD without hyperactivity—how it differs in its academic and behavioral features from ADHD with hyperactivity.

Cantwell, D.P. & Baker, L. "Attention deficit disorder with and without hyperactivity: A review and comparison of matched groups," *Journal of the American Academy of Child and Adolescent Psychiatry*, 31:432-438, 1992.
Describes ADHD with hyperactivity as more impulsive, distractible, aggressive, and suffering greater peer rejection than ADHD without hyperactivity. The latter has an increased incidence of learning disorder, pure language disorder, depression, and "sluggish" tempo.

ADHD and intellectual disability
Handen, B.L., Breaux, A.M., Janosky, J., et al. "Effects and noneffects of methylphenidate in children with mental retardation and ADHD," *Journal of the American Academy of Child & Adolescent Psychiatry*, 31(3):455-61, May 1992.
In children with intellectual disability, the proportion who respond to Ritalin (64 percent) is close to that in children of normal IQ.

ADHD in Preschoolers
Mayes, S.D., Crites, D.L., Bixler, E.O., et al. "Methylphenidate and ADHD: Influence of age, IQ and neurodevelopmental status," *Developmental Medicine & Child Neurology*, 36(12):1099-107, December 1994.
Ritalin is effective in preschoolers.

ADHD in other cultures
Leung, P.W., Luk, S.L., Ho, P., et al. "The diagnosis and prevalence of hyperactivity in Chinese schoolboys," *British Journal of Psychiatry*, 168(40):486-96, April 1996.
An epidemiological study of Hong Kong Chinese schoolboys indicating that the prevalence of ADHD is similar across Western and Eastern cultures.

Drugs used in the management of ADHD
Fox, A.M. & Rieder, M.J. "Risks and benefits of drugs used in the management of the hyperactive child," *Drug Safety*, 9:38-50, 1993.
A detailed look at the use of stimulants and antidepressants.

Gadow, K.D. "Pediatric psychopharmacotherapy: A review of recent research," *Journal of Child Psychology and Psychiatry*, 33:153-195, 1992.
Focuses on recent developments in drug therapy for childhood disorders including ADHD and learning disability.

Stimulant medication in ADHD
Wilens, T.E. & Biederman, J. "The stimulants," *Psychiatric Clinics of North America*, 15:1912-22, 1992.

Jacobvitz, D., Sroufe, L.A., Stewart, M. & Leffert, N. "Treatment of attentional and hyperactivity problems in children with sympathomimetic drugs: A comprehensive review," *Journal of the American Academy of Child and Adolescent Psychiatry,* 29:677-688, 1990.
The above two articles provide comprehensive coverage of the use of stimulant medication in ADHD.

Rapport, M.D., Carlson, G.A., Kelly, K.L., et al. "Methylphenidate and desipramine in hospitalized children: I. Separate and combined effects on cognitive function," *Journal of the American Academy of Child & Adolescent Psychiatry,* 32(2):333-42, March 1993.
Both medications improved short-term memory and visual problem solving. Only Ritalin improved vigilance.

Growth and the stimulants
Gittelman Klein, R. & Mannuzza, S. "Hyperactive boys almost grown up III. Methylphenidate effects on ultimate height," *Archives of General Psychiatry,* 45:1131-1134, 1988.
Ritalin did not compromise final height, even though it may suppress growth during active treatment. Compensatory growth rate follows discontinuation of stimulant therapy.

Tricyclic Antidepressants
Ambrosini, P.J., Bianchi, M.D., Rabinovich, H. & Elia, J. "Antidepressant treatments in children and adolescents: II. Anxiety, physical and behavioural disorders," *Journal of the American Academy of Child and Adolescent Psychiatry* 32:483-493, 1993.
Evaluates the efficacy as well as side effects of the antidepressants in children and adolescents.

Riddle, M.A., Geller, B. & Ryan, N. "Another sudden death in a child treated with Desipramine," *Journal of the American Academy of Child and Adolescent Psychiatry,* 32:792-797, 1993.
Includes new information as well as references to all previous case reports and commentaries on this topic.

Clonidine & Guanfacine
Steingard, R., Biederman, J., Spencer, T., et al. "Comparison of clonidine response in the treatment of attention-deficit hyperactivity disorder with and without comorbid tic disorders," *Journal of the American Academy of Child & Adolescent Psychiatry,* 32(2):350-3, March 1993.
One of the few papers investigating the role of clonidine in ADHD with or without tic symptoms. ADHD symptoms improved in 70 percent of children studied. Tic symptoms also improved in 70 percent of children studied.

Walkup, J.T., *AACAP News* (The newsletter of the American Academy of Child and Adolescent Psychiatry), Sept/Oct. 1995, pp. 11-12.
A review of four cases of sudden death reported to the U.S. FDA.

Hunt, R.D., Arnsten, A.F. & Asbell, M.D. "An open trial of guanfacine in the treatment of attention-deficit hyperactivity disorder," *Journal of the American Academy of Child & Adolescent Psychiatry,* 34(1):50-4, January 1995.
Thirteen outpatients diagnosed with ADHD were treated with guanfacine. Preliminary results indicate its usefulness in hyperactivity and probably also inattention.

Chappell, P.B., Riddle, M.A., Scahill, L., et al. "Guanfacine treatment of comorbid attention-deficit hyperactivity disorder and Tourette's syndrome: Preliminary clinical experience," *Journal of the American Academy of Child & Adolescent Psychiatry*, 34(9): 1140-6, September 1995.
Guanfacine improved both tics and the symptoms of ADHD. Guanfacine improved omission and commission errors on the continuous performance test (a measure of distractibility and impulse control). Sedation and headaches were its commonest side effects.

Moclobemide (Aurorix)
Priest, R.G., Gimbrett, R., Roberts, M. & Steinert J. "Reversible and selective inhibitors of monoamine oxidase A in mental and other disorders," *Acta Psychiatrica Scandinavica, Supplementum*, 386:40-3, 1995.
Includes reference to the few studies on the use of Moclobemide in ADHD.

Trott, G.E., Friese, H.J., Menzel, M. & Nissen, G. "Use of Moclobemide in children with attention deficit hyperactivity disorder," *Psychopharmacology*, 106:S134-S136, 1992.
One of the first reports on the usefulness of Moclobemide (Aurorix) for the treatment of 12 children with ADHD in an open trial. This documented an improvement in parent assessment of behavior, computer-based assessment of attention and memory function, and overall reduction in frontal lobe delta activity on brain mapping. Moclobemide appeared to be well tolerated with only vague gastrointestinal symptoms reported.

Allergy, food additives, and hyperactivity
Conners, C.K. *Food additives and hyperactive children*, New York: Plenum Press, 1980.
Reports only a 5 percent success rate in the dietary management of hyperactive behaviors.

Egger, J., Stolla, A. & McEwen, L.M. "Controlled trial of hyposensitisation in children with food-induced hyperkinetic syndrome," *Lancet*, 339:1150-1153, 1992.
An exclusion diet (which is nutritionally inadequate and requires vitamin and mineral supplementation) and rechallenge are required to properly diagnose food intolerance in hyperkinesis. This group of researchers previously found that about 60 percent of children with hyperkinetic syndrome responded to an oligoantigenic diet. Because of the difficulties associated with such restriction diets, hyposensitization using a series of injections was suggested as a means of treating the substantiated food-intolerance-induced hyperactivity. This study has created considerable discussion and controversy.

McGee, R., Stanton, W.R. & Sears, M.R. "Allergic disorders and attention deficit disorder in children," *Journal of Abnormal Child Psychology*, 21:79-88, 1993.
Large study of 1,037 children which calls into question the relationship between attention deficit hyperactivity disorder and allergic disorders.

Wolraich, M.L., Lindgren, S.D., Stumbo, P.J., et al. "Effects of diets high in sucrose or aspartame on the behavior and cognitive performance of children," *The New England Journal of Medicine*, 330:301-307, 1994.
Cane sugar (sucrose) was not found to affect children's behavior or cognitive function.

Feingold, B.F. *Why your child is hyperactive*. New York: Random House, 1975.
The original book giving rise to the Feingold diet.

Language-learning disabilities in ADHD

Javorsky, J. "An examination of youths with attention-deficit/hyperactivity disorder and language learning disabilities: A clinical study," *Journal of Learning Disabilities*, 29(3):247-58, May 1996.
Children with learning disabilities alone or learning disabilities in association with ADHD shared common deficits in phonology and syntax. Children with pure ADHD did not have these deficits.

Branch, W.B., Cohen, M.J. & Hynd, G.W. "Academic achievement and attention-deficit/hyperactivity disorder in children with left- or right-hemisphere dysfunction," *Journal of Learning Disabilities*, 28(1):35-43, 64, January 1995.
It has been suggested that attention and arithmetic calculation are localized to the right hemisphere of the brain as opposed to reading or spelling, which are left hemisphere functions. Neuropsychological testing in this study does not support this.

Reading

Rowe, K.J. & Rowe, K.S. "The relationship between inattentiveness in the classroom and reading achievement (part A): Methodological issues & (part B): An explanatory study," *Journal of the American Academy of Child & Adolescent Psychiatry*, 31(2):349-68, March 1992.
The difficulties facing researchers examining the relationship between behavioral disorders and learning difficulties are highlighted and discussed. The authors found that inattentiveness in the classroom had a strong negative effect on children's reading achievement, as well as on their attitudes toward reading and reading-related activity at home. These findings were independent of socioeconomic status, age, and gender.

Pennington, B.F., Van Orden, G.C., Smith, S.D., et al. "Phonological processing skills and deficits in adult dyslexics," *Child Development*, 61:1753-1778, 1990.

Siegel, L.S., Ryan, E.B. "Development of grammatical-sensitivity, phonological, and short-term memory skills in normally achieving and learning disabled children," *Developmental Psychology*, 24:28-37, 1988.
The above two references look at the underlying deficits in reading disability.

Spelling and Handwriting

Resta, S.P. & Eliot, J. "Written expression in boys with attention deficit disorder," *Perceptual & Motor Skills*, 79(3 Pt 1):1131-8, December 1994.
Weaknesses in writing, copying, and composition are demonstrated in boys with ADHD.

Goswami, U. "Annotation: Phonological factors in spelling development," *Journal of Child Psychology and Psychiatry*, 33:967-975, 1992.
This paper emphasizes the importance of phonological ability in spelling proficiency.

Major, S.T. "Written language," in C.T. Wren (ed.), *Language learning disabilities: Diagnosis and remediation*. Aspen Systems Corporation, Maryland, 1983 (pp 297-325).
Discusses the underlying processes necessary for proficient spelling and handwriting and includes a framework for assessment and remediation of written language problems.

Sandler, A.D., Watson, T.E., Footo, M., et al. "Neurodevelopmental study of writing disorders in middle childhood," *Journal of Developmental and Behavioural Pediatrics*, 13:17-23, 1992.
Defines four subtypes of writing disorders.

Arithmetic

Levine, M.D., Lindsay, R.L. & Reed, M.S. "The wrath of math: Deficiencies of mathematical mastery in the school child," *Pediatric Clinics of North America*, 39:525-536, 1992.
Describes the skills required for mathematical proficiency and the approaches to evaluating and managing underachievement in mathematics.

Shalev, R.S. & Gross-Tsur, V. "Developmental dyscalculia and medical assessment," *Journal of Learning Disabilities*, 26:134-137, 1993.
It is suggested that children who are not improving academically in spite of appropriate professional intervention be referred for medical assessment. Certain medical conditions, including attention deficit disorder without hyperactivity, which have a direct bearing on the children's cognitive disability and remedial programs may have been missed.

The study of brainwaves

Kuperman, S., Johnson, B., Arndt, S., Lindgren, S., et al. "Quantitative EEG differences in a nonclinical sample of children with ADHD and undifferentiated ADD," *Journal of the American Academy of Child & Adolescent Psychiatry*, 35(8):1009-17, August 1996.
Referring to the mixed results that have been obtained in previous attempts to use quantitative EEG to characterize ADHD, this study attempts to identify EEG differences in ADHD subtypes as one possible reason for the mixed results.

John, E.R., Prichep, L.S., Fridman, J. & Easton, P. "Neurometrics: Computer-assisted differential diagnosis of brain dysfunctions," *Science*, 239:162-169, 1988.
Describes the methodology used in the creation of topographic brain maps in neurometrics—a computer-assisted quantitative analysis of the electroencephalogram (EEG). Neurometrics may be used as an adjunct to clinical diagnosis.

Nuwer, M.R. "Quantitative EEG: II. Frequency analysis and topographic mapping in clinical settings," *Journal of Clinical Neurophysiology*, 5:45-85, 1988.
A review of the use of quantitative EEG techniques in clinical settings finds that these tests require substantial user expertise in EEG. For dyslexia there was still no consensus about how to use these tests for individual patient care.

Drake, M.E., Jr. "Clinical utility of event-related potentials in neurology and psychiatry," *Seminars in Neurology*, 10:196-201, 1990.
P300 and other commonly described event-related potentials are explained in regard to their origins, the factors which influence them and the neuropsychological processes they are assumed to measure.

Brain networks in ADHD

Mesulam, M-M. "Large-scale neurocognitive networks and distributed processing for attention, language, and memory," *Annals of Neurology*, 28:597-613, 1990.
An in-depth discussion of the relationship between brain structure and complex behaviors including selective attention, memory, and language.

Heilman, K.M., Voeller, K.K.S. & Nadeau, S.E. "A possible pathophysiologic substrate of attention deficit disorder/hyperactivity," *Journal of Child Neurology*, 6:S76-S79, 1991.

Looks at the evidence for the neuroanatomical localization of the features of ADHD to the frontal lobe and striatum.

Comorbidity

Semrud-Clikeman, M., Biederman, J., Sprich-Buckminster, S., et al. "Comorbidity between ADHD and learning disability: A review and report in a clinically referred sample," *Journal of the American Academy of Child and Adolescent Psychiatry,* 31:439-448, 1992.
This contains a review of the studies into the overlap between attention deficit disorder and learning disability. It finds that a wide range of overlap has been reported in the literature (from 10 percent to 92 percent).

Biederman, J., Newcorn, J. & Sprich, S. "Comorbidity of ADHD with conduct, depressive, anxiety, and other disorders," *American Journal of Psychiatry,* 148:564-577, 1991.
Looks at the evidence for the co-occurrence of ADHD with conduct disorder, oppositional defiant disorder, mood disorder, anxiety disorder, and learning disorder in children. Is this a random coincidence or specific comorbidity?

Shaywitz, B.A. & Shaywitz, S.E. "Comorbidity: A critical issue in attention deficit disorder," *Journal of Child Neurology,* 6:S13-S20, 1991.
Examines relationships between ADHD, learning disability, conduct disorder, and oppositional defiant disorder in regard to issues of definition, prevalence, prognosis, and the differences between hyperactive versus nonhyperactive ADHD.

August, G.J. & Garfinkel, B.D. "Behavioral and cognitive subtypes of ADHD," *Journal of the American Academy of Child and Adolescent Psychiatry,* 28:739-748, 1989.
Describes how children with ADHD and reading disability differ in linguistic and cognitive processes from children with ADHD alone. The former exhibit information processing deficits that involve inadequate encoding and retrieval of linguistic information, which are not found in the latter.

Conduct and Oppositional Defiant Disorders

Lahey, B.B., Loeber, R., Quay, H.C., et al. "Oppositional defiant and conduct disorders: Issues to be resolved for DSM-IV," *Journal of the American Academy of Child and Adolescent Psychiatry,* 31:539-546, 1992.
Oppositional defiant and conduct disorders are seen as separate but overlapping disorders. Conduct disorder is more likely to be associated with school suspension, police contact, and a family history of antisocial behavior.

Bipolar Disorder/Mania

Biederman, J., Faraone, S., Mick, E., et al. "Attention-deficit hyperactivity disorder and juvenile mania: An overlooked comorbidity?," *Journal of the American Academy of Child & Adolescent Psychiatry,* 35(8):997-1008, August 1996.

Wozniak, J., Biederman, J., Kiely K., Ablon, J.S., et al. "Mania-like symptoms suggestive of childhood-onset bipolar disorder in clinically referred children," *Journal of the American Academy of Child & Adolescent Psychiatry,* 34(7):867-76, July 1995.
Bipolar disorder is comorbid with ADHD in about 10 percent of children at initial diagnosis, and the occurrence increases with time. The presence of bipolar disorder in ADHD children is associated with more severe psychopathology and dysfunction.

Butler, S.F., Arredondo, D.E & McCloskey, V. "Affective comorbidity in children and adolescents with attention deficit hyperactivity disorder," *Annals of Clinical Psychiatry*, 7(2):51-5, June 1995.

West, S.A., Strakowski, S.M., Sax, K.W., Minnery, K.L., et al. "The comorbidity attention-deficit hyperactivity disorder in adolescent mania: Potential diagnostic and treatment implications," *Psychopharmacology Bulletin*, 31(2):347-51, 1995.
Adolescent and childhood-onset bipolar disorders often meet the criteria for ADHD. This raises the possibility of the co-occurence of both disorders and questions the lack of specificity of diagnostic criteria for each. This has important implications for drug treatment as different medications are indicated for each condition.

Motor vehicle accidents
Pless, I.B., Taylor, H.G. & Arsenault, L. "The relationship between vigilance deficits and traffic injuries involving children," *Pediatrics* 95(2):219-24, 1995.
Children with evidence of hyperactivity and attention deficit are at increased risk of injury in traffic accidents.

"Driving histories of ADHD subjects: Notes and commentary," *Annals of Emergency Medicine*, 29(4):546-8, April 1997.
ADHD is a risk factor for poor driving performance in early childhood. Includes reference to Russell Barkley's two earlier studies on the topic. Barkley et al. found that ADHD subjects know the road rules but do not follow them and are at higher risk for accidents.

Tourette's Syndrome and Tic Disorder in ADHD
Abwender, D.A., Como, P.G., Kurlan R., et al. "School problems in Tourette's syndrome," *Archives of Neurology*, 53:509-511, 1996.
School-related difficulties are strongly associated with the presence of ADHD, not the tic disorder.

Singer, H.S., Brown, J., Denckla, M.B., et al. "The treatment of attention-deficit hyperactivity disorder in Tourette's syndrome: A double-blind placebo-controlled study with clonidine and desipramine," *Pediatrics*, 95(1):74-81, January 1995.
Desipramine was superior to clonidine in the treatment of comorbid ADHD symptoms in children with Tourette's syndrome and ADHD. It is suggested as a useful alternative to clonidine when the two conditions coexist.

Spencer, T., Biederman, J., Wilens, T., et al. "Nortriptyline treatment of children with attention-deficit hyperactivity disorder and tic disorder or Tourette's syndrome," *Journal of the American Academy of Child & Adolescent Psychiatry*, 32(1):205-10, January 1993.
The tricyclic antidepressant nortriptyline significantly improved tics (67 percent) as well as ADHD symptoms without major adverse effects.

Sallee, F.R., Sethuraman, G., Rock, C.M. "Effects of pimozide on cognition in children with Tourette's syndrome: Interaction with comorbid attention deficit hyperactivity disorder," *Acta Psychiatrica Scandinavica*, 90(1):4-9, July 1994.
Pimozide was superior to haloperidol in the treatment of coexisting Tourette's syndrome.

Substance abuse
Schubiner, H., Tzelepis, A., Isaacson, J.H., et al. "The dual diagnosis of attention-deficit hyperactivity disorder and substance abuse: Case reports and literature review," *Journal of Clinical Psychiatry*, 56(4)146-50, April 1995.
Stimulant medication can successfully treat substance abuse in ADHD adults resulting in abstinence from alcohol and other drugs. Includes a literature review of ADHD and substance abuse.

Family-genetic transmission of ADHD
Biederman, J., Faraone, S.V., Keenan, K., et al. "Further evidence for family-genetic risk factors in attention deficit hyperactivity disorder: Patterns of comorbidity in probands and relatives in psychiatrically and pediatrically preferred samples," *Archives of General Psychiatry*, 49:728-738, 1992.
The relatives of children with ADHD with or without learning disability had a higher risk of ADHD, while the risk of learning disability was higher only among relatives of children with both ADHD and learning disability.

Gillis, J.J., Gilger, J.W., Pennington, B.F. & DeFries, J.C. "Attention deficit disorder in reading-disabled twins: Evidence for a genetic aetiology," *Journal of Abnormal Child Psychology*, 20:303-315, 1992.
Analysis of questionnaire data for attention and hyperactivity symptoms suggest that ADHD is highly heritable with a concordance rate of 79 percent for monozygotic twins and 32 percent for dizygotic twins. On a scale of 0-1.00, the obtained estimates of the extent to which ADHD is heritable is 0.98 ± 0.26. (Other studies such as that of F. Levy, personal communication, report 90 percent concordance for identical twins.)

Frontal lobe tests in ADHD
Barkley, R.A., Grodzinsky, G. & DuPaul G.J. "Frontal lobe functions in attention deficit disorder with and without hyperactivity: A review and research report," *Journal of Abnormal Child Psychology*, 20:163-188, 1992.
Some measures presumed to assess frontal lobe dysfunctions were not sensitive to the deficits in ADHD. Both types of ADHD share some similarities in deficits on frontal lobe tests, while the ADHD without hyperactivity group may have an additional problem with perceptual-motor speed and processing.

Shue, K.L. & Douglas, V.I. "Attention deficit hyperactivity disorder and the frontal lobe syndrome," *Brain and Cognition*, 20:104-124, 1992.
ADHD children are found to have frontal lobe deficits in motor control and problem-solving skills.

Executive function
Tannock, R., Ickowicz, A. & Schachar, R. "Differential effects of methylphenidate on working memory in ADHD children with and without comorbid anxiety," *Journal of the American Academy of Child & Adolescent Psychiatry*, 34(7):886-96, July 1995.
Working memory in ADHD children without comorbid anxiety was improved by Ritalin.

Tannock, R., Purvis, K.L. & Schachar, R.J. "Narrative abilities in children with attention deficit hyperactivity disorder and normal peers," *Journal of Abnormal Child Psychology*, 21(1):103-117, 1993.
Narratives by ADHD boys were more poorly organized, less cohesive, and contained more

inaccuracies. Such organization and monitoring of information for narratives are functions of executive control. It was postulated that these deficits in narrative production may reflect underlying deficits in executive processes.

The action of neurotransmitters in ADHD

Shenker, A. "The mechanism of action of drugs used to treat attention-deficit hyperactivity disorder: Focus on catecholamine receptor pharmacology," *Advances in Pediatrics,* 39:337-382, 1992.
The article reviews in depth the role of chemical messengers between the cells of the brain in relation to ADHD. It also describes an innovative method of studying neurotransmitter function in ADHD by observing the behavioral effects of different classes of medication—the so called "pharmacological dissection" of ADHD.

Zametkin, A.J. & Rapoport, J.L. "Neurobiology of attention deficit disorder with hyperactivity: Where have we come in 50 years?," *Journal of the American Academy of Child and Adolescent Psychiatry,* 26:676-686, 1987.
Preview of the studies into the neurotransmitter defect hypothesis in ADHD finds that no single current model can account for the efficacy of all the drugs used in ADHD.

SPECT scans in ADHD

Lou, H.C., Henriksen, L. & Bruhn P. "Focal cerebral hypoperfusion in children with dysphasia and/or attention deficit disorder," *Archives of Neurology,* 41:825-829, 1984.
Using Xenon 133 single photon emission computed tomography (SPECT), focal areas of low metabolic activity were seen in both perisylvian regions of children with dysphasia and in the white matter of the frontal lobes and caudate nuclei region of patients with ADHD. Methylphenidate increased perfusion in the central region, including the basal ganglia, and decreased perfusion of motor and primary sensorycortical areas.

Lou, H.C., Henriksen, L., Bruhn, P., et al. "Striatal dysfunction in attention deficit and hyperkinetic disorder," *Archives of Neurology,* 46:48-52, 1989.
Using Xenon 133 SPECT scans to examine regional cerebral blood flow in 13 children with ADHD, it was found that the striatal regions were underperfused while the primary sensory and sensorimotor cortical regions were highly perfused. Methylphenidate increased flow to the striatal region and decreased flow to the sensory regions.

Note: The above two studies are the original papers on the use of functional scans in ADHD. They reported reversal of the abnormal blood flow pattern in ADHD by Ritalin, findings which have not been fully backed up by more recent work.

Lou, H.C., Henriksen, L. & Bruhn, P. "Focal cerebral dysfunction in developmental learning disabilities," *Lancet,* 335:8-11, 1990.
Xenon 133 SPECT scans differentiated between children with pure ADHD (who had low regional cerebral blood flow to the striatal and posterior periventricular regions and high blood flow to the occipital region) and those with a language-learning disability (who had low blood flow to the left temporofrontal regions).

Sieg, K.G. & Gaffney, G.R., Preston, D.F. & Hellings, J.A. "SPECT imaging abnormalities in attention deficit hyperactivity disorder," *Clinical Nuclear Medicine,* 20(1): 55-60, 1995.

Findings suggestive of decreased metabolism in the left frontal and parietal regions are consistent with previous studies implicating decreased regional cortical perfusion in those areas which are involved in the control of attentional processes.

PET scans

Zametkin, A.J., Nordahl, T.E., Gross, M., et al. "Cerebral glucose metabolism in adults with hyperactivity of childhood onset," *The New England Journal of Medicine,* 20:1361-1366, 1990.
Positron Emission Tomography (PET) was used to measure glucose metabolism in different regions of the brains of adults with histories of hyperactivity from childhood, who continue to have symptoms and who were also the biologic parents of an ADHD child. Glucose metabolism was found to be significantly reduced in the premotor cortex and the superior prefrontal cortex, areas believed to be involved in the control of attention and motor activity.

Pardo, J.V., Fox, P.T. & Raichie, M.E. "Localization of a human system for sustained attention by positron emission tomography," *Nature,* 349:61-64, 1991.
In normal adults the right hemisphere is preferentially activated in vigilant tasks, an indirect piece of evidence for right-hemisphere abnormality in ADHD.

Matochik, J.A., Nordhal, T.E., Gross, M., Zametkin, A.J., et al. "Effects of acute stimulant medication on cerebral metabolism in adults with hyperactivity," *Neuropsychopharmacology,* 8:(4)377-386, 1993.

Matochik, J.A., Liebenauer, L.L., King, A.C., Zametkin, A.J., et al. "Cerebral glucose metabolism in adults with attention deficit hyperactivity disorder after chronic stimulant treatment," *American Journal of Psychiatry,* 151(5):658-66, 1991.
Acute and chronic stimulant administration did not alter regional or global brain metabolism in adults with ADHD.

Zametkin, A.J., Liebenauer, L.L., Fitzgerald, G.D., et al. "Brain metabolism in teenagers with attention-deficit hyperactivity disorder," *Archives of General Psychiatry,* 50:3333-40, May 1993.

Ernst, M., Liebenauer, L.L., King, A.C., et al. "Reduced brain metabolism in hyperactive girls," *Journal of the American Academy of Child & Adolescent Psychiatry,* 33:858-868, 1994.
Two PET studies in teenagers—one finding no change in brain metabolism and the other showing reduced global brain metabolism.

Volumetric MRI

Castellanos, F.X., Giedd, J.N., Marsh, W.L., Rapoport, J.L., et al. "Quantitative brain magnetic resonance imaging in attention-deficit hyperactivity disorder," *Archives of General Psychiatry* 53(7):607-616, 1996.
Comprehensive volumetric measurements of the brain in a relatively pure sample of ADHD documenting the dysfunction in right-sided prefrontal-striatal systems.

Hynd, G.W., Hern, K.L., Novey, E.S., Voeller, K.K., et al. "Attention deficit-hyperactivity disorder and assymetry of the caudate nucleus," *Journal of Child Neurology,* 8:339-347, 1993.

Reversal of the normal pattern of caudate asymmetry is noted on the MRI of most ADHD subjects.

Hynd, G.W., Semrud-Clikeman, M., Lorys, A.R., et al. "Brain morphology in developmental dyslexia and attention deficit disorder/hyperactivity," *Archives of Neurology*, 47:919-926, 1990.
Metric measurements on magnetic resonance imaging (MRI) scans of the brains of dyslexic and ADHD children showed significantly smaller right anterior width measurements than normal. The dyslexics, but not children with ADHD, had an increased incidence of reversed asymmetry of the planum temporale, the auditory association cortex.

Teicher, M.H., Polcari, A., Anderson, C.M., et. al. "Methylphenidate effects on hyperactivity and fMRI in children with ADHD," *American Academy of Child & Adolescent Psychiatry, Scientific Proceedings of the Annual Meeting*, 12, 1996.
Preliminary results using functional MRI indicates that hypoperfusion in the right caudate of ADHD subjects is reversed on optimal treatment with methylphenidate.

Controversial therapies for ADHD
Silver, L.B. "Controversial approaches to treating learning disabilities and attention deficit disorder," *American Journal of Diseases for Children*, 140:1045-1052, 1986.
Reviews the literature related to the generally accepted and the controversial approaches to treatment of learning disabilities and ADHD. The controversial approaches covered include neurophysiologic retraining (patterning, optometric visual training, and vestibular dysfunction) and orthomolecular medicine (megavitamins, trace elements, hypoglycemia, food additives and preservatives, and refined sugars).

Kaplan, B.J., Polatajko, H.J., Wilson, B.N & Faris, P.D. "Re-examination of sensory integration treatment: A combination of two efficacy studies," *Journal of Learning Disabilities*, 26:342-7, 1993.
Sensory integration was found not to have significant therapeutic advantage over the more simple traditional interventions.

Tinted lenses
Cotton, M.M., Evans, K.M. "A review of the use of Irlen (tinted) lenses," *Australian and New Zealand Journal of Ophthalmology*, 18:307-312, 1990.
Finds much confusion and inconsistency between the many research studies (many of which are unpublished) into the efficacy of tinted lenses and colored overlays for the treatment of reading disability. Recent experimental evaluations do not support the use of the lenses as a useful intervention for children with reading disabilities.

Adult ADHD
Spencer, T., Wilens, T., Biederman, J., Faraone, S.V., et al. "A double-blind, cross-over comparison of methylphenidate and placebo in adults with childhood-onset attention-deficit/hyperactivity disorder," *Archives of General Psychiatry*, 52(6):434-43, June 1995.
At a dose of 1 mg per kg per day, Ritalin resulted in a significant therapeutic response in adults with ADHD, whether or not there was coexisting anxiety or depression.

Wilens, T.E., Biederman, J., Mick, E. & Spencer, T.J. "A systematic assessment of tricyclic antidepressants in the treatment of adult attention-deficit hyperactivity disorder," *Journal of Nervous & Mental Disease*, 183(1) 48-50, January 1995.

Retrospective data analysis supports the efficacy of tricyclics in adult ADHD.

Silver, L.B. "Diagnosis of attention-deficit hyperactivity disorder in adult life," *Child and Adolescent Psychiatric Clinics of North America*, 1:325-334, 1992.
Considers the dilemma which faces the physician in making the diagnosis of adult ADHD.

Bellak, L. & Black, R.B. "Attention-deficit hyperactivity disorder in adults," *Clinical Therapeutics*, 14:138-147, 1992.
An overview and suggestions for the diagnosis and management of adult ADHD.

Mannuzza, S., Klein, R.G., Bessler, A., et al. "Adult outcome of hyperactive boys: Educational achievement, occupational rank, and psychiatric status," *Archives of General Psychiatry*, 50:656-576, 1993.
Concludes that childhood ADHD predicts antisocial and drug-abuse disorders but not mood or anxiety disorders. NOTE: A major criticism of this study is that the co-occurrence of conduct disorder was not addressed.

Ward, M.F., Wender, P.H. & Reimherr, F.W. "The Wender Utah Rating Scale: An aid in the retrospective diagnosis of childhood attention deficit hyperactivity disorder," *American Journal of Psychiatry*, 150:885-890, 1993.
An attempt to develop a new diagnostic rating scale for adults to describe their own childhood behavior, so aiding in the retrospective diagnosis of childhood ADHD.

Girls with ADHD

Berry, C.A., Shaywitz, S.E., Shaywitz, B.A. "Girls with attention deficit disorder: A silent minority? A report on behavioral and cognitive characteristics," *Pediatrics*, 76:801-809, 1985.
ADHD in girls was associated with more severe cognitive and language deficits and greater social liability. ADHD without hyperactivity in girls is even more likely to be missed than the equivalent in boys.

Perrin, S. & Last, C.G. "Relationship between ADHD and anxiety in boys: Results from a family study," *Journal of the American Academy of Child & Adolescent Psychiatry*, 35 (8):988-96, August 1996.
There is an increased risk of both anxiety disorder and ADHD in adult relatives of children with ADHD, in particular female adult relatives. However, ADHD and anxiety appear to be independently transmitted in the families.

APPENDIX XVI

Recent Review Papers

Spencer, T., Biederman, J., Wilens, T., et al. "Pharmacotherapy of attention-deficit hyperactivity disorder across the life cycle," *Journal of the American Academy of Child & Adolescent Psychiatry*, 35(4):409–432, 1996.
Reviews the medications used in ADHD, including 155 controlled studies documenting the efficacy of stimulants in the treatment of ADHD.

Wilens, T.E., Biederman, J., Spencer, T.J., et al. "Pharmacotherapy of adult attention deficit/hyperactivity disorder: A review," *Journal of Clinical Psychopharmacology*, 15(4): 270–9, August 1995.
A review of medications in adult ADHD.

Wender, E.H. "Attention-deficit hyperactivity disorders in adolescence," *Journal of Developmental & Behavioral Pediatrics*, 16(3):192–5, June 1995.
A review of the disorder in adolescence.

Cantwell, D.P. "Attention deficit disorder. A review of the past 10 years," *Journal of the American Academy of Child & Adolescent Psychiatry*, 35(8):978–987, 1996.
An easily readable review presenting new information from all areas of ADHD research.

Elia, J., Welsh, P.A., Rapoport, J.L., et al. "Classroom academic performance: Improvement with both methylphenidate and dextroamphetamine in ADHD boys," *Journal of Child Psychology and Psychiatry*, 34(5):785–804, 1993.
Includes a review of stimulant effects on measures of academic achievement.

Castellanos, F.X. "Toward a pathophysiology of Attention Deficit/Hyperactivity Disorder," *Clinical Pediatrics*, 36(7):381–93, July 1997.
A good review of the research into the neurological substrate for executive function. Includes data from studies on neuropsychology, prefrontal circuitry, neuropathology, and brain neurotransmitters.

Goldman-Rakic, P.S. "Cellular basis of working memory," *Neuron*, 14:477–485, 1995.

Goldman-Rakic, P.S. "Cellular and circuit basis of working memory in prefrontal cortex of nonhuman primates," *Progress in Brain Research*, vol 85. Uylings, H.B.M., Van Eden, C.G., De Bruin, M.A., et al. (eds), Elselvier Science Publishers BV, 1990.
Detailed research documenting neuronal networks for working memory.

Denckla, M.B. "Biological correlates of learning and attention: What is relevant to learning disability and attention-deficit hyperactivity disorder?" *Journal of Developmental and Behavioral Pediatrics*, 17(2):114–119, 1996.
Learning disability and ADHD from a cognitive neuroscience perspective, highlighting the role of executive dysfunction.

Shaywitz, B.A., Fletcher, J.M., Shaywitz, S.E. "Defining and classifying learning disabilities and attention-deficit/hyperactivity disorder," *Journal of Child Neurology*, 10 Suppl 1:S50–7, January 1995.
An overview of current conceptual models of learning disability and ADHD. It argues for a normal distribution model for reading disability/ability.

Barkley, R.A. *Attention Deficit Hyperactivity Disorder—A handbook for diagnosis and treatment*. New York: Guilford Press, 1990.

A comprehensive, well-researched overview of the subject. Though now becoming out-of-date, this is still useful, interesting, and highly recommended for those with an academic interest in ADHD.

Rosenberger, P.B. "Attention deficit," *Pediatric Neurology*, 7:397–405, 1991.
Focuses on the neuropsychological testing and neurobiology of ADHD.

Levine, M.D. "Attention deficits: The diverse effects of weak control systems in childhood," *Pediatric Annals*, 16:117–130, 1987.
Includes Dr. Levine's unique description of the observed behaviors and cognitive symptoms in ADHD children which are incorporated into an inventory of symptoms, patented to form the ANSER system questionnaires.

Leffert, N., & Susman, A. "Attention deficit hyperactivity disorder in children," *Current Opinion in Pediatrics*, 5:429–433, 1993.
Focuses on neuroanatomic and genetic linkages, and the effects of medication on school performance, achievement, and social relationships.

NHMRC (National Health and Medical Research Council) (1997) Working party report on Attention Deficit Hyperactivity Disorder AGPS Canberra.
This is the long-awaited report of the expert panel set up by Australia's NHMRC. The panel supports, without reservation, the existence and biological nature of ADHD. This document reviews the international research at the time of publication (August 1997). The panel comments on all methods of treatment and gives strong support to the safety and benefits of stimulant medication.

Help for Parents

ADHD Support Groups
There are many support groups all over the United States. The following is an incomplete list of groups. We are giving information here on the main branches of each organization. Within those organizations, there are usually state chapters which address local needs. We have also found that the Internet is a valuable tool for locating information and support groups.

CH.A.D.D (Children and Adults With Attention Deficit Disorder)
499 Northwest 70th Avenue, Suite 101
Plantations, Florida 33317
(800) 233-4050
Fax: (954) 587-4599

ADDA (National Attention Deficit Disorder Association)
9930 Johnnycake Ridge Road, Suite 3E
Mentor, Ohio 44060
(800) 487-2282
Fax: (440) 350-0223

National Center for Learning Disabilities
99 Park Avenue
New York, New York 10016
(212) 687-7211

Attention Deficit Information Network (AD-IN)
475 Hillside Avenue
Needham, MA 02194
(617) 455-9895

Learning Disabilities Association of America
4156 Library Road
Pittsburgh, PA 15234
(412) 341-8077

Center for Mental Health Services
Office of Consumer, Family, and Public Information
5600 Fishers Lane
Rockville, MD 20857
(301) 433-2792

*TOUGH*LOVE—a Self-Help Program for Parents
Troubled by Teenage Behavior

The *TOUGH*LOVE program was founded by Phyllis and David York in 1972. The Yorks worked as family and youth counselors in Pennsylvania for 13 years before they realized that while understanding and forgiveness may be commendable, when dealing with children who are constantly in trouble, this approach does not always work. This lesson was learned through personal experience with their own children.

*TOUGH*LOVE is a loving solution for families that are being torn apart by unacceptable adolescent behavior. These young people may skip school, run away from home, abuse drugs or alcohol, and get into trouble with the law. Often they act as though they are the only people to be considered when making decisions about their lives. *TOUGH*LOVE encourages parents to allow their children to experience the natural and logical consequences of their actions. *TOUGH*LOVE also teaches parents that constantly rescuing children from these consequences is not helping them to grow and mature. It is in fact hindering the growth of mature, responsible attitudes.

*TOUGH*LOVE is tough on parents. It is recognized that it is hard work changing behavior and habits that have developed over years and that we need the support of others to do this. Parents come to *TOUGH*LOVE because they love their children enough to want to make positive changes in their own lives and in the lives of their children.

*TOUGH*LOVE is not a parenting program; it is a crisis intervention program.

*TOUGH*LOVE is a philosophy based on action. Parents join local *TOUGH*LOVE groups for practical and emotional peer support. Parents provide understanding for one another without becoming involved in blaming. *TOUGH*LOVE is nonjudgmental. Where counseling or therapy is required, parents are referred to professionals while continuing to get support from the *TOUGH*LOVE group.

*TOUGH*LOVE is also confrontational. Parents are challenged to view themselves clearly, to examine their present behavioral responses and ideas, and, where necessary, to make constructive changes. Practical solutions are provided to help change behavior. It is accepted that the only people that we can change are ourselves and that others may, or may not, choose to change in response to the changes we make. Decisiveness and directness are encouraged. Parents are able to call upon other members of the group for practical support at any time. Members have been asked, at times, to take in children from other families and provide them with temporary shelter while a family tries to resolve a crisis.

*TOUGH*LOVE recognizes that it takes a lot of courage to ask for support and that asking is not a sign of weakness. It also requires a degree of commitment so that members give as well as receive. It is recognized that the best solutions to problems come from practical experience. People who have benefited from *TOUGH*LOVE are asked to stay on and help others overcome their problems.

*TOUGH*LOVE is a nonprofit organization offering self-help materials to parents, kids in trouble, and professionals working with them. *TOUGH*LOVE groups are not run by professionals. They are run by parents. People in service roles in society may initiate groups but they only survive if the parents are committed to the group and to each other. For many people, *TOUGH*LOVE provides an extended family of caring adults who are not only ready and willing to listen but also willing to become involved and *remain* involved.

For more information about *TOUGH*LOVE support groups, contact:

*TOUGH*LOVE
P.O. Box 1069
Doylestown, PA 18901
Ph: 1-800-333-1069
Fax: 215-348-9874
E-mail: service @ toughlove.org

Recommended reading
*TOUGH*LOVE by Phyllis and David York, Bantam, 1997

*TOUGH*LOVE *SOLUTIONS* by Phyllis and David York, Bantam, 1997

Index